America's Systemic Psychosis

America's Systemic Psychosis

**How Our Nation Lost Its Mind
and How To Get It Back**

Jack L. Richardson, IV, J.D.

NEW YORK

LONDON • NASHVILLE • MELBOURNE • VANCOUVER

America's Systemic Psychosis

How Our Nation Lost Its Mind and How to Get It Back

Published in New York, New York, by Morgan James Publishing. Morgan James is a trademark of Morgan James, LLC. www.MorganJamesPublishing.com

Proudly distributed by Publishers Group West®

First printing, 2023

Morgan James BOGO™

A **FREE** ebook edition is available for you or a friend with the purchase of this print book.

[ ]

CLEARLY SIGN YOUR NAME ABOVE

Instructions to claim your free ebook edition:
1. Visit MorganJamesBOGO.com
2. Sign your name CLEARLY in the space above
3. Complete the form and submit a photo of this entire page
4. You or your friend can download the ebook to your preferred device

ISBN 9781636984100 paperback
ISBN 9781636984117 ebook
Library of Congress Control Number:
2024936031

Cover and Interior Design by:
Chris Treccani
www.3dogcreative.net

Morgan James is a proud partner of Habitat for Humanity Peninsula and Greater Williamsburg. Partners in building since 2006.

Get involved today! Visit: www.morgan-james-publishing.com/giving-back

CONTENTS

ACKNOWLEDGMENTS

The definition of "acknowledgments" is the acceptance of the truth or existence of something; or the expression of gratitude or appreciation for something. It may seem strange to start a book, or even just the "acknowledgements" page, with a definition, but words have meanings without which we cannot know or communicate truth. You will see this exhibited throughout the book. However, to know the truth one needs to know from whence truth comes, the truth giver, God.

While I could give much credit, attribution, and indeed acknowledgment to many individually in appreciation, (and I do throughout the book), for the truth they have spoken and made available to others through their works (and there are many), I desire to show appreciation for all who are lovers of the truth. I do this by giving acknowledgment to the One without which there would be no truth. My appreciation overflows to God for opening my eyes and ears, enabling me to thrive and flourish with the truth He has provided me, but also the truth He has provided others. It is through building on the truth that others have also discerned, and whose works have brought so much reality to the forefront, that we can prosper and live productive, peaceful, and happy lives. And for that I am appreciative.

To God be the glory.

Disclaimer: *This book contains the personal opinions of the author and should not in any way be construed as the positions or opinions of any of the organizations that the author has been, or is currently affiliated with, or those referenced in the book.*

PREFACE

From Denmark to America

"Something is rotten in the state of Denmark."[1]

This is one of the most famous quotes from Shakespeare's play, *Hamlet*. One of the characters in the play, Marcellus, says this to Horatio as they debate about following Hamlet and the ghost into the dark.

Marcellus means that something bad is happening in the country. The rottenness refers to the body politic. Shakespeare meant it to convey a symbolic and ominous message about the state of the nation. The word "rotten" evokes a sense of corrosion. Marcellus saw that his country was decaying, and a systemically unwell condition was spreading across its people.

Political, societal, and cultural malaise is a significant theme of the play. It's apparent in the characters' actions and the dialogue, as Shakespearean language conjures vivid imagery of corruption. Decay and disease repeatedly appear throughout the play as rottenness is found everywhere, spreading like gangrene.

It's a bleak but frank assessment. Denmark *was* rotting. We must ask ourselves: Are things any different in America today?

America today is in much the same condition as Denmark in *Hamlet*. There is an unmistakable decay throughout the country, manifesting itself in our body politic in profound ways. Regardless of your political persuasion, most people know something is gravely amiss. Even the progressive talk show host, Bill Maher, shows increasing alarm and concern about the mental insanity gripping our nation. He has, of late, had some

---

1   William Shakespeare, *The Tragedy of Hamlet Prince of Denmark* (New York: Simon & Schuster, reprinted 2012), 104, Scribd.

logical diatribes pointing out the inexplicable incongruity in the stance taken by those on his own side of the political spectrum, earning him derision from those who would rather indulge their feelings than think or seek the truth.

I've spent my life as a lawyer, political activist and leader, and student of history. You would be wise to heed the fact that there has never been such chaos in American culture and society at its very core as there is today. While we have been through a civil war and two world wars, what is occurring today is the intentional, contrived moral death and decay of America as we know it. The societal fabric has been torn, and the rip is rushing across the rest of the nation. Think I'm overstating the case? We don't even know the differences between men and women anymore and are castrating young boys. This is truly a case of the "barbarians at the gate."

What is this affliction? What's causing the rot in 2023 America? Make no mistake, this goes deeper than political division and Republicans vs. Democrats. This goes broader than even the widespread media manipulation, though that's a key piece of the problem. The lie cannot survive the light, which is why the light is hidden.

What's happening is that the country is suffering from a profound mental dysfunction affecting every segment of the culture and society. It is so pervasive that many of those who should know better don't. It was, and is, a planned deconstruction—not just of the foundational pillars that once made the country so strong and great, but of the truth itself.

We have become a nation disconnected from life-giving truth. We are suffering from a taught, insidious, cognitive disease of the mind rendering our citizens incapable of seeing and knowing the truth. And if they do, they are demoralized, unable to summon the will to do anything about it.

In his book, *The Psychology of Totalitarianism*, Dr. Mattias Desmet foreshadows the future for those who become detached from the truth. I will be referring to Desmet again, but here he gives a reason for why he wrote his book. Desmet was worried that: "The dystopian vision of the German-Jewish philosopher Hannah Arendt loomed at society's horizon: the emergence of a new totalitarianism, no longer led by flamboyant 'mob leaders' such as Joseph Stalin or Adolf Hitler but by dull bureaucrats and technocrats."[2] He goes on:

> That November morning, I drafted the blueprint for a book in which I would explore the psychological roots of totalitarianism. At the time, I wondered: Why did totalitarianism as a form of statehood emerge for the first time in the first half of the twentieth century? And moreover: What is the difference between it and the classical dictatorships of the past? The essence of this difference, I realized, lies within the field of psychology.[3]

He's right. The issue here is, in large measure, psychological. However, it isn't *only* psychological.

What renders a people so warped in their thinking and actions that it sets a country off on such a steep trajectory of decline, and one that leaves them open to totalitarianism? Dr. John MacArthur, pastor and theologian in California, calls it a "depraved mind," that is, a non-functioning mind, incapable of normal thinking ("normal" meaning conforming to a standard, or in this instance, functioning properly in relation to reality).

Depraved people have historically and inexorably delivered themselves into the hands of their captors, prisoners of self-selected bondage. They live a miserable existence. A depraved mind is blind; it cannot process facts or understand reality in a normative way such that its chosen outcomes are not destructive, and those outcomes have reasonable predictability. The depraved mind does not and cannot see that its decisions and conduct are leading to its demise and the demise of society.

Given this abnormal behavior, depravity is a good word for it—a deeply theological term. It speaks to the sickness caused by sin. In this book, I want to use a different term, a medical term, that captures the essence of "what is rotten in the state of America." That term is *psychosis*.

---

2   Mattias Desmet, *The Psychology of Totalitarianism* (London, UK: Chelsea Green Publishing, 2022), 9, Scribd.
3   Desmet, *The Psychology of Totalitarianism*, 9.

That's right—America is psychotic. It has lost its connection to truth and reality and therefore has entered a state of psychosis. Like a malignant tumor, if not cut out by the scalpel of renewed truth, the psychosis will spread and spread, ultimately destroying the social fabric of the country and its people. America is in its decline and close to the climactic moment where there is no return.

Historically there have always been the depraved in society, but not aided by and merged with the Orwellian type of technology of today. This combination has created a nearly impossible and poisonous concoction, such that given the existential denial of reality and the slothful character of those who do think more normatively and rightly, recovery is nearly impossible. With every slip further away from reality, America is pulling the plug on itself. There have always been moral reprobates amongst us, but never without overwhelming and countervailing opposition and rejection. The immune system of our American body politic is failing, our checks and balances are no longer working, and America does not appear to be self-correcting anymore.

There have always been those suffering from psychosis, but they weren't behind every major news desk, or even worse, behind the Resolute Desk in the Oval Office. There is one common denominator among those in government, media, the classrooms, and our corporate board rooms, and that is they are mostly godless and morally bankrupt, doing only what they think is right in their own blurred eyes. They grew up as wild weeds, detached from any ethical moorings making up their morality along the way, and now they have ascended where they are forcing their anti-religion upon the rest of us.

Both sides in our American conflict are to blame but to differing degrees. For convenience's sake, I refer to the opposite sides of the spectrum here and throughout the book in more political terms as "Left" and "Right" which many identify or relate to simply because of their common usage. However, there are other more descriptive and characteristic terms they possess which I will allude to later. However, for now, it's Left and Right.

The power-hungry progressive Left drives the psychosis, aided and abetted by the media and most major American institutions. It's truly not a stretch to say that Democrat policies and preferences are making us all go insane—and it needs to stop.

However, the pusillanimous character of those on the political Right (granted, many do not fit this characterization but haven't the resources to do otherwise), fostered by their addiction to convenience and comfort, renders them useless. They are too fat and comfortable, too ensconced in their sloth, to engage in any effective extraction from the inevitable collapse within the country.

The wealthy elites are to blame as well. With the advance of technology and the power and influence of the mega-rich who have become countries in themselves (above the law and wholly hedonistic, if not occultists), they manipulate and control the narrative and public opinion. They have effectively destroyed the one-man, one-vote system, eliminating the checks and balances of those who could and would do something to bring about a correction but find themselves "socially exhausted" (which is one of the goals of the neo-anarchist, for only they know how to navigate their web of chaos, deceit, and deception). If the average voter spent $10 in the 2020 election, the sum that Mark Zuckerberg spent was the equivalent of over 35 million votes. This kind of spending is insane, as are the billions from corporations whose last interest is you.

The average American is to blame too. Far too many "average Joes" refuse to wake up to the fact that they are living in a lie. They are like a balloon floating away in the breeze, totally untethered to anything real. The reason I know regular Americans are increasingly untethered is that far too many are content to look reality in the eye and still say things like "Lia Thomas is a woman" because they don't want to suffer the social cost. If you aren't willing to pay the price for the truth, you will pay with the truth. Now, I do not know what Thomas "truly" thinks or believes, but I do know what science says. Biologically, and by every measure and metric, Lia is William, and William is a man. It's never a good sign when your average citizen starts denying reality because they have been gaslighted into doing so.

As more evidence comes out about Thomas, it appears that, in the psychosis of the Left, who push every deviance known, Thomas may have AGP (auto gynephilia) which is a male's propensity to be sexually aroused by the thought of himself as a female and gets a thrill out of making you play along with his fetish. So now the question is: does Thomas really believe he is a woman or is he playing out a fetish? He now apparently claims to be a lesbian having relations with another male who claims to be a woman. There are more salacious details out there, but this is the important point of this discussion; it is less about Mr./Ms./M. Thomas and more about those on the Left who shamefully and psychotically gaslight the public and insist that you accept the deviance of Thomas' condition as normative. They don't believe he is, but he's a tool in their authoritarian toolbox to create a chaos that advances their quest for power.

Right, Left, Republican, Democrat, rich, poor, and everyone in between is suffering from delusions of wokeness in America. We have been disconnected from the truth and reality. As I defined it in my previous book, *Hey Teachers, Leave Those Kids Alone*, "woke":

> ...is a mindset and posture of those who, in their delusion, see a reality in which everyone else, they think, is asleep, particularly as to the inequities, systemic injustices, and broad racism they emptily claim exists. They don't believe it either but hope you do to advance the hidden agenda they have. Most of these inequities are created or conjured up by the self-ordained woke person. They create a problem, designate themselves as the leader and then implement the solution and consequential outcome they desire. These self-ordained "woke-priests," project upon others what they, the radicals, are most guilty: the sins of envy, hatred, and resentment. These woke-priests have a hatred for those who have made something of their lives. Woke-priests want the consequences of their bad choices in life to be subsidized by those who are reaping the benefits of a more disciplined life – they want total control. There is not a single cell of concern in their minds for those suffering the conjured-up inequities they espouse. Don't go looking for any Mother Theresa types in this group. These woke priests have preyed upon the church with accusations and guilt, and have succeeded in distracting, sidelining, and dividing congregations.

The recently released movie, "Enemies Within the Church," explains the dilemma using WOKE as an acronym for "Willfully Overlooking Known Evil." Visit their website at EnemiesWithintheChurch.com for resources to awaken your church.[4]

As Dr. Owen Strachan noted in his book *Christianity and Wokeness*, "Woke ideology is not made for the classrooms. It is made for revolutions."[5] Or, like Elon Musk said of wokeness in an interview with the Babylon Bee, "Wokeness gives people a shield to be mean and cruel, armored in false virtue."[6]

They are so correct as to the effect and symptoms of Wokeness, but that is not what is at the core of the problem. Whether you are a doctor or a lawyer or anyone else in a profession that deals with complex problems, when a problem is presented, you see the symptoms, but you know that is not at the core of the illness; it's only a by-product. Many, including me, have sought to define and help explain "wokeness," but I think that Dr. James Lindsay has summarized it the best: Wokeness is Marxism. That is why I devoted so much of the book and particularly one chapter on Marx to connect these dots.

Again, Lindsay gives one of the most succinct summaries and explanations of the chaos in the West. He addresses the smorgasbord of problems that seems to have suddenly engulfed us, whether it is feminism, white privilege, queer theory, critical race theory, racism in general, etc. All these perceived problems Lindsay likens to the relationship between a "genus" and a "species," as we learned in school in explaining the biological world in which we live. Let me explain.

The house cat is of the genus *felis* and its species is *felis catus*, of which there are over 30 different breeds. So, to put it another way, the genus is like a cold, and the runny nose, sneezing, coughing, headache, and feeling terrible are like the species. The cold is the core of all the other

---

4   Jack L. Richardson IV, Esq., *Hey! Teachers, Leave Those Kids Alone: Critical Race Theory and Wokeness in a Nutshell, A Condensed Tutorial for Moms, Dads, & Legislators* (Louisville, KY: V.G. Reed and Sons, Inc., 2021), 21.

5   Owen Strachan, *Christianity and Wokeness: How the Social Justice Movement Is Hijacking the Gospel—and the Way to Stop It* (Washington, D.C.: Salem Books, 2021), 45-46, Scribd.

6   Elon Musk, "FULL INTERVIEW: Elon Musk Sits Down with The Babylon Bee," Youtube.com, accessed October 28, 2022, https://www.youtube.com/watch?v=jvGnw1sHh9M.

problems. You cure the cold, and you get rid of all the other problems. Wokeness is nothing other than another word for Marxism. Marxism is the genus and all the problems being experienced in society are the species that are spawned from Marxism. Marxism has morphed from trying to control the means of production to controlling the culture, and under the genus of Marxism comes the plethora of symptoms as just stated causing all the chaos in the West.

Within the last couple of decades, but going back nearly 100 years, Marxism has been on the move to destroy the West, and it is reaching a climactic point. Marxism is behind the woke mindset and in all the cultural appropriations such as I mentioned above: the transgender movement, the LGBTQ (which I'm tired of spelling out) agenda, white privilege, the "everything is racist, even roadways" mentality, identity politics, etc. It is rampant in the schools and is destroying your children. It is all by design to confuse you and create social exhaustion with the multiple waves of what most of us see as complete departures from reality and normalcy. Marxism does not appeal to happy people which are created by capitalist economies. So, Marxism cannot prevail unless it creates divisions and false narratives, fake problems, and false guilt so you become unhappy, and then it poses as your savior.

The West has been in the midst of a global totalitarian revolution for decades, and only in the last couple of decades has it reached a fever pitch, leaving you scratching your head wondering what has happened and why is all this occurring at the same time. You have been asleep. It was designed that way. That is why I have identified this psychosis as inorganic or planned and intentionally implemented. All I can do is warn you of the danger. If you don't wake up and reform your thinking, voting, inactions, and conduct, then you will suffer a bondage that will never end in your lifetime. Yes, this is a direct threat to your life, liberty, and happiness and you had better get a sober grip on that reality. Psychosis is a detachment from reality and the core is Marxism which has produced an intended mass psychosis within the country in furtherance of its goal of redefining society and humanity.

These are hard and pithy truths that the psychos on the Left hate. Nevertheless, while there are voices out there telling the blunt truth, they are smothered and drowned out by the psychos in control.

We are suffering from psychosis. We are rotting, and we must be cured, or we will be destroyed, which clearly serves the agenda of our adversaries, both foreign and domestic. Throughout this book, words will be defined, like *psychosis*. This is critically important because the psychotic, agenda-driven, moral reprobates running this country have cleansed words of any meaning, bleaching our dictionaries like a Clinton email server.

The purpose of word and definition appropriation is to deceive and manipulate. It has returned us to a precarious time, similar to the one found in Scripture right after the Tower of Babel. God confounded and confused those taking counsel against Him by causing the people to speak in different languages such that they could not understand one another, so they dispersed. There was no way for them to communicate, much less know the truth. Watch five minutes of the media today and ask yourself if it sounds like they can speak the same language that truth speaks.

Now, I'm not asking you to believe in the Babel story, that's on you, but you get the point. We are losing a common language—one of truth and reason—and in this rotted state of America, the perpetrators of our mass insanity sow the confusion of corrupted terminology. Make no mistake about it. It is agenda driven, intentional, and destructive. You had better be asking what their plan is.

This may sound nefarious, but it's almost impossible *not* to discern if you are disciplined. On the Left, many think chaos must be embraced as a means to an end and see it as providing an opportunity for the leftist psychotics of society to seize control. They create chaos and try to seize control, but they have no idea how they are going to get there without destroying millions of lives along the way. They are just making it up as they go, foolishly thinking they can avoid the horrors of the past.

Over thirty years ago, I embarked upon a new business venture with a friend. I prepared all the corporate papers and got the structure of the business in place. My friend was to take care of sales and run the day-to-day operations. On the first day, I accompanied him on his first call. As we drove up to the business, I asked him, "What are you going to say?" He said, "I don't know, but I will figure it out between here and the door." This is where the Left is today as they dismantle society. They are clueless, and if they are wrong, and they are, you will pay the price. Too much is at stake for them to try to figure it out on the way.

The psychotic detachment from reality on the Left side of the spectrum is characterized by those who are the least committed to a moral code, obsessively resentful, envious, hedonistic, anarchical, and lost in their delusion of a utopia. If I were that deluded, I suppose I would be looking for a utopia as well. If that were not bad enough, the Left is supported by the occultic "demi-gods" of society, people who, in their delusions, think they can escape their mortal demise. If you have ever watched leftist demonstrators being interviewed, you will see that upon the first question, they immediately resort to violent rhetoric and recoil from any logic and reason. The reason for this is obvious. They have no answers and cannot win the argument with coherent, logical, and fact-based reasoning. They have completely overdosed on emotion; and if you persist, they will physically remove you, shove you, and place placards in your face and your camera. They cannot tolerate the light of truth.

Matt Walsh, of "The Matt Walsh Show" podcast, and others, have referred to this rottenness as a "mass psychosis" or "mass formation psychosis."[7] These are good descriptors. For the most part, it is inorganic; that is, it is being intentionally taught and imposed on people, and it is not simply developing naturally in our society. It's not the same as ignorance or stupidity. Ignorance is merely a lack of knowledge—I'm ignorant about how to perform brain surgery, so ignorance is not the issue. Stupidity, on the other hand, is a horse of a different color. It is the lack of good sense or judgment. That would look like me trying to perform brain surgery even though I don't know how to, or, even worse, a brain surgeon getting drunk the night before a serious operation.

The psychosis plaguing our society is more comprehensive and sinister than either ignorance or acts of stupidity. The psychosis I'm addressing in this book is the product of a massive social engineering effort. More than making people stupid, it zombifies people into a non-analytical mindset where other points of view are not tolerated, or even capable

---

7   Matt Walsh, "Mass Formation Psychosis Is Real and We're All Living Through It | Ep. 870," Youtube.com, accessed on October 28, 2022, https://www.youtube.com/watch?v=O4l4m-dbA_k.

of being processed. In more sane times, this kind of cognitive malfunctioning would have been diagnosed as a mental disorder. It is an inability to deal with reality. Another way to refer to it is as "planned reflexive noncognitive conduct." What I mean by that is as follows: millions of people are being programmed to respond to certain triggers and stimuli without even thinking about what they are responding to or what a reasonable, sane, and truth-based reaction would look like.

Dietrich Bonhoeffer reasoned that the root of all the malevolence in Germany during the time leading up to and during World War II was stupidity. Stupidity was seen by him as more dangerous than malice. The stupid person is self-satisfied. This is not an intellectual defect but a moral one. People are made stupid or have allowed it to happen to them. And the stupidity of others forms the foundation of the power of political demagogues. It has never been more prevalent than in today's America with the chaos gripping the nation. Slogans and catchwords possess the stupid person. They are mindless. Abandon attempts to reason with them.

Like I said: Psychosis. This is where we are today. Something is rotten in the state of America. Few are blameless either on the Left or the Right, which will be further developed on several fronts herein as we specifically point out current issues that exemplify not only the decay in the country but also the root from which it stems.

We must recover the truth. After all, it is the truth that will set us free.

INTRODUCTION

"He who is not angry when there is just cause for anger is immoral. Why? Because anger looks to the good of justice. And, if you can live among injustice without anger, you are immoral as well as unjust."
Thomas Aquinas

Like Shakespeare said, something was rotten in Denmark. I'm no Shakespeare, but I am here to warn you that something is rotten in America too. We no longer resemble the country our Founders envisioned, the land of life, liberty, and the pursuit of happiness. The causes for our American rottenness are many. Even worse, they are not accidental. Those intent on bringing about the "rotten" situation planned and implemented their agenda with patience and precision. The architects of this decay pursued their goal methodically. In many ways they were assisted by the indolence and indifference of the rest of us. When you realize what's happening, there is every reason to be angry about it. If you are not, given the conditions facing our country today, then as Aquinas said, you may be immoral.

How did this happen? Immorality, borne of a departure from God, gave us over to disorder and so many ills, not the least of which is the loss of our freedoms. We tolerated what should not have been tolerated. Hypocrites were admired and elevated in stature, not punished. We lost our discernment as to the encroachment of evil. We lost our understanding of cause and effect. We became lazy and apathetic. We became cozy with the lie and began to live out our lives in a lie. We overlooked injustice and found so many ways to suppress the condemnation of our own guilt by redefining sin. In the chaos we asked "why," when we knew why and at the core was a church that had gone astray. That too was planned while so many within were asleep. In a world governed by evil there is never time for sleep, sloth, or indolence. Evil never sleeps.

This book addresses all the areas wherein we, as a nation, as a society, have gone astray, as well as discussing the *what, when,* and *where.* There is no cure within, but there are things of which we must be aware and things that can and should be done, if not for the sake of the country, then for the sake of your own soul.

The core of the problem, the rot, if you will, in America is often misunderstood by those wondering what has happened. However, the core of the problem is not by accident or by simple miscalculation, but rather one of design and intentional implementation. The first part of the book deals with the core, the second part deals with all the symptoms and connects the dots, and the third part deals with the cure and the way back, if possible.

However, I am not here to preach down to you or sound like I've never suffered from the serious confusion that is plaguing our nation. So, to begin, let me share a personal story about a time when I was misled by some of the architects of rottenness—and what it took for me to see the light.

Feasting on the Truth: How One D.C. Dinner Party Changed My Life

Looks can be deceiving. Of course, we all know that—or at least we tell ourselves that we do. Still, it's an essential truth to state clearly at the very outset. In this book, I will make some direct and blunt statements supported by facts and evidence. Even as I plan to put my finger right on the beating "heart of darkness" animating our current social and political crisis here in America, I want to acknowledge and recognize that as a young man, I myself had fallen victim to misinformation.

I've been around the sun—and the courtroom, and the political world—enough times that I've learned how to spot the lies and the incongruencies characteristic of various players. One story from my many years of fighting for truth, the absolute truth, helps to illustrate what I mean. Hopefully, you will relate as you journey back with me to a remarkable moment in my career.

The year was circa 1997. The scene was our nation's Capital. I had traveled to Washington, D.C. with my friend, Colonel Ronald D. Ray. Ray was the recipient of the Purple Heart, served as a Deputy Assistant

Secretary of Defense under President Ronald Reagan, and was appointed by President George H.W Bush to serve on the American Battle Monuments Commission. But Col. Ray was also a mentor and close friend; by his invitation, I accompanied him and his wife, Eunice, to D.C. as he had a scheduled appearance on one of the nightly ABC news shows for an interview.

During that trip, we went to a mutual friend's house in the Georgetown area for dinner. To grant the family privacy, I will refer to the friend as Pam. Pam was a socialite and conducted a salon for political soirées. There were about ten people present (an intimate gathering), including Admiral Thomas Moorer, who was chairman of the Joint Chiefs of Staff from 1970 to 1974, and Mr. G., whose identity I will disclose later. Also present were Col. Tom McKenney and Monica Jensen Stevenson, an Emmy Award-winning producer of 60 Minutes. After cocktails, we settled down for dinner in front of the fireplace for the most engaging conversation I can ever recall, and an evening I'll never forget.

The military brass delivered detailed play-by-plays about their encounters with President Nixon (whose inaugural committee I worked in 1973). It was equal parts gripping and gruesome. They shared some of the most intimate details about decision-making surrounding the Vietnam War; how it was done and how the Democrats played into it. If there was any virginity of my ears left, it was lost that night. Not in a profane way, per se, but I learned things about the world and our government I had never known before, and, specifically, how evil corruption cost so many lives. I never saw things the same again. Indeed, if there is any ultimate justice in this existence, there must be a blast furnace in hell loaded with politicians (not all, there are some good public servants, but sadly I'd say most).

The pivotal point in the conversation was when they recounted how Nixon cried over the boys left behind in Vietnam. Nixon wept over the fact that he knew some of our troops were getting left behind, but the Marxist cabal in the Democrat party was too fixated on eliminating Nixon to care about such things. They wanted to take him out, not for a crime but for a cover-up. Yet this was when the Democrats were also engaged in profound corruption. One of those corrupt but ruthless figures at the time—who put Nixon in his crosshairs—was none other than our current president, Joe Biden.

Be that as it may, Nixon was too wrapped up in Watergate to be able to salvage our men, and the Democrats couldn't care less as they were of the same ideological mentality as the forces that took over South Vietnam. They knew there was blood in the water and wanted the head of the President, who gained fame in his younger years by rooting out communists within our government. At the end of the day, the Democrats, who had dominated Congress at the time for decades, cost the lives of over 50,000 men. Psalm 109 is a fitting prayer for politicians who commit such heinous acts.

As mentioned, Monica Jensen Stevenson was there, too. She had written a book called, *Kiss the Boys Goodbye: How the United States Betrayed Its Own POWS in Vietnam*. My conversation with her was riveting. She had produced a masterful piece of investigation that was so piercing and revealing. Her book was a best seller. She exposed the flaw and the coverup and how our men were left behind only to suffer at the hands of communists.

Now, this is important for you to know: The last POW to come home was a man named Bobby Garwood. From all the news accounts on TV and in the papers, I had been convinced he was a traitor, and I loathed him from afar.

Thankfully, Monica had not taken the news about Garwood at face value; considering she worked in that industry, she knew better.

Along with *Kiss the Boys Goodbye*, Monica had recently finished a second book, *Spite House: The Last Secret of the War in Vietnam*, wherein she told the story of Marine Private Bobby Garwood.

One particular review summarizes *Spite House* incredibly well:

> This book uses impressive spadework to tell the story of what its subtitle calls "the last secret of the war in Vietnam," namely, what really happened in the case of Marine Private Bobby Garwood, the last soldier to return from the war alive. He returned in 1979, after 14 years missing in action. Jensen-Stevenson, a former Sixty Minutes producer, managed to get on the record people who have spent years staying off it: several well-placed military

intelligence figures and Garwood (court-martialed for consorting with the enemy upon his return) himself. The main contentions of the book are that Garwood didn't desert but was captured after a firefight, that despite the sorts of lapses that virtually all Vietnam POWs fell prey to from time to time, he remained a loyal American throughout an incredibly arduous captivity, and most explosively of all: that before his return, based on the idea that he was a defector, there was an organized effort by U.S. forces to assassinate him. Readers will conclude that the Garwood case needs re-opening.[8]

Just like McKenney was once convinced Garwood was a traitor, I had been fooled as well. However, that night, in stunned amazement, I learned the truth as I was sitting across from both having dinner.

That's right. Garwood (Mr. G.), and McKenney (target and alleged assassin appointee) were both there, in front of me, as close friends. And yet just a few years earlier, McKenney believed that Garwood was worthy of death for desertion, all because of a government psychological operation and misleading media reporting.

Monica's reporting uncovered the truth. And the truth set McKenney free. That night, it set me free as well. I remember standing in the archway between the living room and the hall with Monica for the longest time, shocked as I heard what telling the truth had cost her. I also talked with Bobby for quite some time as I battled the guilt of my previous feelings toward him. I was not only fighting the guilt of my former ill will toward him, but I was outraged at the lies that were told and how I had been deceived. I realized I was a victim of a sophisticated deception. Like you, I hate being lied to. When you discover it, you are enraged.

There I was, having dinner with Mr. Garwood, and his once-appointed nemesis, McKenney, surprisingly now the best of friends. I saw a divine and cosmic force at work on display right in front of me. Here was McKenney, and his target, a soldier who suffered torture for 14 years

---

8   Editorial Review of *Spite House: The Last Secret of the War*, by Monica Jensen, Amazon.com, accessed on December 12, 2022, https://www.amazon.com/Spite-House-Last-Secret-Vietnam/dp/0393040410.

for a country indifferent and hostile to him as well as many Vietnam War Veterans. This country, at the time, was unworthy of the protections he and others were providing it. I know it all too well as I lived through the hell of radical protesters and the lack of respect for those who came back after the war. They were just young men, serving to protect their country.

This is an important aside. The media was complicit in the loss of the Vietnam War—even though there was a point when we already had it won, despite the gross mismanagement. One of the primary sources that turned public opinion against the war was in fact one man who was then known and considered as the "most trusted man in the news"—Walter Cronkite. Since enough already has been written about him, I'll leave you with this quote from Cronkite and let you decide what to think:

> I'm in a position to speak my mind and, by God, I'm going to do it. First, we Americans are going to have to yield up some of our sovereignty. That's going to be for many a bitter pill.

> Today, we must develop federal structures on a global level to deal with world problems. We need a system of enforceable world law, a democratic federal world government. Most importantly, we should sign and ratify the treaty for a permanent international criminal court. That is now at the core of the world federalist movement's drive. That court will enable the world to hold individuals accountable for their crimes against humanity...

> ...Our failure to live up to our obligations to the United Nations is led by a handful of willful senators who choose to pursue their narrow, selfish political objectives at the cost of our nation's conscience. They pander to and are supported by the Christian Coalition and the rest of the religious right wing. Their leader, Pat Robertson, has written in a book a few years ago that we should have a world government but only when the Messiah arrives...He (Robertson) wrote, "Any attempt to achieve world order before that time must be the work of the devil."

Well, join me. I'm glad to sit here at the right hand of Satan.[9]

I think Cronkite most likely got his wish. Who knows, maybe what we suffer today in this nation is a divine judgment, and considering our collective moral corruption, one that we deserve.

And this is important to know about me and this book. Hearing Garwood's story, and having my eyes opened that night, helped me realize just how far down the rabbit hole the media and government lies went, and how these kinds of lies were disconnecting Americans from the truth. Perhaps the politicians and their proxies in the media can be roommates in hell.

Garwood's poor, tragic life could be seen in his face and the way he walked. Once a young man, doing his duty and full of hope for the future, became imprisoned and tortured for 14 years—only to be betrayed by his own country because of the optics, because of corrupt politicians playing God. He was an uncomfortable truth and proof that men were left behind. Garwood was apparently a scapegoat. I know this all too well from the accounts of the time. I was traumatized by the notion that our men were being left behind in the hands of communists and I was enraged that the Democrats would sacrifice them over their lusts and fixations to bring Nixon down. Not much has changed today as we recall how President Biden left many Americans and allies behind in his hasty and disastrous withdrawal from Afghanistan.

I will never forget the time I spent with Garwood. I was humbled by his presence. He lit a fire in me to oppose the corruption within our system of government and seek justice. And McKenney's story—from purported assassin to friend—lit another fire in me. It wasn't enough to know the truth, I also had to help make sure the truth was known by others. Furthermore, I realized that the men and women in the media and the government who ascend to power without any moral compass cannot be trusted and must be held accountable. However, my wrath is

9   Walter Cronkite, "1991 Norman Cousins Global Governance Award Speech," Investment Watch Blog, accessed December 12, 2022, https://www.investmentwatchblog.com/one-world-government-walter-cronkite-im-glad-to-sit-at-the-right-hand-of-satan/.

hottest against those who allowed them to ascend to such positions of power and influence.

This was a night that I never wanted to end. My head was about to explode with all the revelations, facts, and truths which were revealed by this stellar group of people in the know and at the highest levels of their professions. Before that night, I never knew what I didn't know about Bobby Garwood—or for that matter our government and media. I thought I had the facts and the truth. Why would anyone lie about that? I had bought the Big Lie that he was a deserter and a traitor, hook, line, and sinker. Why didn't I seek out the truth myself? At first, I was naïve and had misplaced trust in the government. Then I realized that this was happening all over our nation, at a much deeper level than previously anticipated. No more would I blindly trust. The lies had to be fought— and I was going to fight them, both for my life and for others.

As I left Georgetown that night, I knew then that life was going to be a fight. It was truly a Matrix moment. I took the red pill (more on that later) and I haven't been the same since.

Clearly the government, media, and now big corporations, at any level, could not be trusted. Even worse, it was apparent from the candid stories I heard that the government (for the most part) attracts the worst of humanity. I was awakened to the whorish hell of this world and particularly in politics and the lies of the media, who only serve themselves while the people go neglected.

To that end, I have given my life in pursuit and defense of the truth. I have done this in the courtroom, the classroom, and the public square. I've worked to elect state and federal officials who believe and are committed to the truth, stand on principle, and are willing to push back against the darkness of lies and propaganda.

I've been in this fight for decades. Now, I want to help others get their footing in this fight for the truth. I want to help you understand what the fight *really* is, how you are being manipulated, how to counterpunch, and how to win. Because today we face delusions on a mass scale and with much more sinister consequences. Right now, there are millions walking around America, willing to commit violence based on total lies. The McKenney of yesteryear believed the lie and was operating in good conscience considering that false belief. Today, some are acting in good conscience as well, but the majority are acting in bad faith with a corrupt agenda based upon a pathological ideology stemming from hate and resentment of who you are and what you have. They are manipulating you with lies, grooming you, and detaching you from reality.

What lies at the root of this mass delusion is what I develop in this book. And after you are done reading, I hope you are willing to disabuse yourselves of the lies, question everything, and join the fight for truth and be willing to live in the truth as well. The very future of our nation depends on it. Your very life, liberty, property, and happiness depend on it, as does your soul.

PART ONE

CHAPTER 1:

Our American Psychosis

"He who dares not offend cannot be honest."
Thomas Paine

Attention: As is the habit of so many, they skip the preface and introduction and dive into the main content of the book. Don't do that here, because it will be like starting to watch a movie in the middle. If you haven't read the preface and the introduction, let me recommend going back and doing so now.

Reality Seekers Wanted

Thomas Paine's quote is so appropriate for today as so many feign offense as a means to block the truth. Truth by its very nature is offensive because we live lives of lies in this fallen world. However, before we go dissecting the lie and the truth, let's talk about the lovers of truth and the lovers of lies, and that leads to the audience this book will and will not appeal to.

Most books have a specific audience (except for the Bible, which is for all of mankind). Writers write to hit a target. Not every book is universal in appeal and application. This book is no exception (though I hope the truths contained herein are universal). My audience is a particular crowd—and I do hope you are a part of that crowd. I aim to write to those who are lovers of life, liberty, and happiness, which only the truth can provide. Now, we live in a day and age full of contested truth claims.

3

However, there is still "true" truth—grounded in objective and verifiable reality, not the subjective and postmodern kind of truth, "my truth," "your truth," etc. Pope John Paul II reminded his listeners of this at an outdoor mass in Poland in 1991. He said, "We cannot simply possess freedom; we must constantly fight for it. We fight for it by putting it to good use and using it in the cause of truth."

I aim to write as part of those working for the cause of truth. And I aim to write to those who still maintain and exercise some degree of critical thinking, common sense, and a moral compass. I'm writing to those who are still capable of connecting the dots and bringing clarity to the situation in which they find themselves (even if that clarity doesn't bring comfort). I hope that it will motivate others, give them direction and insight as to who their real enemies are (and yes, "enemy" is a real word because there is such a thing and the word means someone or something that harms or weakens someone or something else), and provide a roadmap to a better future. This book also, unapologetically, intends to shame some of those who know better but don't, could do better but aren't, yet may still be motivated to change their indolent ways.

In a not-so-subtle way, this book will castigate and offend those who are evil and endeavoring to destroy people's lives. Yes, good and evil exist, and evil people exist. You spend billions on movies every year where you watch good and evil battle it out. If evil people pick this book up and read it, I hope they find a sharp rebuke for their efforts to destroy the liberty and happiness of their fellow countrymen. They are trading it all for a dystopian delusion where they become the oppressive controllers of others' lives in pursuit of permanent power. By doing so, they hope to salvage their own wretched existence. That is the group that desires to become, at any cost, a permanent governing elite. They are dysfunctional, resentful, self-loathing and will do you harm. So, this book is not for them because they won't accept its diagnosis nor take its prescription for a cure. They are fools, the fools of Proverbs—and fools never listen.

So, I have the lazy critical thinkers on the Right and active fools on the Left. However, another audience for this book is those in the middle who are not engaged in the fight as it stands today. They live their daily lives not knowing that those lives are about to be permanently interrupted (though they got a good preview with the fake COVID lockdowns). They probably could do something and would if only they knew. However, they don't join the fight because they don't know. I'm here to let them know—starting now.

Some people I will write to. Others I will be writing about. Another purpose of this book is to further identify and expose those who do (or should) know better. They are people in positions of leadership but have failed or are failing in the face of our civilizational collapse. These people are cowardly and not engaged in this existential fight. They are blind guides who refused to act to save themselves and those they took an oath to protect. Hopefully, connecting the dots for that group, and pointing the finger of shame at those who should do better, will motivate them both to reform their conduct and start acting commensurate with the responsibilities of their position and power.

A few years back I was having a conversation with one of our U.S. Senators, a Republican, and I asked in frustration, "What is wrong with Republicans, particularly ones like Liz Cheney and Mitt Romney?!" And he told me, "Jack, there are two types of Republicans: one is an opportunist, and the other is philosophical. The philosophical will hold to their professed conservative principles, and the opportunist will never risk his or her position for a principle." Several years ago, I would have said that dichotomy probably applied only to the Democrats, but they have become such a homogenized group that there is no distinction or independent thought amongst them as they vote collectively only for their self-interests.

In addressing the premise of this book with others, there was a not-so-unexpected response, and that was, "Wow, you're right but won't that be controversial?" My response was, "Exactly, and that is how you get a conversation started." For the most part, those on the Left never want to dialogue, since that requires dealing with facts that refuse to align with their narrative.

For as long as humans have occupied this world there have been arguments and disagreements. Usually, the psychos win. Those in the wrong usually win the war of ideas, often with terrible consequences like Neville Chamberlain's pacifism that allowed Hitler to grow stronger and eventually start World War II. Lenin, Stalin, and Mao Zedong also won the "argument," but they were grievously wrong. Many of those who believed them and followed them died. Castro was wrong but won the argument.

Dr. Anthony Fauci was wrong but he and his companion, Dr. Deborah Birx, won the argument. They were wrong, but millions followed them, and millions died. To make this even richer, Birx wrote a book, *Silent Invasion: The Untold Story of the Trump Administration, COVID-19, and Preventing the Next Pandemic Before It's Too Late*, essentially admitting they lied. Biden and his entire team of clowns (just look at their pictures and listen to them talk and you will see the term clown is not ad hominem) won the argument on Afghanistan, Ukraine, shutting down oil production, spending trillions, etc. They were wrong and you paid for it.

So, you can take issue with the premise of the book if you wish, but facts are facts. The trajectory of the country is clearly in decline, and the policies and plans of the Left are not normative, they defy reality—they are *psychotic*.

Normal vs. Deviant: Understanding How the Psychosis is Sold

Before we delve into systemic psychosis, it's worthy of note that two words must be understood. The first is *normal* or *normalcy* (the condition of being normal) as it relates to the human condition and society. "Normal" refers to that condition, which is healthy, usual, productive, thriving, and necessary for the prospering of humanity, particularly as humanity is organized into countries with their own cultures. The second word is the opposite of normal, and that is *deviant* or *deviancy*, that is, abnormal. Deviance is that which is bizarre, idiosyncratic, and strange. It is unhealthy.

For example, the Left has focused the nation's attention, promulgated legislation, and developed policies forcing 98% of the nation to conform to only 1.6% of those in society who are deviant, as if it were normative. That would be the self-identified transsexual portion of the population. Let's make this clear, 98% is the normative, and 1.6% (which is probably high), by definition, obviously deviates from the norm. They are not the norm in society; and if you are not the norm, then you are, by definition, deviant from the norm. It is not normal thinking. Therefore, it is irrational that some want to treat 1.6% of the population as if they were the norm of society.

As a quick sidebar, for those who legitimately have gender dysphoria (and I say legitimately because it is so subjective) their mental dysfunction may be a real deviance, but it is a psychological condition from a medical perspective, not a physical condition. Nevertheless, it is still a deviation from the norm. It is contrary to reality and therefore a psychotic condition that leads us to systemic psychosis. To twist the definition of deviance in such a way as to make it normative is psychotic. That is a departure from reality. That's not to say that all those struggling with gender dysphoria are experiencing something that is not "real" (it's only a reality in their minds), but that it is not normative for society at large and you don't force society to restructure to accept deviance as normative.

Where is this heading? Dr. Jordan Peterson equated those who indoctrinate small children with gender theory and encourage the mutilation of their bodies or the use of puberty blockers as demonic. He even likened it to the sacrifice of children to Molech. More and more people are seeing the demonic character and influence behind the psychotic mindset of so much of the chaos that has erupted in this country and throughout the west in the last decade. It's as if the gates of hell were opened and demons flooded the world; there is no other explanation for the mass onset of insanity and human destruction going on. This is not a new science or discovery of fact or reality that society has stumbled upon. It is the very evil that has brought down great civilizations in the past and it happened in large part because the good guys simply did nothing. However, this is how psychosis is sold. The deviant becomes redefined as normal. The danger to society is that with that kind of mental dysfunction, judgment is impaired; and those with impaired judgment should not be allowed in areas where society could be harmed. Just like we don't allow alcoholics to be airline pilots, we should never let pedophiles be daycare workers.

Systemic Psychosis

The focus of this book is the pervasive and underlying cause of the chaos being experienced in the country. Many on the Right seem perplexed at the insanity, hypocrisy, and radical measures proposed by the Left. The Right incessantly asks why. They do so because they can't seem to come to grips with the core of the problem. The Left is metaphorically forcing everyone to accept that the moon is made of green cheese; that 1.6% is greater than 98.4%. This has been the unchallenged modus operandi of the Left for decades. They are dishonest with the numbers. They disingenuously and falsely extrapolate the size of deviant parts of society and attempt to get the normative to accept and conform to the deviant. They often create the deviant in society, making them a class of victims as well as making victimhood something they all have in common. The Left weaves this patchwork of deviant victims into a voting majority. They have done this through intersectionality wherein they create a psychotic fraternity, mobilizing them to come together as a voting bloc.

The psychosis on the Right is shown by how, time and time again, they fail to educate society as to the reality of a situation. While they fail on this front, the Left presses on because they are master provocateurs. It leaves many people stunned that any rational human could lie to such a profound degree and not suffer humiliating ostracization from normal society. However, that is exactly what is happening. The more profane and absurd the Left gets, the more the Right becomes paralyzed in their foolhardy attempts to analyze and understand the (insane) reasoning behind the Left's actions. The Right has a "paralysis induced by analysis." What they need to do is to stop asking "why" and start fighting back (more on this later).

In law school one is taught to sift through a plethora of extraneous facts that don't have any relevance to the primary issue to be addressed and the problem to be solved. If you can't do that, or if you are easily distracted and confused by the out-of-place facts and issues thrown your way, you will never make it as an attorney, much less pass the law exam.

By God's grace, I have been gifted and trained with the ability to tune out the noise and focus on the signal, and the relevant data dealing with the issue at hand. I'm here to help us sift. There is something at the center of our national issues that needs to be exposed and addressed. In many ways, the Right has been hitting the target but missing the bullseye. However they need to get right to it and deliver the kill shot if they are going to help our country avoid devolving into a dystopian nightmare.

So, here we have the Right side of the body politic confused and wringing their hands as the Left is taking the country over the proverbial cliff. The Right is seemingly impotent to do anything about it. And they can't do anything if they don't even know what is at the core of the problem.

Too often the Right acts like a doctor (ineffectively) treating a patient with aspirin when the patient's core problem is cancer. The Right simply cannot keep up, spinning its wheels trying to address the litany of symptoms created by the Left's false narrative assembly line. The Right keeps barking about what doesn't work, what is unconstitutional, what is immoral, what is fiscally irresponsible, etc. But they haven't figured out that our body politic has *cancer*. As long as they keep focusing on the symptoms, i.e., the false narratives, they will never address the cause of the problem. And by doing this they are almost as much a part of the problem as those who are intentionally creating all the problems and chaos. The Right wastes time trying to figure out the Left. That gets no one nearer to fixing the problem. So, what is the Right to do? I will address that later in the book.

Let us cut through the chaos—the issue is *systemic psychosis*. What do I mean by that?

Psychosis Defined

Psychosis is a severe mental disorder in which thoughts and emotions are so impaired that contact is lost with external reality. In short, psychosis occurs when people lose contact with the truth and the world as it really is. Not all psychosis renders one nonfunctional, often just unpredictable and dangerous. This is the real pandemic of our time. We have lost contact with reality. The psychotics have been allowed to occupy the stage of life and governance.

This isn't a condition that is confined only to the occasional weak-minded individual who has fallen into a state of mental illness. This can and has occurred to entire cultures and societies. That happens through something known as a "mass formation psychosis."

Here are some examples of the symptoms of psychosis as it has played out in our country and has been encouraged by the leftist cabal through their agenda. However, the psychosis doesn't end with the Left. It includes all of those who, with the exercise of common sense and diligence, could have avoided acting out in a psychotic way but didn't.

We saw this very clearly with behavior during the COVID-19 "pandemic." Dr. Robert Malone, an American biochemist and one of the inventors of the mRNA vaccine technology addressed this issue. He explained how this mass-scale societal delusion is what happened in Germany when the Nazis were taking over. The same thing happened in America with our reaction to COVID. Malone said the condition occurs when a society "becomes decoupled from each other and has free-floating anxiety and a sense that things don't make sense…And then their attention gets focused by a leader or series of events on one small point, just like hypnosis."[10] Now you can see the strategy and necessity for the government to lock you in your homes.

Sound familiar?

Think about the stories of people disinfecting the mail. Look at the people still wearing masks alone in their cars. Does that sound like what normal people who know the truth and are connected to reality do?

As recently revealed by the "Twitter Files," the FBI and the government were complicit in suppressing the truth about COVID and even censored top scientists and medical doctors just to keep the lie alive. Economies collapsed. Hundreds of thousands died because of the planned and coordinated agenda of the psychos in charge of your life. The utter absurdity of it was seen in how the "medical establishment" that was on board with the government agenda did things like make up a random unit of distance—"six feet"—and we all obliged by standing dutifully on those stupid circles on the floors of stores.

It was madness. It was *psychosis*.

While many often think being "psychotic" is something horrible that happens just to a random person or someone with a severe mental illness, the truth is far more ordinary. However, when it occurs on a mass scale due to unchecked, undisciplined behaviors manifested in a compounding sequence, that becomes a perfect societal storm. It starts with a drift from a moral compass, objective principles, accepted norms, the rule of law, and a common language in the form of fixed meanings, given words, and terms.

---

10   Robert Malone, "#1757 - Dr. Robert Malone, MD," The Joe Rogan Experience, Spotify.com, accessed October 28, 2022, https://open.spotify.com/episode/3SCsueX2bZdbEzRtKOCEyT.

And that's what is happening in America today.

I want to be clear: There are two kinds of psychosis with which we are dealing. You could call it "naturally occurring" vs. "manufactured." However, given we are dealing with a matter of the mind, I think "organic" vs. "inorganic" is a better framing.

Systemic Psychosis: Is It Organic or Inorganic?

The question now is whether nationwide psychosis is organic or inorganic. Some have said that a psychopath is *born*, but a sociopath is *made*. However, I think that we can make psychopaths too, whether we mean to or not (and mark my words, some people certainly mean to make them). The Left loves creating a new victim class that they can add to their voting bloc.

Remember, psychosis is mostly referred to by the medical community as an organic (that is, naturally occurring) mental disease. In individual cases, that is certainly true. However, if people like Robin DiAngelo can peddle books with made up terms like "white fragility," selling thousands of copies in her woke grift, then there is no reason that I can't try to provide a helpful, pithy description of our current ailment (to which DiAngelo has certainly contributed).

Here, I am primarily using the term inorganic psychosis to refer to a manufactured systemic psychosis (it couldn't be widespread any other way). The indoctrinations being implemented and forced upon children in schools today are mentally disabling future generations from being able to separate fact from fiction, or reality from fantasy. Our country is mass-producing psychotics.

It is being foisted upon even the adult population, much like communist re-education camps. The result is a person is rendered incapable of processing facts in relation to reality or deductively reasoning to proper conclusions. These are conclusions that have beneficial results for the individual and the community in which he or she lives, both now and in the future. In other words, conclusions connected to the truth are unreachable for those who have been indoctrinated into a psychotic state of mind.

We are not dealing with organic psychosis here but an inorganic, manufactured psychosis that vitiates the mental faculties through deception, fear tactics, disinformation, and paranoia. The results of such a disability are seen in how those affected by it think, act, and behave.

As a backdrop to the analysis of the organic or inorganic nature of the systemic psychosis in this country, one need only look at the consequences and stark contrasts in the short period between 2020 and 2021.

Examples of the Spread of Psychosis

In less than two years, America has gone from the most economically prosperous, militarily strong, and at-peace country in the world, to one that is in economic collapse, with wide open borders, and facing a resurgent Russia and an ascendant Imperial Chinese Communist Party poised to invade Taiwan. Our markets lost trillions, wealth evaporated, and instead of focusing on our national problems, we are instead shipping billions overseas to fund the corrupt kleptocracy of Ukraine. Make no mistake, I'm no Russian apologist, but your government has lied to you about Ukraine. Look into the eyes of both the Ukrainian and Russian young soldiers on TV. You can see they want none of this, they don't want to kill anyone, and they just want to be left alone to live their lives. It's now estimated that at least 400,000 Russians and Ukrainian soldiers (combined) have died, and that's not counting civilians, a true tragedy. Whatever the total number is, there has been a massive and needless loss of life.

This may be a difficult truth to contemplate, but in 1963 when Russia attempted to put nuclear missiles in Cuba, we nearly had a nuclear war as we blockaded Cuba and were not going to allow Russian nukes 90 miles from our shores. We stared the Russians down—and they backed off. After the collapse of the Soviet Union in the 1990s, the West made certain implied promises to Russia regarding the limits of future NATO expansion. In our modern moment, in many ways, Ukraine is to Russia what Cuba is to the U.S., except this time we are feeling all the costs on the home front. The war has caused hyperinflation, food shortages, and energy shortages. It has cost the American taxpayer tens of billions of dollars and the inflation-equivalent of a full month's worth of income from each American citizen. If this sounds insane and counter to American national interest, that's because it is. However, this is what we get when we have psychotics running the country and controlling our foreign policy.

Prior to Biden's election, it was widely known in the Senate and broader foreign policy circles that all of Biden's foreign policy positions in his forty-plus years in the Senate were total disasters and utter failures, without exception. Yet, the public voted for him anyway and are now paying for it dearly.

How could this happen? How could people select one over the other? Because they no longer realize that their decisions have consequences. We have lost the understanding of cause and effect. The people of this country selected the misery they are now experiencing. They voted for it. Normal critical thinkers would not do this. Why did they vote for "Hidin' Biden" over Donald Trump? Forget the personalities. I'm not making any apologies for or promoting Trump but simply stating the facts. Look at the policies and how they affected your lives. You were gaslighted, lied to, and manipulated to vote based on personality or perceived personality as opposed to the issues that affect your daily life. You are now paying the consequences of an imposed psychosis. This is the political version of a personal "cutting" disorder—willfully inflicting harm upon oneself.

Recent polling data reveals that those who had been living in the most prosperous period of this country's history, having broken all measuring data for economic performance, chose to kick out of office the man and his team *responsible* for such astounding performances. Give me a robot who exercises decisions based on the overall good of the people. I don't need to be in love with or even like my president or leaders. I just want them to make good decisions based on facts and reality.

So many have this bizarre need for a human god, a king, or a demigod that they can love and adore. Had they not forsaken the God of the universe, they would be more focused on selecting leaders as employees, expecting good performance based on their job description, not someone worthy of their adoration. Instead, they fall for these false gods which always disappoint and bring destruction.

Now, lest I be guilty of psychosis and seemingly looking for a utopia myself, I acknowledge that having a robot to serve us in dispassionate and purely logical ways beneficial for all would be asking for a perfect world, and it won't happen this side of heaven. However, it serves to exemplify how irrational it is to vote for someone who will deplete your wealth, indoctrinate your children, diminish your standard of living, and threaten your life with increased crime and nuclear war. Ask yourself, did you really just do that to yourself and the nation? If so, you may want to consider that you are not correctly processing reality like someone living in the real world.

Recall how the English kicked out Prime Minister Winston Churchill immediately after he won World War II and saved England. In the 2020 elections we hoisted ourselves upon our own petards, voting for a cognitively impaired, near octogenarian figurehead who is not in control. Look at the disaster that has occurred in just two years.

How could this be? One word: psychosis.

Instead of keeping the much-needed American boom going, the people elected a man clearly in cognitive decline with a moron (from the Greek μωρός, meaning foolish, dull, stupid, idiotic) for a Vice President. Even among the Left, she gives them a painful cringe factor when she tries to piece together a coherent thought. And when Biden speaks you can see in the faces of his staff that they are suffering from hypoxia, holding their collective breaths in fear of what he is about to say. Even they know he's not all there. He's just a useful puppet.

Of course, there are lingering and substantial questions as to the legitimacy of that election, but suffice it to say, whether it was won or lost by one percent or by hook or crook, that is not the issue here, but rather the conduct of the people that is most alarming. The cognition (or lack thereof) that has caused them to act as they did, against their own self-interest, resulting in the abject disaster in which we all now find ourselves, can only be described as evidence of mass, inorganic psychosis. Under the circumstances, one cannot be too sympathetic.

Polling from October of 2022 (less than two years after electing a clearly mentally disabled man for President) revealed that nearly 75% of the respondents disapprove of the direction of the country, and 60%+ disapprove of President Biden's performance and think he is not fit for office. The country is in chaos on every front. One would think that this is a good poll, for it would seem to reveal that the people have awakened to their error. Not so fast. Let's not look at the 75%. Let's look at the 25%. That's an amazing number given the chaos and decline in the country.

That is a most troubling number. I can be 75% free of cancer but the 25% will surely kill me. It's that nasty, abnormal, non-functioning 25%, a permanent, embedded, noncognitive, non changing, irrational segment of society that will eventually destroy the 75%. This was the concern of Socrates about the dangers of democracy. Democracy has embedded within it the seeds of its own destruction because it always trends toward tyranny. Let me clear this up for some: We have a democratic republic, not a pure democracy (God forbid). Far too many lazily refer to America as a democracy as opposed to a republic—stop it.

This general survey regarding the President's approval and the direction of the country is even worse, as most polling in advance of the November 2022 midterm elections showed a 45/55 split or closer across the country in various jurisdictions. This is a major incongruity that can only be explained by mass psychosis. Nearly 1/2 of the country, despite the overwhelming evidence of societal collapse, is willing to vote for more of the same. It is a collective national suicide.

And make no mistake, through mass unchecked illegal immigration, fake news media programming, and government lies, the purveyors of this inorganic psychosis plan to turn that 25% into a permanent ruling majority. The native population is being replaced by another culture, one wholly unfamiliar with the principles that made America great.

Millions of illegal immigrants are refusing to assimilate into our American way of life. Even worse, they seem oblivious to the proliferation of the same tactics here in America, pushed by the Left, that the socialists and Marxists used against them to turn their own formerly prosperous nations into poor, failing dictatorships. The same ideological forces that drove millions of immigrants out of their homes in South America are at work today in Texas, New York, and California. We are gaslighted with emotional appeals that it's only fair and compassionate. They're playing on our emotions, the noncognitive part of our brains, as they further their hidden agendas.

However, what causes 25% or more of the people, during such dire conditions as we are in now, to still think things are well? I'm reminded of a story that Dr. R. C. Sproul used to tell, that makes the point of irrationality.

Once there was this couple, and one morning the wife goes to wake up her husband for work. She walks into the bedroom and says, "Charlie, get up you have to go to work." Charlie says, "I can't." The wife replied, "Why can't you?" Charlie answered her, "Because I'm dead." The wife says, "Don't be silly, I'm talking to you, get up!"

However, Charlie stubbornly insisted that he was dead. So, the wife called the doctor, and the doctor came over. He took all of Charlie's vital signs and pronounced to Charlie that he was alive and well. Yet, once again, Charlie refused to get up, insisting he couldn't since he was dead.

So, the doctor said to Charlie, "Ok. I will prove to you that you are alive." The doctor and Charlie's wife took Charlie down to the morgue and pulled out a cadaver. He takes a pin, sticks the cadaver in the toe with it, and then says to Charlie, "See Charlie, dead people don't bleed." Then the doctor took the pin and stuck one of Charlie's fingers and he bled. The doctor said to Charlie, "See you're bleeding. So, what do you think now?"

Charlie replied, "Wow, I guess dead people do bleed after all."

The moral of that humorous story is no matter how much evidence exists, some people, in fact, *many* people, will refuse to be rational; they have an endless reservoir of excuses and reject all truth that is inconvenient to their cognitive dissonance, their psychosis. I'm sure most of you have dealt with this type before.

Some want to say, "Well it's a matter of opinion." To that, we must say, "No, not all opinions are equal." And this is not just a matter of a benign difference of opinion, this is a terminal disagreement. There is a malignancy that is killing the host. The host is the nation. And this inorganic psychosis is spreading. There can be no co-existence with those voting so irrationally. If we were talking about something isolated to just a person, just one blind fool, then fine. I wouldn't be writing this book. However, it's not. And when it affects others, then that opinion has no right to be on the platform, and undoubtedly so when it is killing the country in which we all live.

Karl Marx had an opinion that should have been snuffed out over 150 years ago. It wasn't. Consequently, well over 100,000,000 people lost their lives,[11] and 2 billion were enslaved because of the mental defect of this one perverse man. The right to act on an opinion with these kinds of consequences is not justified.

The psychosis may be inorganic—but that doesn't make it any less infectious or deadly. Mental illness is dangerous and most often it involves others close to the one that is ill.

Consider the tragic happenings in Uvalde, Texas. A mentally ill eighteen-year-old shot and killed 19 children and teachers. What was the response? The Left and the media, devoid of reason or facts, leaped to the opportunity that chaos always brings. They did so for the sole purpose of making another attempt to confiscate everyone's guns instead of focusing on the grieving families and the problem of the mental illness of the shooter. They feign concern but they care for no one. They care only for that which advances their authoritarian agenda.

A gun has no will of its own. The mental illness of the shooter is being ignored. The lack of understanding of cause and effect is on full display as well as the dishonest agenda of the Left.

The transparent agenda here by American authoritarians (akin to those in Russia, China, Venezuela, Cuba, North Korea, etc.) is that they don't like anyone having guns but them. Why? They know their policies don't work. They fear the eventual uprising of armed citizens, who would throw them out of office. As the saying goes, you can vote your way into socialism, but you'll have to shoot your way out. Of course, the would-be socialist dictators know that too, and so they want to get your guns. Many people fall for it! Why? Because they engage your emotions and disengage your mind. There is no syllogistic or deductive reasoning, no logic, and no common sense.

Here again, the people have been conditioned away from critical thinking. They cannot even *reason* since that has been, by design, educated out of them. It's called educated ignorance. It is a conditioning that leads to inorganic psychosis.

This is why I contend that with such a significant amount of perpetually irrational people in the country (approximately 25%+ and many

---

11   David Satter, "100 Years of Communism—and 100 Million Dead," *Wall Street Journal*, accessed October 28, 2022, https://www.wsj.com/articles/100-years-of-communismand-100-million-dead-1510011810.

of which I have dealt with in my profession), ultimately the psychotic behavior must be inorganic, albeit many are the "educated stupid." A small amount of it may be organic – people born without the capacity for reason – but with the great majority of the actors, it is inorganic, being manufactured through education, news reporting, social media, etc. A scene in the movie "Tár" with Cate Blanchett illustrates this well when responding to a belligerent woke student. After he verbally assaults her for not buying into his psychotic view of the world, she says, "The architect of your soul seems to be social media." This is where we are today as a country.

The overall point here is that this psychosis is both taught and caught. I would argue that we see evidence of the transmission of inorganic psychosis in the indifference toward the millions being allowed to illegally immigrate to this country. The open-borders Leftists allow this to happen, as stated, in hopes of creating a majority of easily controlled and dependent drones. This furthers their efforts to usher in an authoritarian, "uniparty" government with a select governing elite in permanent control, thus destroying this nation. It is not just the Left that is guilty. The Right, when they had control of all branches of government, failed to do anything about the immigration problem thanks to the pusillanimous opportunists who co opted the party and sold their souls to big corporate America. The country is being overrun and the indifference to the existential consequences is staggeringly psychotic.

In a conversation with an Uber driver who had escaped from Cuba, I asked, "Well, I guess you are glad to be free of the Castros?" He responded, "Oh, the Castros are great people." Surprised by this, I replied, "Well if they are so great why did you have to escape?"

I pressed no further, realizing from Proverbs you don't argue with a fool lest you become one. You say, "well his attitude is irrational and insane." Yes, it is. And that is why he was a slave in a communist state for most of his life, and his and other illegal immigrants' votes will make us all slaves.

This inorganic psychosis is also seen most profoundly in our education system. It is intentionally targeted at our school children. As Lenin once said, "Give me a child until he is five, and the seed that I plant will never be uprooted." That subject could be another book on its own but consider the moral deformation of our American public-school students. Throughout history, the purpose of education was to form and shape virtuous citizens who pursued the best thing in life, the good of themselves and their fellow man. However with radical gender theory, pornified sex education, and Critical Race Theory flooding the classrooms, not to mention decades of the failed experiment with Common Core, our nation has not been making citizens, but misshapen mental malcontents who hate their family, religion, and nation. Again, this didn't happen by accident. This didn't occur organically.

Now we see mothers across our country fighting back despite being labeled by the former Obama Supreme Court nominee and now Attorney General, Merrick Garland, as potential domestic terrorists. The question is how many of them voted for the Left? Is it too late to reverse the madness? Time will tell, but the prognosis is dim.

The bottom line is this: The evidence is in, and the psychosis is inorganic. It has been (and is being) manufactured, manipulated, and released into our society like a contagion, or a mind virus. It is also intentionally taught to our school children. And it is all part of a plan and agenda that has been implemented for decades. The long slow march through our institutions by the cultural Marxists has been amazingly successful. In the wake of their silent coup, those who look to the corrupted institutions for information receive poisoned transmissions of psychosis instead. Doubt me? Just try to find any diversity of thought in the media, higher education, Hollywood, Big Tech, and major corporations. Good luck.

Neurosis: The Fertilizer of Psychosis

Some people might argue that psychosis is too strong of an assessment and that what many of these "non-thinkers" are really dealing with is more of what you might call neurosis. I want to address this point because they are indeed related. They are so closely related it's like asking "Which came first, the chicken or the egg?"

Let me put it this way: Neurosis is to psychosis what socialism is to communism. It's the onramp, the gateway drug to our systemic psychosis. Consider how Merriam-Webster defines neurosis: "a mental and emotional disorder that affects only part of the personality, is accompanied by a less distorted perception of reality than in a psychosis, does not result in disturbance of the use of language, and is accompanied by various physical, physiological, and mental disturbances (such as visceral symptoms, anxieties, or phobias)."

Carl Jung, a Swiss psychiatrist and psychoanalyst who founded analytical psychology, explains neurosis in very similar terms. He argues that neurosis is a condition of overall anxiety and fear of life that is often accompanied by depression, phobias, obsessions, and endless ruminations, etc. Like psychosis, as I am defining for this book, it is also inorganic, but not as severe, because neurosis doesn't fully separate one from reality. Those who suffer from neurosis are useful tools for aspiring totalitarian governments due to their high levels of anxiety which produces in them a desire for safety and a willingness to conform.

You can observe great similarities between neurosis and psychosis. It destroys potential, instills false guilt, cowardice, laziness, and a debilitating paralysis from anxiety. Neurotics are often hypocrites (like psychotics) because their condition leads them to project their own failures or guilt upon others. You see this very clearly in the younger generations today.

The point here is that neurosis serves as the fertilizer of our mass psychosis today. People can only live in severe anxiety for so long until they seek refuge and relief in total delusion. And that's when a neurotic becomes a psychotic.

The chaos of today and the stew of neurotics and psychotics are kept in their state of mind through their addiction to technologies and the screens before which they waste their lives. They accomplish nothing and rely on a paternalistic government to do everything for them, not realizing that those we put in charge are the least capable and most corrupt. This elixir keeps people from accepting self-responsibility. We see this in today's generation as well as a lot of the left-over hippies of the 60's, many of whom never mentally grew into adulthood. Add to that the epidemic of drugs and a moral system that has collapsed with the absence of the church. This leaves no guidance to the virtues of self-reliance, courage, and an independence which is an essential to be cured of neurosis.

Many in this country are rightly concerned about the ongoing slide into Marxism or totalitarianism, but what they might not realize is that this is a form of "collectivism," and that is a direct byproduct of neurosis and what Jung calls "atrophied collective adaptation." These people (today's youth in their parents' basements) stand outside of life, neglecting many normal duties, whether in social achievement or day-to-day human tasks. In many of his lectures, Peterson preaches this when he tells young men to get out of bed and clean up their rooms in order to get control of their lives.

The government and education system today are designed to create mass conformity and obedience. However they also destroy the one thing neurotics need to become well, and that is the development of their individuality. As I say in this book, there is no greater freedom than between your ears, and there is only room for two there, God and you. Expel all else.

Jung says individuality is indispensable for healing, and as I address in the chapter, "Addiction to Convenience and Comfort," to be healed the neurotic has to break the addiction of what seems all too comfortable. Without doing so the individualism of one's nature cannot emerge.

Risking some social rejection and discomfort is a necessary part of normal life (as I also reference in the chapter, "Stop Asking Why and Start Fighting Back,"). As Jung also suggests, "to cure neurosis you have to risk something." There are so many examples of where those who succeed first had to risk something, whether it was injury in pursuit of athletic excellence, or financial failure in pursuit of business success. The neurotics and particularly those with psychosis, are created by the hypocritical Left. Those who dare to succeed are hated by the Left, as they can't be controlled and are not conformers.

In today's world some of us who dare to be mentally healthy cannot be normal in comparison to modern day standards. Looking at the chaos in the world today and the cultural collapse around us a healthy person would need to be abnormal in today's world in order to remain salubrious and succeed.

CHAPTER 2:

The Psychology of Psychosis and Totalitarianism

"Remember what Hannah Arendt said when she was talking about fascism and totalitarianism. She said thoughtlessness is the essence of totalitarianism. So, all of a sudden emotion becomes more important than reason. Ignorance becomes more important than justice. Injustice is looked over as simply something that happens on television."

Henry Giroux

Having established that the systemic psychosis plaguing America is primarily an inorganic psychosis that is manufactured and produced, now I want to explore some of the psychological factors related to mass systemic psychosis and its relationship with totalitarianism. My characterization of the decay in America as coming from an inorganic psychosis has been addressed by many other thinkers and philosophers as well. In their studies they have found strong links between its insidious nature and how societies drift into totalitarianism. So next, let's look at how they have summarized the situation.

The Psychology of Systemic Psychosis

French psychologist Gustav Le Bon in his book *The Crowd: A Study of the Popular Mind* said, "The masses have never thirsted for truth. They turn aside from evidence that is not to their taste, preferring to deify error, if error seduces them. Whoever can supply them with illusions is easily their master; whoever attempts to destroy their illusions is always their victim."

Similarly, Carl Jung has warned that "Man's greatest danger is to man, for the simple reason that there is no adequate protection against psychic epidemics, which are infinitely more devastating than the worst of natural catastrophes."

The problem and danger of mass formation psychosis has been around for a very long time, and we have seen its horror play out time and time again. Each time it rears its hideous face, it becomes a little more sophisticated. With the advent of new technology, social media, and the use of algorithms, your mind is being so controlled that Descartes would have to rethink his famous quote of "I think, therefore I am." The state, with the aid of technology, technocrats, bureaucrats, and malevolent corrupt politicians are in far greater control of your mind, decision-making, and opinion formation than you realize.

As Carl Jung defined it, mass psychosis is "an epidemic of madness, and it occurs when a large portion of society loses touch with reality and descends into delusions."[12] Furthermore, a lecture series from the Academy of Ideas on the topic of mass psychosis summarized, from a number of sources, the thoughts and analysis of others who also studied this phenomenon of mass psychosis and how it has proven so deadly in the past.

As noted, this psychological condition has manifested itself in the past and was seen particularly in Europe and America in the 1600s with the witch hunts and in the 20th century the rise of totalitarianism.

Many of us who took a history class when they were still taught in school can recall how insane people became during the witch hunts and trials, when thousands, mostly women, were killed. They were scapegoats. As recounted in the lecture by the Academy of Ideas, in some Swiss villages there were only few women left alive. These witch trials, as

---

12 Academy of Ideas, "Is a Mass Psychosis the Greatest Threat to Humanity?," Academy of Ideas. com, accessed on March 3, 2023, https://academyofideas.com/2021/02/mass-psychosis-greatest-threat-to-humanity/.

I recount elsewhere in the book, had nothing to do with justice or reality—they were the result of a mass psychosis. We are beginning to repeat the same hysteria today with climate change, gender dysphoria, and a plethora of other issues over which we have been fooled into believing are an existential crisis. All the foundations have been poured and the army of useful idiots is in place.

As the Academy of Ideas warns:

> When mass psychosis occurs, it is devastating. Those individually infected by psychosis become morally and spiritually inferior and they sink unconsciously to an intellectually inferior level. They become unreasonable, irresponsible, and emotional, erratic, unreliable, and worst of all, commit crimes that the individual could never stand or freely commit.[13]

We are seeing this play out now and at an increasingly faster pace by the day.

Those infected with a cognitive disability, and easy prey for the manipulators, cannot collectively see their madness. All the players are in place. You have those designing and plotting the psychosis because it aids their permanent ascendancy to power. Then you have the compliant ignorant masses that give their votes to the cause. And then you have the violent radicals like Antifa that burn down cities causing chaos which is the perfect smoke screen for what is going on behind the scenes. Simply recall how the leftist mayor of Portland, Oregon simply let the riots and burning go unabated. It's as if Emperor Nero was resurrected. It happened city after city and the leftist "Neros" in power just stood down and let them burn. And they were all Democrats. Every major metropolis in America's decaying cities is completely Democrat controlled and has been for decades. Let that sink in as I develop the psychosis theme further in this book.

So, what causes mass psychosis? As the Academy of Ideas analysis continued, "There are physical triggers that can cause psychosis, but this

---

13   Academy of Ideas, "The Manufacturing of a Mass Psychosis – Can Sanity Return to an Insane World?," AcademyofIdeas.com, April 24, 2021, https://academyofideas.com/2021/04/manufacturing-of-a-mass-psychosis-can-sanity-return-to-an-insane-world/.

is psychological or psychogenic. Mass psychosis is triggered by fear and anxiety that drives a person into a state of panic. When in that state one will seek relief, as it is too draining to exist in this hyper emotional state. (They enter a psychotic break but not one of disorder but a reordering of one's experiential world.) It blends facts and fiction into a delusional reality so as to end the panic."[14]

When one enters the phase of panic, they become confused. Then it morphs into a warped view of reality, a psychotic insight, in an attempt to explain the experience they are having. Delusions give relief to the individual but at the cost of living in reality. This is an abnormal way of dealing with anxiety. The lecture contends, and I agree that "the mass psychosis state can be reached when a mass of people is driven into a state of panic, real or imagined or fabricated. In the modern era it is the mass psychosis of totalitarianism that is the greatest threat." We are in the midst of it now.

Systemic Psychosis as the Foundation for Totalitarianism

According to Arthur Versluis, Department Chair of Religious Studies in the College of Arts & Letters at Michigan State University, "totalitarianism is the modern phenomenon of total centralized state power coupled with the obliteration of individual human rights. So, there are two classes: those in power and then the objectified masses, the victims."[15] As the Academy of Ideas lecture explains, "In a totalitarian society the population is divided into two groups, the rulers and the ruled, and both groups undergo a pathological transformation. The rulers are elevated to an almost God-like status which is diametrically opposed to our nature as *imperfect* beings who are easily corrupted by power. The masses, on the other hand, are transformed into the dependent subjects of these pathological rulers and take on a psychologically regressed and childlike status."[16]

---

14 Academy of Ideas, "Is a Mass Psychosis the Greatest Threat to Humanity?"
15 Arthur Versluis, "The Manufacturing of a Mass Psychosis – Can Sanity Return to an Insane World?"
16 The Academy of Ideas, "The Manufacturing of a Mass Psychosis – Can Sanity Return to an Insane World?"

If you have been paying attention to all the events of the last decade, what many have been observing and warning about has now collapsed into almost a singularity in that there is very little time between the events (waves) for one to get a grasp on what is happening and to give it sober reflection so as to see its cloaked agenda and those implementing it.

As I have said elsewhere this is a planned transformation and deconstruction of human nature itself. We are seeing this with the deconstruction of the biological foundations of life via the confusion of what is a man and woman. This transformation destroys individual thought and makes normal, sound minds into sick ones. Don't miss the point that Versluis makes of us being imperfect beings. This is of great significance; and had the church not collapsed, the people would know that we are all imperfect (having depraved minds, as Dr. MacArthur contends) and thus need to be governed by a moral code, not trusting any man or government to be God. Instead, the psychotic Left believes in the perfectibility of man which always leads to tyranny and totalitarian dictators. The loss of this simple truth has brought deadly and disastrous consequences.

As noted by Dutch psychologist, Joost Meerloo, in his book, *Rape of the Mind*, "There is in fact much that is comparable between the strange reaction of the citizens of totalitarianism and their culture as a whole on the one hand and the reactions of the sick schizophrenic on the other."

Building off what Meerloo argues, the Academy of Ideas explains, that;

> "the social transformation of totalitarianism is built upon and sustained by delusions as only deluded men and women regress to the child-like status of obedient and submissive subjects. They hand over complete control of their lives to politicians and bureaucrats. Only a deluded ruling class believes they have the knowledge and wisdom and acumen to control an entire society from a top-down manner. Only while under the spell of delusions would anyone believe that a society composed of power-hungry rulers on the one hand and a psychologically regressed population on the other will lead to anything other than mass suffering and social ruin."

The permanent irrationality of the 25% of the population, combined with the psychotic conduct of the rest, both Left and Right, has made for a compliant and submissive society ripe for totalitarian dominance. They not only give up their rights, but they also drag you and yours with them.

Meerloo goes on to discuss what triggers the mass psychosis of totalitarianism. He claims,

> It begins with a society's ruling class. They are prone to delusions that augment their power. They believe they can and should control a society…. (We see this in the Left today and their obsession with power) …. When a ruling elite becomes possessed by an ideology of this sort, the next step is to induce a population to accept their rule by infecting them with a mass psychosis of totalitarianism. It is simply a question of reorganizing and manipulating collective feelings in a proper way.

They organized and activated teachers and professors to spread the totalitarian message to the youth in this country such that now nearly half believe communism to be a good thing. They think not because they were taught not. They will buy the lie and live a miserable life. Unfortunately, so will the rest of us, since so many parents were clueless about what their children were being taught.

I have a good personal anecdote about the conduct of citizens under a totalitarian governance/culture. I was the Chairman of the Jefferson County Republican Party, in Louisville, Kentucky after the fall of the Soviet Union. At that time, Russia was attempting a transformation and a reunion with the rest of the world, particularly economically, and moving toward a free market system. However, they were running into problems with starting businesses and getting people to work together and form reliable contracts with each other. Why? Because in the totalitarian state there is no truth. Lying is a way of life and a means of self-preservation. This created a lot of chaos when entering capitalism, and having greater freedoms, because the old habits of trust, contracts, and the expectation that people would honor their word had been erased. How does one instill an ethical code, a moral code, that has been eradicated after decades of suppressing freedom and religion?

In my role as Chairman, I was asked to meet with a delegation of Russian dignitaries who were interested in building a free enterprise and economic system. However, like I mentioned, they were running into issues. Amazingly, they also knew what the answer was, and asked for help to re-create a society built on a more biblical model. They asked me for Bibles and even accompanied me to church. They understood that to be able to compete with the west and to have capitalism flourish they had to have certain ethical principles instilled in the people to which they would adhere, because contracts create stability of relationships and there is no prosperity without. Totalitarianism had eradicated this concept, which was why it failed.

What's most interesting is the term Meerloo used to describe how a people become so demented that they lose their ability to think. The way the ruling class accomplishes totalitarian psychosis is through "menticide" meaning a "killing of the mind." Or, as Merriam-Webster dictionary defines it, it is "a systematic and intentional undermining of a person's conscious mind also known as brainwashing. Mwalimu Bomani Baruti also defines it in stark terms. He says that menticide occurs "when you willingly think and act out of someone else's interpretation of reality to their benefit and against (another's) survival." It's an old system of psychological intervention and judicial perversion in which a ruling class can imprint their own opportunistic thoughts upon the minds of those they plan to use and destroy.

The Academy of Ideas explains that:

> The priming of menticide is by inducing fear. When one is subjected to negative emotions then they are very susceptible to a descent into delusions and madness. The ruling class use waves of fear and terror followed by a calm (as previously mentioned). Morality declines and with each new wave of the propaganda campaign the rulers become stronger. The public is then softened up. The media and the government conspire to keep the population confused and make it easier to control them.

This act has been unfolding before our eyes for years. If you have not seen it or don't recognize it, then it is amazing that you have made it this far into the book! Congratulations on taking the red pill. Many others have seen it, but are suffering what is called, "social exhaustion," which is designed to wear down the sane portion of our population.

What we saw during the COVID pandemic, with the lies and inconsistent regulations, is that, as Meerloo explains,

> Logic can be met with logic, while illogic cannot. It confuses those who think straight. The big lie and monotonously repeated nonsense have more of an emotional appeal than logic and reason. While the people are still searching for a reasonable counter-argument to the first lie, the totalitarians can assault them with another.

The Right, in futility, rushes to address each new lie but can't keep up. This was an incredibly poor strategy as the lies would come off the conveyor belt faster than the Right could explain what they were. Instead of going to the source and pulling back the curtain on the Wizard of Oz, they worked in vain trying to explain to those who really have no thirst for truth, those like Charlie who insisted he was dead, but really part of that 25% perpetually irrational group.

The implementation of totalitarian psychosis is aided by technology, phones, media, and the internet in conjunction with algorithms which quickly censor the flow of unwanted information that allow those in power to control the mind of the masses. This observation from the lecture was not so profound, as those caught in the addiction know it but haven't the strength to resist it. It is just easier to go along.

Meerloo, again, puts it well. He explains that:

> Most of us by now would admit to the addictive nature of social media and technology today. With today's technology there is no rest, no meditation, no reflection, no conversation. The senses are continually overloaded with stimuli. Man doesn't learn to question his world anymore. The screen offers him answers already made.

I contend we have already lost autonomy over our own minds and are thus already enslaved.

As the Academy of Ideas further explains, and as we have experienced with COVID,

> Another step that the 'rulers' take is to force people into isolation. In such a state one is more susceptible to delusions and manipulation. What does this accomplish? First, they don't see a positive example in others from whom they are isolated. Second, humans are more easily conditioned into new patterns of thought when isolated. As Pavlov stated, "conditioning is more effective when one is isolated from other stimuli."

Totalitarians know this and so they isolate their political victims or the target to be conditioned by isolation. Alone, confused, and battered by waves of terror, a population under the attack of menticide descends into a hopeless and vulnerable state. It destroys rational thought. However, when you own the space between your ears, you are the ruler of your mind and immune from manipulation.

This is why I rejected isolation. I resisted the mask mandates and had to endure endless debate with idiots. I was right then, and I am right now, but nevertheless I had to endure the inane insanity and stupidity of so many. I also refused the vaccine. Yes, I got COVID, but that was inevitable with or without the vaccine. I knew this would happen but also knew that the vaccine was useless insofar as preventing infection and dangerous as far as it being another unneeded risk. I was proven correct there as well, but through those two hellacious years I stood my ground and am likely alive today because I did. You must fight for your mind and with your mind against the menticide.

Throughout the 20th century, we have seen the masses cede control of nearly all aspects of their lives, including their freedom, to the ruling class. This is a capitulation in a desperate attempt at regaining some order and relief in their lives. This is the new dependent class who no longer are self-reliant, and they become obedient and submissive, not the fiercely independent and self-reliant American of the past.

Meerloo explains that:

The totalitarian systems of the 20th century represent a kind of collective psychosis whether gradually or suddenly. Reason and common human decency are no longer possible in such a system. There is only a pervasive atmosphere of terror and a projection of the enemy imagined to be in our midst. Thus, society turns on itself, urged by the ruling authorities.

We have seen this play out with Antifa, and with those who will confront you if you don't wear a mask or don't wear it in a way pleasing to them.

As the lecture comes to an end, it discusses how totalitarianism can be prevented. There are many different approaches that I will cover in more detail in Part Three, but for now, here are some ways to begin resisting those who seek to control your life:

Bring order to your own mind and be inspiring to others. Show others your own emancipation. Be a beacon of light. I establish this further in the last chapter in discussing steps to take to regain our minds.

Information that counters propaganda should be spread as far as possible, as others are doing in various articles and books and as I am doing in this book. Charlie Kirk has been doing this very effectively through Turning Point USA. Truth is powerful and truth is education.

Also, one must use humor and ridicule and point out the absurdity of the corruption to delegitimize the ruling elite. This is so effective and is basically using the playbook the Left has been using. I'm astounded by the ineptness of the Right who simply have been blind, if not just stupid, to such a simple exercise. This was in part revealed in Confrontational Politics written by H.L. Richardson, a former assemblyman in California years ago. He used it and it was very effective. Delegitimizing humor, as with anecdotes, finds that open door in an otherwise locked mind that can set people on a course of thinking for themselves, questioning everything and discarding the compliant mindset so needed by authoritarians.

The Academy also suggests a means of escape or resistance, of which I have spoken, by creating parallel structures outside of the ruling classes' moral void. The former president of Czechoslovakia, Vaclav Havel, discussed this in his book The Power of the Powerless. He confronted the communist regime in his country; and while it was a struggle, he won, and the authoritarians collapsed. (I recall his courage and his efforts, and he became a force and movement.) When enough of the parallel structures are created, a separate society and entity is created within the totalitarian world. Here a different life can be lived with its own aims and structures. It will eventually collapse the totalitarian delusion. Some of this is being done now but must be enhanced and expanded exponentially.

As I have preached for decades, you must encourage as many as possible to take action. Insist on your rights and freedoms. Stand your ground. Be that needed example to others. As Thomas Paine said in American Crisis: "Tyranny, like hell, is not easily conquered, yet we have this consolation with us, that the harder the conflict, the more glorious the triumph." Triumph can be had, but not from the couch.

The truth is buried. However, I brought a shovel. And I have an extra one if you are of the kind that is willing to dig down deep enough to find it again. Some see that this is happening, but far too few, as those on the dark side are better chess players and move quickly to control the flow and dissemination of information.

What's rotten in America today? It's a systemic psychosis. Where did it come from? I turn to that next.

CHAPTER 3:

Origins of America's Systemic Psychosis

"Those of us who live with peace in our hearts can barely face the shock of this existence, as the pain of our collective experience exceeds the scope of our comprehension. We watch news reports and conclude that the world is tragically insane."

Michael Ronin, Author

The Origins and Historical Roots of our Systemic Psychosis

A nd insane we have become, as Ronin contends, because so many of us simply would not and did not do what we knew needed to be done. Instead, we ceded power to the most incompetent, evil, and corrupt amongst us.

Sadly, many were asleep at the switch over the last century. We let the seeds of the psychosis pass undetected through our intellectual and spiritual "Customs and Border Patrol," after which the seeds quickly sank deep roots into our national soil and started spreading like a fungus.

Then, in the last decade, it broke out above ground in full force. In 2022 we observed the then-nominee for Supreme Court, Justice Ketanji Brown Jackson, who, when questioned at her confirmation hearing, claimed she could not define a woman.[17] It was shocking. It was a "pause the tape and hit rewind moment." This was pretending. This was acting. This was an Academy Award-winning moment for dishonesty by a Supreme Court nominee. She was confirmed by 53 "Democrats" (that is, 50 Democrats and 3 "Republicans") to 47 Republicans. How did we get here? While the differences between the political parties could not be any more opposite, they both failed us. One is totally evil and corrupt and the other living in their own utopia of denial.

After all, isn't the process supposed to be about what is in the best interest of the country and finding the most qualified jurist in the country? No! It's about what is in the best interest of advancing a pathological ideology, Marxism, and judicial perversion (which occurs when judicial appointments are selected not based upon their legal qualifications or commitment to the Constitution and upholding the rule of law, but rather to fill the seat with an ideological ally of the Left). This is the result, as Senator J.D. Vance said, "we are being ruled by unserious people who are worried about fake problems."

If you want to know how we got here, it is a simple matter of connecting the dots and tracking the progression of societal decay. However, that doesn't answer the question of why it was *allowed*. That will be explored later. So far, we have named the malady within the body politic. Let us now consider where it came from.

Systemic psychosis is in part a product of one of America's most deadly imports. Much (though not all) of the foundational ideology and worldview that produced the disease is not native to our soil or our intellectual tradition.

The decay didn't happen overnight. At some point, it reached critical mass wherein it took on a life of its own. That is exactly what has happened in America.

---

17   Caroline Downey, "Judge Jackson Refuses to Define 'Woman' during Confirmation Hearing: 'I'm Not a Biologist'," National Review Online, accessed October 28, 2022, https://www.nationalreview.com/news/judge-jackson-refuses-to-define-woman-during-confirmation-hearing-im-not-a-biologist/.

Psychotic Commies

The origin of the psychosis goes back to a man named Karl Marx. If Helen of Troy was the "face that launched a thousand ships," then Marx's anti-God and anti-human screed, *The Communist Manifesto*, was the "book that planted a thousand seeds of psychosis." Although the workers never seized the means of production, Vladimir Lenin seized the seeds of the revolution he found in Marxism. In the revolution of 1917, he established the communist Soviet Union.

However, it didn't take long for the communist revolution in Russia to metastasize. During the revolution, there was a window of opportunity for the West to help prop up and support a more democratic form of government that existed in Russia after the fall of the Czar. As usual, the west was indolent and missed its chance. As a result, the fledgling communist experiment hadn't even gotten their governmental seats warm before they started spreading the poison of their ideology to other countries.

As you look back on the last 100-plus years of communist terror, it is an established historical fact that it is a profoundly corrupt, evil, and deadly ideology and form of governance. Born in hell, it should have been outlawed worldwide at its inception, back when the West had the opportunity to do so. For it was not merely a new idea for governing, but a design for the enslavement and dehumanization of the human race.

Sadly, as a result of the Right's psychosis of denial in the face of an existential threat, tens of millions of people have been tortured, executed, and exterminated—all under the flag of communism. In retrospect, the Nazis were amateurs compared to what communism did during the last century. Isn't it interesting how those so influenced by Marxist thought and theory today instantly deflect to the evils of Naziism, using the term to demean the Right as if their brand was not historically proven even more deadly.

And the point is this: Communism succeeded because it induced and then operated on psychosis. One could come up with a number of other valid contributors, but at the core when the individual or a society operate outside reality, the psychosis is almost always deadly. Evil opportunists prowl around looking for opportunities to seize power and destroy anyone or anything that gets in their way. You would think that by now we, as a collective human race, would have smartened up. You would think wrong.

All too often those who run the government are not the brightest of the lot, but merely the most egotistical, appearing to have a competence they truly lack. As the communist regimes sent spies to undermine this country's foundations, many were asleep. The Marxists went unchecked as they infiltrated the churches, seminaries, government, and courts.

In the 1950s there was the Red Scare and the government held hearings and uncovered the surreptitious activities of the communists within. This is how Richard Nixon rose to fame, but the investigations did not go far enough or long enough. The undermining was underwritten by the then-elite who feared not the Marxists (since they planned to be the ones in control), but rather the masses and wanted authoritarian control to protect their riches and status.

One foundation after another was infiltrated, gatekeepers installed, and the decay went mostly unchallenged. The psychosis of communism had spread, in function if not in name.

Consider how in the 1930s we saw the entire nation of Germany devolve into a mass psychosis and indoctrination preceded by a moral collapse, decay within the church, and suppression of not only the truth but a proliferation of false and fake news. The people were conditioned, and the children were groomed in school. The same occurred in Russia, China, Cuba, North Korea, and the list goes on. When truth dies, so do the people, so does the culture, and the country.

While the Allies ultimately defeated the German Nazis, the Italian fascists, and the Japanese imperialists, the communists marched on—in both Russia and China. And soon enough—even in America—we now find ourselves in an existential fight for our freedoms. Marxism today is cloaked in many deceiving titles and terms such as "Black Lives Matter" (BLM). By the time the people catch on to all the variants of the Marxist disease, it has already done its damage and raised tens of millions to finance other destructive missions. As of 2023, nearly all of South America has Marxist or leftist governments. What a sad commentary for our once revered Monroe Doctrine.

This is a tale as old as time. While Adam and Eve were real people, metaphorically one could see Eve as today's Left, having no love for the truth she knew, and Adam as the Right, being so desperate for Eve he turns a blind eye to the truth and lives in denial—all for the sake of one more day of comfort with Eve. They both died as a result, and now our nation and world are dying too.

Psychotic Courts

Coming off WWII, America was suffering a hangover from our celebration of defeating the Nazis. We were filled with false optimism and thought that our constitution immunized us from bad governance and leaders. People thought it didn't matter who got elected as President, so they went with a celebrity in the form of a general trained in warfare but not governance. We had false security. It didn't last.

Generals don't make good presidents. Such was the case with President Eisenhower. It was this general, lacking in any knowledge of jurisprudence, politics, or governance, who appointed the disastrous Earl Warren to the Supreme Court.

And Justice Warren ruled like a communist. President Eisenhower would later admit that Warren was his biggest mistake as president.

Warren eroded the influence of the church and removed its stabilizing influence over schools and education. Prayer, the Bible, morality, the Pledge of Allegiance, faith in God, and respect for our country would eventually begin to fade. The outcome of the rulings of the Warren court is that every form of perverseness became tolerated, and the degeneration continued manifesting itself in the most profound ways.

This rotted state of America today is a result of the outright suppression of truth over time. Facts are distorted daily by news outlets and are displaced by a systematic, agenda-driven, pathological ideology bent upon the restructuring of society. As truth became inconvenient to the "dystopians," it was redefined, and it became relative. Truth has become like beauty in our culture—found only in the eyes of the beholder. Truth has ceased to reside in the individual. Truth (facts and fixed law) was relinquished by lazy people to a central source. You were told what the truth was, and you were expected to accept it. Thus, there were no givens, no standards, and no fixed points of reference.

As Dr. James Lindsey puts it, we have a psychopathic ideology within the country. It is a culturally fatal phenomenon and has two protagonists, a militant Left and a paralyzed Right. In the moral void of today, there is not much we can count on to help correct the ship of state.

While there are more roots to pull up, for now, know that psychotic communists (which is almost a redundancy) and psychotic court rulings, starting specifically with the Warren court and his successors, are what landed us in the mess we are in today. While Warren poured gas on the fire, it started with what is now known as one of the most wicked presidents we have ever had, Woodrow Wilson. Even Wilson acknowledged that he thought he had destroyed his country before he went insane (which resulted in his wife practically becoming the de facto president). Wilson's Marxist revolution was followed by the disaster of the socialist president, Franklin Roosevelt. Between the two of them laying the foundation for radical social change, and the evils of the Warren court, our nation was hurled headlong on a path toward psychosis. Yes, the church abrogated its responsibility too, but we will get to that later. Those are the historical roots. Now let's consider some modern consequences and examples.

Examples of Modern Systemic Psychosis

Rational and normative thought processes, if operative, would never allow the profoundly irrational behaviors seen in our culture today on such a broad scale. There are many examples, but three of the most glaring at the present are: 1) The transgender deceit that has taken our nation by a gruesome storm; 2) The historical acceptance and impact of Darwinism; and 3) The rise of climate change ideology. I will now consider each of these examples of widespread psychosis in more detail.

Psychotic Trannies

The transgenderism craze is, again, a perfect example of modern systemic psychosis. They constitute only 1.6% of the population, if that. How could this tail wag the dog? There is a core cause. Other powerful forces along with other extreme minorities, ones which are experts in the dark arts of redefining what is normal, are weaponizing the trans-ideology tail so as to wag the national dog. Yet again, the leftist psychos want to define the normal by the abnormal.

What once was confined to the psychologists' and psychiatrist's offices for treatment now has been declared by fiat as normal. Built on the lies of radical gender theory and the pseudo-science of the notion of gender dysphoria, all of a sudden, our society is doing truly insane things. We are calling men, "women." We are allowing for the irreversible genital muti-lation of minors. Doctors are claiming boys can menstruate and tampons are being placed in boys' bathrooms. Pronouns are being changed and required, if not compelled, and freedom of speech is violently opposed on campuses and within our major corporations. The profane list goes on and on and there are tens of millions of dollars for those pushing this agenda.

Transgenderism is the seminal example of ingratitude for the physi-cal body you have been given by God. The transgender mental illness is destroying perfectly healthy bodies and consigning those who mutilate their bodies to a lifetime of physical and mental illness. It was never a malfunction of the body but rather of the mind. Knowing that those who transition will regret their decisions later and have a lifetime of physical illness, I imposed upon lawmakers to pass legislation to allow minors who are mutilated to be able to sue their parents, doctors, hospitals and clinics after the minor becomes an adult (some legislation simply outlawed the procedure completely). This would shut down the medical cash register, as no insurance company would cover such procedures knowing that their insured is likely to get sued after a child becomes an adult and real-izes they made a youthful mistake – an indiscretion (which all children do), and that the adults should have known better and protected them.

Nearly every deviance and perversion you can imagine is being found acceptable or normalized today. The created order and normal function-ing of the human, physically and mentally, is being distorted and becom-ing dysfunctional. This is the product of a depraved and psychotic mind.

In 2021, two top-notch collegiate female swimmers, Olympic med-alists at that, were defeated by a male who now calls himself Lia Thomas, claiming to be a girl.[18] As a male swim team member, he was a loser. That's not ad hominem; it's an established statistic and fact. That's not the only way he was a loser. Genetically he is a male. From his bone and muscle structure, and genitalia, all the way down to his DNA. The only thing missing in Mr. Thomas appears to be a functional mind congruent with his biology in the normative sense.

---

18   Guardian Sport, "Lia Thomas' victory at NCAA swimming finals sparks fierce debate over trans athletes," The Guardian, accessed October 28, 2022, https://www.theguardian.com/sport/2022/mar/21/lia-thomas-victory-at-ncaa-swimming-finals-sparks-fierce-debate-over-trans-athletes.

His decision to race against women gave him notoriety and a platform because of a dysfunction on the opposite side of the spectrum. With Mr. Thomas, the dysfunction is clearly in the mind of the boy because biologically he is a male. Worse are those who condone and accommodate the deviance by enabling and normalizing it and forcing society to conform to the abnormality. The lack of outrage is also glaring and either missing or takes an inordinate time to materialize before society corrects the injustice. This perversion was countenanced, aided, and abetted by many, including elected officials.

I do not care about what Mr. Thomas wants to think of himself or call himself. Just don't force the rest of the normative culture to accept your descriptions and desires or think or tell us our eyes are lying to us. Of course, I hope he doesn't do himself harm, as so many in this situation ultimately do, but instead gets the real help he needs. The hard truth is that those who are his caretakers have done him a great disservice. The statistics don't lie, and those enabling him and others to mutilate themselves physically and permanently are hurting, not helping, them.

The people, many who think the whole transgender matter is insane, nevertheless voted people into office that went along with the insanity of the transgender movement. There is a *disconnect*, a clear incongruity. Those voters fit into one or more categories. They want something for nothing (another government handout) and are willing to tolerate the absurd, or they are indifferent and lack any understanding of cause and effect. As Bertrand Russell once said, "Most people would die sooner than think—in fact, they do so."

Several states have begun to counter this trans madness by limiting participation in sports based on the gender assigned at birth. Even that is technically wrong, as gender is determined at conception, not birth. However, be that as it may, the correction of these dysfunctional fires seems to come only after half the forest has been burned.

Viewing it scientifically, Mr. Thomas has the genetic makeup of a male and has male DNA. That's not my opinion; that is a medical and scientific fact. Allowing anyone to suggest that, despite his male DNA, he could be a "woman," is the definition of psychosis (departing from reality). Furthermore, one nasty little trick the Left always uses is pure sophistry, with both word appropriation and redefinition. They separate the term "gender" from "sex." This never has been the case throughout human history, and it is intellectually dishonest. Don't buy into that narrative. Don't even allow it on the platform as a matter of discussion. There is no difference between gender and sex. They are synonymous, always have been, and always will be unless you buy into the false narrative that was created by the Left. They had to change the definitions, as they always do, just to have a chance at justifying transgenderism as normative, as well as the surgeries they wanted to perform on children (making millions along the way). Take caution: Children always have been the target and they are coming for *your* children, too.

Psychotic Darwinism

Another current example of psychosis is the ongoing acceptance of social Darwinism. This reality-denying theory teaches us that we are all the product of random chance and natural selection, having evolved out of the primordial goo and then miraculously gained sentience along with unbelievably intricate, complicated, and fully functioning human bodies.

The truth is that there is no Darwinian evolution, but rather what we are seeing is a *devolution*. It's not that Darwin had any answers, nor was he endowed with any genius or special insights – he didn't. He's not so unlike others throughout history who came up with absurd ideas that took root, but only because he was at the right place at the right time. He got traction and became as famous as the Kardashians (in his day and age) for what was nothing more than an unproven theory, one that remains unproven to this day.

In fact, Darwin's theory is increasingly under attack within the scientific community since the evidence is showing more and more that the theory is improbable, if not impossible. Nevertheless, I'm not getting off onto an evolutionary sidetrack or debate but only mentioning it and referencing him since we, as a country and world have devolved, not evolved, mentally. If you want a thorough analysis of the failures of Darwin, then look up Dr. James Tour, one of the world's leading and published scientists, who deals with this issue and exposes the lies of evolutionary theory in a devastating way.

As it relates to Darwin, how interesting it would be to have Darwin's take on the claim now circulating that there are now something like 100 genders. Devolution is occurring, and all one needs to do is look at the test scores of students coming out of public schools today.

Darwin claimed that natural selection favors the strong. However, interestingly, researchers from the University of East Anglia found that "natural selection" (again, not a real thing) is favoring poorer people with little education. The study "shows how natural selection effects are stronger in groups with lower income and less education, among younger parents, people not living with a partner, and people with more lifetime sexual partners." On the flip side, natural selection "is pushing against genes" associated with highly educated individuals, people who have more lifetime earnings, those who have a low risk of ADHD or major depressive disorders, and those with a lower risk of coronary artery disease.

Researchers analyzed the polygenic scores of more than 300,000 people in the United Kingdom. (Polygenic scores estimate a person's genetic liability, a prediction of their health, education, lifestyle, or personality.) They then used data on two generations of people living in the U.K. by looking at their number of siblings and number of children. They "found that 23 out of 33 polygenic scores were significantly linked to a person having more or fewer children over their lifetime," explains Hugh-Jones. "Scores which correlated with lower earnings and education predicted having more children, meaning those scores are being selected from an evolutionary perspective." So, in conclusion, the "Polygenic scores prove natural selection is no longer valid."[19]

Despite being invalid, social Darwinism continues to induce psychosis in many. What does that mean? According to Oxford Languages, social Darwinism is the "theory that individuals, groups, and peoples are subject to the same Darwinian laws of natural selection as plants and animals." This theory is now largely debunked even in the secular scientific community, as you can imagine. In some ways, believing that this earth, its inhabitants, and everything we see in all its wonder and glory are just the product of random chance over time is one of the most psychotic things imaginable. Darwinism didn't need a scientific study to prove that it was false—common sense tells us as much. Biases then, as now, always

---

19 Matt Higgins, "Darwin's theory upended? Natural selection may be making society more unequal," Study Finds, accessed on October 28, 2022, https://studyfinds.org/charles-darwin-natural-selection-society-unequal/.

favor the profane, the fake, the false, the lie. Of course, it has only taken over 200 years for genetics and societal changes to rudely smack us in the face, awakening us to our utter stupidity, not to mention the incredible loss of time, talent, and treasures in pursuit of a false narrative and theory.

Psychotic Climate Change

Another example of the surreal nature of life in America today is climate change conversation and rhetoric. Radical claims are made, and many people just fall in line. ("Radical" means affecting the fundamental nature of something, a departure from tradition, unorthodoxy.)

We have been conditioned to "look to the science," or "follow the science." In other words, they want you to surrender your own logic, reasoning, and common sense to the "experts." The "experts" here are people who have been responsible for these glaring examples of their *lack of* expertise.

During the Trump administration, for the first time in my lifetime, America became energy independent. We were a net energy exporter, particularly in oil. But once upon a time, it was predicted we would reach our peak production in 1943. The scientists were wrong.

The United Nations predicted via their scientific sources that there would be a famine in 1967. It never happened. Then, in 1969, it was predicted that within 20 years we would all disappear in a cloud of blue steam. Last I checked, we are still here.

The Washington Post and Time Magazine in the early 70s predicted the world would soon flood. They ignored the fact that the earth was warmer in the 1930s. Clearly, it has not happened, and those who denied that it would happen were attacked then as they are today. Reason is always attacked by those whose agenda it does not suit.

There were examples of flood disaster predictions in 1989 and that countries would drown by 2000, twenty-three years ago. In fact, lower Manhattan was to be underwater by 2018. I've yet to hear any apologies. You never do. These doomsayers are never held accountable. "That's the problem with experts," says Dr. Thomas Sowell, "they are frequently wrong without consequence or accountability."

One of the "best" false claims came from the self-proclaimed "inventor of the internet," former vice president Al Gore himself. In 2009 Al

Gore said that by 2013 there would be no more ice in the arctic. Thank God he was never president! Statistics show that in 2012 there were 1.67 million square miles of arctic ice, and by 2013 it was 2.25 million square miles. Wrong again!

How many of you recall Dr. Spock (Leonard Nimoy) of Star Trek fame, who starred in a 1979 video claiming that, according to his sources, i.e., "scientists," we would have an ice age during the time of our grandchildren? Well, those grandchildren are here. Where is the ice?

That reminds me, before the current scare about global warming, they tried to tell us we were heading for a "new ice age." That's right, in the 1970s, climatologists predicted that a "new ice age" was right around the corner. *Newsweek* even published an article called "The Cooling World." Even the History Channel ran a series with a video warning that bitter Buffalo, New York-style, cold winters could soon cover the entire United States. When that didn't come true, they decided to try "global warming" instead. That didn't work either. It statistically couldn't be established with any significance and, humorously, in a series of conferences they had planned back in the 80s and 90s, it just so marvelously happened their chosen venue was experiencing some of the coldest temperatures on record. This occurred several consecutive times such that it was becoming an embarrassment and discrediting. It was a PR nightmare. Fear not, the Left, as always, owns the dictionary so they change the definitions or change the terms, at will, and they did, to "climate change" so anything and everything can or will now be blamed on human-caused climate fluctuations.

God was mocking the fools who were trying to create a new religion out of the goddess of weather, as if mankind had more effect upon the climate than Mount Saint Helens, or the recent explosion in Tonga, the largest explosion ever recorded, equivalent to 100 atomic bombs. Yes, the climate fools and the gaslighted are the acolytes of a new religion. To some, it is part of a larger agenda that has nothing to do with climate. Other worshipers in need of a new religion, are primed to believe anything and are intolerant of any inconvenient fact. The facts and reality be damned, they reject any truth that runs counter to their Alice in Wonderland pre-drawn conclusions. They are the judgment-first, trial-later crowd.

The climate radicals are today's Jacobins, like the French radical anarchists who brought down the French monarchy followed by the reign of terror and violence where people were indiscriminately accused and beheaded. It's also reminiscent of the Salem Witch Trials in the 1600s. They would submerge you, and if you drowned, you were innocent. We, as a nation and world, are regressing into a period of darkness. We are not that advanced. Technology will not be our savior; it will be the guillotine in the hands of those infected with psychosis.

What is lacking in the climate debate is a rational, factual, and unbiased analysis of the evidence not cooked up by some so-called scientist trying to qualify for his or her next grant from conflicted groups poised to get rich off climate fear and legislation. It is nothing more than a mass redistribution of wealth with the uninformed consent of the people and their equally uninformed representatives.

When history was taught, most of us mused over how the Romans and Greeks could be so insane as to have so many gods. You need not wonder any longer as history is repeating itself and we are creating these gods all over again. We are looking to them to control the weather just like the pagans of old. Only we don't call them "Zeus" or "Ares" we call them "carbon neutral" and "green energy" and "global warming."

Again, when the climate wouldn't cooperate with the Left's narrative, the terminology had to change. So, we went from "global warming" to "climate change." How deceitful. They are the masters of sophistry. It is so patently wrong. If the climate didn't change then we would all be in trouble. Climate was changing before man inhabited the world. Thank God for the seasons! It will continue regardless of what we do.

Change is a natural cycle. It is a process beyond our control, though this fact has been obscured by the ruse that man alone has or can impact it in any significant way. In fact, looking at the numbers, they show that regardless of what we do and are currently doing, it will be at least 30 to 40 years before anything would have even a detectable impact. Also, you have been deceived by the fact that the world does not have a singular climate zone. There are nearly two dozen separate climate zones around the globe. Take Alaska and Florida for example. They operate separately and are completely different. Further, our biosphere, weather, ocean salinity, etc. has a magical self-correcting mechanism that scientists cannot explain and don't like to talk about. Hmmm. How about that? I guess there is no profit in that. In the meantime, we are destroying economies, businesses, and countries.

I'd welcome some palm trees in the Arctic. The polar bears would probably love it too. They seem to do well in zoos around the world. What a novel observation. How that observation was lost is befuddling. Maybe it wasn't lost, just suppressed and ignored.

Climate worshipers always default to emotion and hyperbole. They vacuously claim that all the polar bears will die off but are not confronted with such an obvious truth of all the polar bears living and thriving outside the Arctic. If it's not the polar bears, then the seas will rise, and we will all be flooded. Scientists cannot predict global flooding. They engage in gross speculation and unjustified exaggerated extrapolations. No one can agree. All they do is speculate and instill fear for something that will not occur until far after our lifetimes, if at all. So, we have suffered with over 50 years of speculation which consistently has been proven wrong. As for the scientists 50 years ago, I'd like to ask, where are the glaciers that were supposed to cover the U.S. Those who are wrong on mass scales are never held to account.

This discussion about climate change is warranted, not for the purposes of getting into a scientific analysis, but rather to connect it with the psychosis attached to it. It is one of the most devastating and destructive false narratives on the world stage today, ravaging everything in its path because people are detached from reality. They are the most psychotic in this one area that is destroying societies and countries. With the hysteria over all the varying "predictions," and they do vary widely, you would be wise to focus on the word, "prediction." You know, as in your weatherman accurately predicting weather, or predicting the stock market a year from now, or predicting who is going to win next year's Super Bowl. You don't trust any of them implicitly, nor should you.

Now that you are thinking about the word "predicting," your subliminal consciousness, if not conscious mind, should be processing another word—" skepticism." The two words usually go together, as they should. Predicting involves tremendous variables and assumptions that can radically alter a prediction or conclusion and they almost always do. The point here is that we are all skeptical about predictions on a regular basis, and we should be. All I am asking is that we apply that same skepticism to climate predictions (because so far, they all have been wrong).

Let's start with this fact about current weather, sea level, and other climate "predictions." When you average all the prognostications, findings, assumptions, predictions, etc., no one alive today will notice any difference. The changes in sea levels, temperature, and glacial melting are negligible and the so-called experts disagree with one another to varying extents.

Here are some fun facts. CO_2 is an essential element for plant growth. Plants produce oxygen. That's good. I'm sure you like breathing. CO_2 is converted or destroyed by H_2O (water). Eighty percent of the world's surface is H_2O. The southern hemisphere has less people than the northern hemisphere but is warmer and has more CO_2. See the problem? Where there are more people on the planet, there is less CO_2 (northern hemisphere) but where there are less people, there is more CO_2 (southern hemisphere). Funny how facts don't ever seem to help the climate alarmists!

The sea level rises differently in Alaska than on the east coast of America or in Vienna. Some land plates are rising, and others are sinking. Where are they taking sea level measurements? Okay, enough of science measurements that are dramatically impacted by the hundreds of variables. Before I get to the point of tying this all into the theme of this book, suffice it to say that heat and warmth brings forth life. Cold does not.

What's the point? You will not need Noah's ark in your lifetime. You will not need a space suit or fireproof clothing. You are going to have the occasional heat wave in summer, or snow blizzards like we saw in 2022 in Buffalo, N.Y. during the winter; but not much is going to change in your life, at least weather-wise. So, stop ruining your life now with all the unsubstantiated "predictions."

You don't trust the weatherman's predictions, or the stock market gurus, or the sportscasters, and you view things with healthy skepticism. So, stop being manipulated by those getting rich over their climate fear mongering as did so many over COVID and the vaccines. I am all for clean water and air, but I'm not going to destroy all mankind and sentient life so that the animals can roam free and alone. Nor am I going to hermetically seal myself in my home and live in such a way that my existence is never detected or felt by the Left's earth goddess, Gaia, known in mythological times as the goddess of chaos. How fitting a name for these times!

The facts are out there. With a little less TV, sports, video games, and amusement you might just learn something. Get control of your life and take it back from those who want to control it, you, your votes, your money, and freedom. If you don't, the climate change priests, who have created a new religion, will force you to bow and be obedient in order to have anything resembling a life.

So, as it relates to the premise of this book, the facts which you have ignored or denied have caused you to act in psychotic ways that are detached from reality. It is to the detriment of you, society, and the nation. Stop being gaslit by the Left and those making a fortune over your decisions. Wake-up. Become a skeptic. Question everything. Stop being psychotic. You will be happier, freer, and richer. Think about it: If you ask anyone alarmed about the climate to cite one established fact conclusive of a disastrous climate catastrophe that is about to kill us all, you will not get an answer. Instead, you will be screamed at, called names, and (if they could) burn you at the stake like they did the witches in the 1600's. This is psychosis.

The Psychology of Obedience

Before we leave the origins of psychosis it is important to understand one of the most potent mechanisms causing people to live detached from reality and that is a profound incongruency as it relates to obedience. Man finds it impossible to obey God, but irresistible to obey man, particularly the tyranny of man.

In a discussion by the Academy of Ideas addressing the psychology of obedience from March 2017, the concept is further developed.[20] As Sigmund Freud stated, "Never underestimate the power of the need to obey." We see this playing out in all the lemmings of society. The lonely driver in his car is fully masked. Even in 2023, nearly a year after all mandates had lifted, there are people who wear the mask. This is even

20 The Academy of Ideas, Lecture, "The Psychology of Obedience and the Virtue of Disobedience," accessed on January 20, 2022, academyofideas.com, https://academyofideas.com/2017/03/psychology-of-obedience/.

after the mountain of evidence has been revealed that the masks are use-less. Nevertheless, there are those mindless robots who desire control and subjugation; and need to be obedient to something even if it is wrong.

As the Academy explains, "This is true even if the authorities demand one go against his or her own morality or beliefs. There is a strong bias toward conformity and the status quo."[21] So many are guilty of complicity with tyranny as seen in the psychosis of the suffering electorate in the 2022 midterm elections in America.

People are their own worst enemies and are aided by a multiplicity of virtue-less characteristics such as laziness, cowardice, fear, stupidity, lack of discipline, moral debauchery, a falling away from religion and its moral codes, and an embrace of hedonism. As we find ourselves caught up and victims of our own choices, we become depraved, mentally func-tionless, and ripe for our oppressors.

The lecture continues:

> Self-education is crucial in escaping the indoctrination and propaganda that has kept us in a state of obedience. This will bring about disobedience but only aided by moral conscience. When the conflict between the immorality of the state and its requirements and the moral code that one may have becomes too dissonant or in conflict, will one begin to question the state and its commands. However, the state, knowing this as an eventuality, will destroy the foundations of morality with its own moral code and eliminate its competition: religion.[22]

It has occurred for decades in America. The surest tool used by the Left is sex, sex, sex. In every form, it is thrust upon the people. It is as powerful, if not more so, than any addictive drug in distracting people from what the Left is up to. It's Caligula all over again. Ply the public with wine and entertainment and you can get away with almost anything.

If sex addiction is not enough, "then surveillance will be imposed to control all thought. Tyrants have never had such a degree of control

---

21 Academy of Ideas, "The Psychology of Obedience and the Virtue of Disobedience."
22 Academy of Ideas, "The Psychology of Obedience and the Virtue of Disobedience."

over the populace as they do today as a result of technology and social media."[23] It is wrapped up in so many conveniences that the people willingly surrender autonomy over their own minds, thoughts and emotions. They are easy prey for the mind control being exerted today. The most popular term in 2022 was the word "gaslighting," that is, manipulating someone, by using psychological methods, into questioning their own sanity or powers of reasoning.

Just ask the man or woman on the street some of the most basic questions about their government, history, society, or their leaders, and it will reveal a profound ignorance, if not stupidity. Those living in third world countries have a greater chance of survival because of the cognitive skills forced upon them by their situation than those living in the industrial and modern first world. Today people have been largely rendered helpless drones, dependent upon a central government; and are obedient to the point of committing and going along with some of the most perverse and immoral dictates of their rulers.

Those with courage are the only ones that can save themselves and others. Sadly, it is most likely too late for America, and its restoration will only come about by the grace of God in giving us courage to disobey these tyrants. Erich Fromm, in his book *On Disobedience and Other Essays*, notes that "Man has continued to evolve by acts of disobedience." This evolution comes about particularly when man rebels against tyrannical governments. Whether that can be done today, with the kind of technology in place to hold us down, is probably a coin toss.

Coinciding with the rise of the technologically advanced security state has come the devolution of America's critical thinking skills and overall education. John Taylor Gatto, in his incisive work *Weapons of Mass Instruction*, wrote about what happens in "the dumbing down of a country." He explains that:

> It is easy to enslave idiots as they haven't the cognition to think and reason, making them readily and blindly obedient. In such a condition you lead them to think that Democracy is a good thing and that by Democracy they have the right to control their own

---

23   Academy of Ideas, "The Psychology of Obedience and the Virtue of Disobedience."

destiny through the exercise of a vote that is really owned and manipulated by the governing elite. The governing elite accomplish this through a public education system not designed to create citizens to think and deduce things on their own but to fall in line with an instilled group think taught in the schools. This is the Prussian system designed to create mediocre intellects, weak and ineffective leadership skills, and most importantly docile and incomplete citizens.

In 1971, the English novelist C.P. Snow said, "When you think of the long and gloomy history of man, you will find more hideous crimes have been committed in the name of obedience than have ever been committed in the name of rebellion." Or, as Voltaire said, "so long as the people do not care to exercise their freedom, those who wish to tyrannize will do so; for tyrants are active and ardent and will devote themselves in the name of any number of gods, religious or otherwise, to put shackles upon sleeping men."

I want to help Americans avoid this future—one of enslavement, with shackles, and perpetual horrors committed under the banner of unending obedience enforced by a surveillance state. If you think this sounds far-fetched, then you clearly haven't been paying attention to how the Communist Party of China has been treating their citizens during COVID. You don't even need to look as far west as China; just look north to Canada. The transgender madness, social Darwinism, the climate crisis insanity, and the blind obedience of the multitude, are a few key examples of our modern psychosis. Next, I want to help you see how this leads to a Marxist totalitarian state and the evil man behind it.

CHAPTER 4

Marx Resurrected: The Godfather of Psychosis

"We have no compassion, and we ask no compassion from you. When our turn comes, we shall not make excuses for the terror."

Karl Marx

I t's time to meet Karl Marx, Satan's footprint, if not incarnation, on the world today. I have mentioned his enduring legacy, Marxism—and cultural Marxism—multiple times in this book. To fully grasp the psychosis gripping our nation today we need to meet the man whose pathological ideology, erroneously believed to have been defeated with the fall of the Soviet Union, is at the core of the rot in America today.

Along with his ghost, we are also looking down the barrel of a world-wide, one-world form of governance where the government becomes "God," and we live at the pleasure of the incompetent and maniacal elite class that run it. While Marx died in 1883, his rotten spirit lingers on, just like the ghost in Hamlet.

Karl: The Man

Karl Marx was born in 1818 to Prussian (German) parents. According to the Stanford Encyclopedia of Philosophy, "Karl Marx was...one of nine children. The family lived in the Rhineland region of Prussia, previously under French rule. Both of his parents came from Jewish families with distinguished rabbinical lineages. Marx's father was a lawyer who converted to Christianity when it became necessary for him to do so if he was to continue his legal career. Following an unexceptional school career, Marx studied law and philosophy at the universities of Bonn and Berlin."[24]

What's particularly fascinating about Marx, given how evil his ideas were and how awful he became personally, is that he apparently showed signs of a Christian faith in his earlier years. In his book, *Marx and Satan*, Wurmbrand writes that "In his early youth, Karl Marx professed to be and lived as a Christian. His first written work is called "The *Union of the Faithful with Christ*" and that "Marx started out as a Christian believer."[25] However, something happened. Wurmbrand records that "Shortly after Marx received this certificate [the equivalent of his high school diploma] something mysterious happened in his life: he became profoundly anti-religious. A new Marx began to emerge."[26] Marx wrote these stark, blasphemous words: "I wish to avenge myself against the One who rules above."[27] This dark change was obvious to his friends, one who noted that "One has to worship Marx in order to be loved by him. One has to at least fear him in order to be tolerated by him. Marx is extremely proud, up to dirt and madness."[28]

Throughout his life Marx moved around, from Paris to Brussels to London, involving himself in political activism and philosophical writing. He was a student of the philosopher G.W.F. Hegel, and worked closely with his friend and colleague Friedrich Engels, both Satanists. His two most well-known contributions are his massive economic treatise, *Das Kapital*, and of course *The Communist Manifesto*.

Before we move on to the main point of his ideas, it's worth noting that Marx, along with his suspicious satanic behavior and beliefs, was

---

24 Stanford Encyclopedia of Philosophy, "Karl Marx," accessed on December 15, 2022, https://plato.stanford.edu/entries/marx/.

25 Richard Wurmbrand, *Marx and Satan* (Bartlesville, OK: Living Sacrifice Book Company, 1986), 11.

26 Wurmbrand, *Marx and Satan*, 12.

27 Wurmbrand, 12.

28 Wurmbrand, 13.

truly a terrible person. He grifted off others, refused to work, and scalped inheritance money from others.

The Mises Institute quotes Carl Schurz, who describes Marx like so:

> But never did I meet a man of such offensive arrogance in his demeanor. No opinion deviating in principle from his own would be given the slightest consideration. Anybody who contradicted him was treated with barely veiled contempt. Every argument which he happened to dislike was answered either with biting mockery about such pitiful display of ignorance or with defamatory suspicions as to the motives of the interpellant. I still well remember the sneering tone with which he spat out the word 'bourgeoisie.' And as bourgeois, that is to say, as an example of a profound intellectual and moral depravity, he denounced everybody who dared to contradict his views.[29]

Sounds like today's Left labeling everyone and everything as racist, doesn't it?

If I had not prefaced this paragraph with the name Marx, one would think I was describing today's liberals and leftists. It's the product of a twisted mind born in the depths of hell. Nothing is redeeming about it. Today's Left and liberals are pseudo-intellectuals parading around as God's gift to man. Yet the evidence reveals otherwise, because absent truth you have no true intellect. To fill out this dark picture, here is Brandon Howse, writing for the WVW Broadcast Network, detailing the depths of Marx's degeneracy:

> Marx hated the free market and capitalism—and their roots in the Protestant Reformation—perhaps because he was a lazy slob who wanted other people to take care of him. He lived largely off his friend Friedrich Engels, who drew an income from the family business. How perversely ironic is that? Marx spread his hatred of capitalism while drawing his livelihood from the fruits

---

29 Erik von Kuehnelt-Leddihn, "Portrait of an Evil Man," The Mises Institute, accessed December 15, 2022, https://mises.org/wire/portrait-evil-man-karl-marx.

of capitalism. Isn't that always the mode of operation for those who follow the economic philosophy of Communism, the most virulent form of Socialism?

Marx was such a reprobate that out of his six children, three died of starvation while still infants, two others committed suicide, and only one lived to become an adult. The Marx family was often hounded by creditors. Yet, when Marx received a gift of 160 pounds (about $500), he neglected to pay his bills, his rent, or to buy food for his starving family. Rather, he went on a two-month drinking binge with his intellectual buddies while his wife and infant children were evicted from their apartment. Marx, the parasite, also spent his wife's inheritances from her mother and uncle, causing his family to live on the edge of financial ruin for years.[30]

The bottom line is this: Marx was the king of reprobates. He was psychotic. Historically, the roots of most of today's chaos can be traced back to the self-avowed satanist, Karl Marx, who lived off inheritances, would not work, and would not bathe all because he saw bathing as bourgeois. Yet, this reprobate and his malignant theories are seen as acceptable by millennials and Gen Zers today. Marx's metaphorical progeny are alive today in the Left and the institutions they inhabit. Make no mistake, there are those today that are so base and fundamentally evil they are mentally subhuman and toxic to mankind. Having plumbed the depths in my research, let me assure you: You haven't even begun to imagine the horrors of which these people are capable.

Any cognitively sound person today cannot escape the strong parallels between the thinking and behavior of Marx and today's liberals and the Left. We have been cleansed of history by design. Society today is embarking upon repeating the horrors of history. It's as if human nature has a default to dysfunction and destruction.

30   Brannon Howse, "Karl Marx (1818-1883) and His Stated Desire To Dethrone God and Destroy Capitalism," Worldview Weekend, accessed December 15, 2022, https://www.worldviewweekend.com/worldviewpedia/transcript/karl-marx-1818-1883-and-his-stated-desire-dethrone-god-and-destroy.

Any adult blind to the self-evident evil of those in power today deserve their sufferings since they had an opportunity to avoid them. My heart goes out to the children and how they are being abused in so many ways. Thank God that He has a plan and has said for those who harm an innocent, "it would be better that they never had been born," referring to the judgment they face.

Marx is facing a blow torch for the rest of eternity, if for no other reason than he let three infants starve to death. The next time you hear a youth spout off that they think communism is a good thing you need to shove this brief history in their face along with the fact that 100 million were slaughtered by communists due to idiots like them. As I mentioned elsewhere, one of the cures for the mass psychosis we are in that leads to Marxist totalitarianism is to delegitimize and humiliate those who ignorantly, and in some cases, wickedly, promote such a scourge upon society.

Bad ideas need to be extinguished at their inception and never given a platform. Ideas, as do decisions, have consequences. However, you say, we can't ban bad ideas – that's against freedom of speech. Oh yes, we can, and yes, we must, as should be "self-evident" by now. The Left has been imposing censorship and suppressing free speech for decades, most recently revealed by the Twitter document disclosures by Elon Musk. This is an existential fight, and there is not much time left. It is clear as to what is right and wrong, and as just listed in the previous chapter, the wrongs ("wrong" is not a relative term) are overtaking the country. When ideas are patently wrong, they must be stamped out before we can turn another wrong into a right or a lie into a constitutional right.

Rotten roots yield rotten fruit. Marx the man was truly a rotten root. His life, beliefs, and behaviors were antisocial and psychotic. It is the rotten fruit of his ideology that we turn to next.

Karl: The Marxism

The main tenets of Marxism can be found in *The Communist Manifesto*. At its most basic level, Marxism promises utopianism—a "perfect" communist society where everyone shares everything, no one owns anything, and no one must work more or less than anyone else. Given Marx's behavioral history, this was very self-serving.

Marx and Engels make this perfectly clear, arguing that, "The theory of the Communists may be summed up in the single sentence: Abolition of private property."[31] As Marx contended, the only thing preventing the advent of this utopian society is the oppression of the proletariat, the working class, by the bourgeois. To usher in the revolution, the working class must rise up. They go on, arguing that, "The history of all hitherto existing societies is the history of class struggles. Freeman and slave, patrician and plebeian, lord and serf, guildmaster and journeyman, in a word, oppressor and oppressed."[32]

Marx wasn't oppressed. He was, like today's Left, virtue signaling and trying to enhance his debauched reputation by clothing himself as a working man, which he was anything but. He was excusing and justifying his depravity. So are the woke today.

Note those two words: oppressor and oppressed. That is the key to understanding Marxism and what we see the Left doing today. They have created a victim class for their use in the revolution they conceal.

In *American Marxism*, Mark Levin explains the allure of the utopian promise of Marxism, a future when all the oppressed are freed forever. He says,

> What, then, is the appeal of Marxism? American Marxism has adopted the language and allure of utopianism…It is "tyranny disguised as a desirable, workable, and even paradisiacal governing ideology. There are… unlimited utopian constructs, for the mind is capable of infinite fantasies. But there are common themes. The fantasies take the form of grand social plans or experiments, the impracticability, and impossibility of which, in small ways and large, lead to the individual's subjugation.[33]

However, to achieve heaven on earth, in the Marxist scheme, we must first go through hell and then be ruled by demons. Marx envisioned a single political party exercising total control over every aspect of life in a

---

31   Karl Marx and Friedrich Engels, *The Communist Manifesto*, trans. Samuel Moore (NY: Pocket Books, 1964), 64, Scribd.

32   Marx and Engels, *The Communist Manifesto*, 45.

33   Mark R. Levin, *American Marxism* (NY: Threshold Books, 2021), 5.

communist system. That is exactly the Democrat party's goal today—and that's not a theory or opinion. They don't even hide their agenda anymore. This has been spoken about and planned since President Kennedy's time.

This is exactly what happened in Russia when Vladimir Lenin instituted Marxist-Leninism after the Revolution of 1917. This is how Joseph Stalin led, implementing policies that resulted in the deaths of tens of millions. The same was true in China under Mao and the Chinese Communist Party. Or in Cambodia under Pol Pot. Everywhere that Marxist communism was implemented, a single, brutal, bloody, and totalitarian party crushed all opposition. There was never a utopia—only bloody nightmares and insane death counts.

This is what the psychotics want to bring to America today. It is already here and is the root of our psychosis in many ways. The revolution is already underway. The Left, Socialists, Progressives, Marxists and Democrats (peas in a pod) are the party of death. They speak glowingly about being the party that is preserving Democracy, but that is a linguistic trick. Historically, Democracy almost always leads to tyranny as you have the most illiterate electing other illiterates deluded with a psychotic and pathological ideology.

Marxism in America Today

Levin, again, provides a perfect description of the problem in America. He writes:

> In America, many Marxists cloak themselves in phrases like "progressives," "Democratic Socialists," "social activists," "community activists," etc., as most Americans remain openly hostile to the name Marxism. They operate under myriad newly minted organizational or identifying nomenclatures, such as "Black Lives Matter" (BLM), "Antifa," "The Squad," etc. And they claim to promote "economic justice," "environmental justice," "racial equity," "gender equity," etc. They have invented new theories, like Critical Race Theory, and phrases and terminologies, linked to or fit into a Marxist construct. Moreover, they claim, "the dominant culture" and capitalist system are unjust and inequitable, racist and sexist, colonialist and imperialist, materialistic and destructive of

the environment. Of course, the purpose is to tear down and tear apart the nation for a thousand reasons and in a thousand ways, thereby dispiriting and demoralizing the public; undermining the citizenry's confidence in the nation's institutions, traditions, and customs; creating one calamity after another; weakening the nation from within; and ultimately, destroying what we know as American republicanism and capitalism.[34]

This is the core of the whole problem. We were asleep at the switch. We went to sell our Democratic-Republic house and discovered that the foundation had been eaten by Marxist termites. The systemic psychosis is Marxist all the way down. The factories of inorganic psychosis are built on Marxist foundations.

History is repeating itself because we refuse to teach it accurately. Historically, Marxism has been and is the deadliest dehumanizing governmental and economic construct in human history. It is a fact over which there is no debate. Marxism is at the core of all these pandemics, whether biological or not, for its core purpose is to destabilize a culture so it will collapse into a freedomless society dependent upon a corrupt authoritarian, elite, ruling government. So how do normal, mentally functioning humans accept such governance? They don't. Those who do, die.

This pandemic thrives off a lack of discernment, a moral collapse, an addiction to convenience and comfort, and planned grooming and conditioning, which is exactly what the COVID Pandemic was all about. It tested people's pliability and how far they could be pushed and controlled.

When the authoritarians go to take over, they destabilize the target. If you look at *The Communist Manifesto*, the goal is to infiltrate, weaken, and deconstruct a country–our country. Its errand boys are the psychotic Left and its pamphleteers the media. This is what Democrats are doing and have been doing. Levin explains it like so:

> The Democratic Party seeks to empower itself by breaching constitutional firewalls; skirting if not eradicating rules, traditions, and customs; adopting Marx's language of class warfare;

---

34 Levin, *American Marxism*, 2.

and aligning with certain avowedly Marxist groups and ideological causes, among other things. Moreover, it is using the instrumentalities of the government for its political empowerment and purposes. The truth is that the interests of the Democratic Party come before those of the country.[35]

They have been doing this for decades now. Putting their interests, Marxist interests, before the country. At first, it was an economic project, but it didn't stay that way.

The Frankfurt School took Marxist economic theory and transformed it into social and cultural terms and language. This is what is known as "cultural Marxism" or "critical theory." My good friend Dr. James Lindsay explains what this is:

> Critical Theory in the narrow sense designates several generations of German philosophers and social theorists in the Western European Marxist tradition known as the Frankfurt School. According to these theorists, a "critical" theory may be distinguished from a "traditional" theory according to a specific practical purpose: a theory is critical to the extent that it seeks human "emancipation from slavery," acts as a "liberating ... influence," and works "to create a world which satisfies the needs and powers" of human beings (Horkheimer 1972, 246). Because such theories aim to explain and transform all the circumstances that enslave human beings, many "critical theories" in the broader sense have been developed. They have emerged in connection with the many social movements that identify varied dimensions of the domination of human beings in modern societies.[36]

We see critical theory playing out in all the conversations about queer theory, Black Lives Matter, feminism, the #MeToo movement, and now, of course, transgenderism. These wicked schemes are all the ideological

---

35   Levin, *American Marxism*, 7.
36   James Lindsay, "Critical Theory," New Discourses, accessed December 15, 2022, https://newdiscourses.com/tftw-critical-theory/.

offspring of Marxism mutated into cultural issues and flash points. This is how they advance the revolution.

Fruits Of Marxism

The fruit of Marxism is chaos. This chaos takes many forms, but it is all designed to destabilize society and destroy what is normative. For example, we've seen the horrible pattern unfold so clearly with transgenderism. This was all predicted decades ago in the 60s for those who had the ears to hear and the eyes to see. When we ask how this could happen, we must answer in one word: Marxism.

Our forefathers referred to "self-evident" truths in the preamble to the Constitution. There are bad ideas in this life that need no debate and should be immediately and reflexively dismissed and outlawed. Nazism, communism, and socialism are all deadly. If we could go back in time, no one armed with the knowledge of today would hesitate to eradicate those ideas at their inception. Their ideas were borne of greed and envy, and were pushed by wicked people. This should have been self-evident. What do you do with weeds? Kill them before they sprout. Pull them out by the roots. The same goes with these deadly ideas. You must expose and kill them before they spread and ruin humanity. You do it with the truth.

The blame lies not with Millennials and Gen Z. It lies with the prior generations. It lies primarily with the generation that defeated communism, or thought they did, while at the same time allowing:

The seminaries, Catholic and Protestant, to be infiltrated by Marxists in the 30s, 40s, and 50s.

Marxist college and university professors were allowed to indoctrinate the children and given tenure to continue their wickedness without accountability.

Nongovernmental organizations (NGOs) with Marxist ideologies influenced our elections and institutions, most notably coming from NGOs operated by the likes of George Soros and Claus Schwab. (Even though neither one of them personally claims to identify as a Marxist, their fundamental philosophy is no different and the results are the same.)

The election of a Marxist president whose parents, grandparents, and mentor were avowed Marxists and members of the American Communist Party.

The media is so nakedly biased, yet allowed to continue their unabated war on our freedoms of speech, bearing arms, religion and worst of all, truth.

The incongruity goes on and on. Cognitive dissonance defies all reason and logic. Just like Marx.

Who was at fault in the examples listed above? Church leaders and slumbering Christians. Trustees of universities who were more interested in esteemed titles than doing their job of oversight. Elected officials who were always seeking re-election and NGOs whose agendas were unconstitutional invasions into the freedoms of the citizens. They are the true insurrectionists. And granting the news and media essential immunity from accountability is exactly how we ended up with a Marxist President in 2008 and now his demented sycophant in 2020.

What has occurred in the rotted state of America is that government has morphed into something endemically evil. As is seen without contradiction around the world, as nations become detached from religion, as they become more atheist, the natural offshoot is nihilism which means that life has no meaning. You are born, you die, and you disappear—so your life is meaningless no matter how high you rise as a star or celebrity. Atheism creates mental illness and today it is on a mass scale.

Atheism leads to totalitarianism, because the state becomes a religion, a god, and your worth is measured by your obedience to the state as if it was your sanctification. The result, without exception, has been the extermination of hundreds of millions. A hell on earth ensues, and men, Left and Right, the sadist and masochist, the activists and the indolent, have all played a part in creating this collective hell. All this has come about because of their individual sin and departure from truth, the loss of a moral code and compass that once safely ordered and ensured a prosperous society.

The Marxist Agenda in America has Never Been a Secret

Yuri Bezmenov, a Russian KGB agent who defected in 1970, was featured on Jesse Watters Prime Time on April 14, 2023; Clips of Yuri were featured from back in 1984 explaining how the communists planned the destruction of the U. S. with psychological warfare. He began by stating that it was a slow process. This is not new news, as Yuri's revelations were made known decades ago.

According to Yuri, the Marxist plan starts with ideological subversion or active measures to change the perception of reality of every American such that no one can come to a sensible conclusion in defending themselves, their community, or their country. (This is the psychosis of which I speak of in this book.) He said it takes between 10 to 15 years to demoralize a nation because this is the number of years it takes to educate one generation of students in the country and expose them to the ideology of the enemy. This has been done so in the open, and it's criminal that our leaders did not protect the country from it. In part, we can blame former President Jimmy Carter and the Department of Education which has polluted our youth's minds. Compulsory education historically has been about mind control and creating a compliant citizenry.

Yuri declared that by 1984 the Communist ideology already had been pumped into the heads of three generations of Americans without being challenged or counterbalanced by American patriotism.

Yuri said in 1984 it was already too late, and we were well on our way towards national decay. He outlined four stages of ideological subversion, or a way of having enemy nations commit cultural suicide:

1. **Demoralization**. The children are taught to hate America and slowly chip away at patriotism and family values. We have seen so many attacks on patriotism, including on the pledge of allegiance.
2. **Destabilization**. According to Yuri, this takes 2 to 5 years in sensitive areas such as defense and the economy, but is not done by spies or sleeper cells, but instead by Americans to Americans through a lack of moral standards. It's the Left and professors who are instrumental in subverting the population. When this started it was face-to-face, but now with the internet we have a wildfire out of control.
3. **Crisis**. Promise people everything. Put a "big brother" government in DC to control everything. Have you ever heard the Left say no to something that is perverse, unsustainable, or unaffordable? Can you recall an entitlement the Left didn't say yes to

even as deficits (debt) in this country reached $31 trillion (about $95,000 per person in the US)?

4. **Normalization**. Everything is normal. Like the pagans of the past, anything goes. Look at what we are normalizing in this country which has been deviant and dangerous throughout human history.

While Yuri was off by about 20 years in his predictions as to when America would be impacted, it is happening now and being implemented.

The cultural revolution has been underway in this country, and they target the kids. Separate the family first and get to the children so when they grow up they will accept any bad idea. Remember Lenin's famous claim, "give me a child until he is five and the seeds that I plant will never be uprooted.

Conclusion

Marxism is like a hydra. We thought we had defeated it, but it is still very much alive. If you don't know this is at the core of all the symptoms of psychosis, you won't be able to effectively fight it. You will keep asking "why" instead of "what must I do to stop it." In order to stop it, you must spot the false promise of perfection, of utopia, at its root. As James Lindsay and Helen Pluckrose warned, "As ever, the perfect is the enemy of the good including the unrealistic expectation that a good system should have been able to produce better results by now. This is what makes Theory seductive—or populism, or Marxism, or any other form of Utopianism that looks good on paper and is ruinous in practice."[37]

We must purge the psychosis of Marxism from our country. To do this requires sacrifice, engagement, and action. Use the same tools of the Left: Vote them out, cancel them, boycott, push them out of the public square. We need to trust-bust the media and the woke corporations. And we must know the truth. Living in the truth is the biggest antidote, the single biggest cure, to authoritarianism and communism, as they exist

---

37 James Lindsay and Helen Pluckrose, *Cynical Theories, How Activist Scholarship Made Everything About Race, Gender, and Identity—and Why This Harms Everybody* (Durham, NC: Pitchstone Publishing, 2020), 344, Scribd.

and are built upon lies. They flourish the more you surrender your mental autonomy.

The starting point is with the individual. Purge yourself of lies and live in reality. The authoritarians are only a symptom, a reflection of the condition of the individual's soul. Suppression of the truth and the departure from reality begins with the individual. The rottenness in the state of America today is with the people. They are choosing the chains of their bondage as they love their sin. The things they claim they desire contrasted with the actions they take are cognitively dissonant. It's an incongruity that is only explained by the sin within. They love lies more than they love the truth.

Marion Smith, executive director of the Victims of Communism Memorial Foundation, said:

"The historical amnesia about the dangers of communism and socialism is on full display. When we don't educate our youngest generations about the historical truth of 100 million victims murdered at the hands of communist regimes over the past century, we shouldn't be surprised at their willingness to embrace Marxist ideas. We need to redouble our efforts to educate America's youth about the history of communist regimes and the dangers of socialism today."[38]

In summary, systemic psychosis is an outgrowth of welcoming Marxism into America. This evil ideology has literally cost tens of millions of lives. It has no business being tolerated in the land of the free and the home of the brave. It has no business on this earth. To end our systemic psychosis, we must purge the Marxists and Marxism from our midst. Nothing less than total defeat will suffice. At this late stage I'm pessimistic about the prospects; I know human nature too well. However, I also know God, and that's who I am counting on to deliver us from Satan—and Marx. My active participation and yours is required.

---

38   Marion Smith, "Fourth Annual Report On U.S. Attitudes Toward Socialism," Victims of Communism Memorial Foundation, accessed December 15, 2022, https://victimsofcommunism.org/annual-poll/2019-annual-poll/.

PART TWO

CHAPTER 5:

Psychosis and Hypocrisy— a Match Made in Hell

"Hypocrisy is the homage vice pays to virtue."
Francois de La Rochefoucauld

A Tale of Two Candidates

This chapter is about how systemic psychosis and unashamed hypocrisy goes hand in hand. First, I want to begin to demonstrate the danger of this deadly combination by contrasting two candidates from the most recent 2022 midterm elections. Consider this: John Fetterman, who is a career politician, lived with his parents until he was almost 50 years old, and is an unrecovered stroke victim who is severely cognitively impaired, now a U.S. Senator. And the voters knew this—the stroke happened before his election! Even though a majority in Pennsylvania oppose Biden's policies and even think that Biden is mentally unfit to be president, they still elected a person to be a senator who is not only mentally impaired but will also be a rubber stamp for Biden's policies that the majority in Pennsylvania say they oppose.

The voters knew all this going into the voting booths. The leftist Democrat's star is the equivalent of the movie, "Waking Ned Devine," where the main character dies upon learning he won the lottery. The town's folk want to get their hands on the winnings so they devise a scheme to fool the lottery officials that Ned is still alive. Just as the town's folk cared nothing about Ned, neither do the Democrats in Pennsylvania care a damn about Fetterman or the proper representation of the state in the U.S. Senate. They wanted a rubber stamp for their socialist agenda. This is cognitive dissonance at the extreme, at the party level, as well as for the voters. It's hypocrisy—it's psychosis.

Now, the media is totally fine with the fact that Fetterman cannot string together a single coherent sentence, because he will work to advance their shared Marxist worldview and end goals. Consider our second candidate: Hershel Walker. In the Democrat's typical hypocritical fashion, the Left attacked Herschel Walker in Georgia for being "inarticulate" and a "bad candidate," yet they excused Fetterman. By any objective standard, Walker was clearly a more competent and qualified candidate than Fetterman. So why did the Left excuse Fetterman's glaring inability yet attack Walker? Because they are hypocrites. They care nothing for the truth, only that which advances their agenda. If you are on the Left, then nothing you say or do is ever wrong. If you have beliefs like Walker's, even the slightest flaws are unforgivable. If you are a rubber stamp like Fetterman and do as you are told, they will turn a blind eye to all your shortcomings. This is the ugly face of hypocrisy and the ugly face of the Left.

The incongruent results of the midterm elections, from the standpoint that the results contradicted the stated will of the people, revealed that systemic psychosis in the country has infected at least 45 to 50% of our population. This was shown by the fact that they voted for what they had said in countless polls they were dissatisfied with. They are still suffering the consequences of their 2020 vote and yet they did it again in 2022.

The Symbiotic Relationship of Psychosis and Hypocrisy

Here is what is happening. Truth is easily blurred in a morally rudderless world. The mass psychosis from which the nation suffers stems from, among other things, the intentional suppression of the truth. And this suppression of the truth empowers hypocrites in all areas of life. What should be self-evident and axiomatic is rejected, if understood at all. It's as if the people have pseudobulbar affect disorder, where they cry when they should laugh and laugh when they should cry. Except, in this case, they vote for those causing them so much suffering instead of voting them out. They claim to deplore those in leadership but turn around and vote for them and their kind again. This irrationality is on clear display, but the issue goes deeper than that.

The country is so off course that conduct which should be described by words such as "wrong," "bad," "evil," "wicked," "sinful," and "corrupt" cannot be employed when appropriate. They are dusty from disuse or forbidden by the P.C. (politically correct) Police. Not only have words lost their meaning from disuse, but some have lost meaning from over-use, like racist, etc. If you disagree with the Left, you are called a racist regardless of how unfitting the term is for the situation. The Left has even made inanimate objects capable of being racist, such as roads, at least according to the leftist Secretary of Transportation, Pete Buttigieg, who was picked for the position not because of any expertise in trans-portation, but because of his identity as a homosexual. His short stint as Secretary has been an unmitigated disaster, racking up one failure after another and prompting calls for his resignation. The indifference and desensitization of the people to the meaning and impact of words is such that they no longer communicate in a way that would or should impact thought and conduct appropriately.

In the past, if a pejorative term were used with empirical propriety, the characterization of what the word implied would significantly impact the target. It provided some degree of accountability. If used accurately the target reaped the consequences and if used wrongly the accuser suf-fered. Words used to serve as a stoplight to bad thoughts and conduct, but no longer.

So now let's consider, very closely, "hypocrisy." Hypocrisy used to have many powerfully negative and demeaning connotations. If a target fit the description, they would not be trusted nor given any credence again. Once a hypocrite, always a hypocrite. At least, that's how we saw things when we used to think more clearly and rationally as a society.

What is a hypocrite? A hypocrite is someone with an inflated sense of ego and self-righteousness coupled with an inability to admit their mistakes and live an honest life. It's also a form of projection wherein you accuse someone of doing or being what the accuser is guilty of them-selves. Chronic hypocrites are liars, deceivers, and not to be trusted.

Another definition of hypocrite or hypocrisy is the practice of claiming to have moral standards, virtues, or beliefs to which one's behavior does not conform. It's pretending to be what one is not. It's when someone puts on a false appearance of virtue. That's called "woke" today.

The hypocrisy of many politicians is what I would call a "double hypocrisy." They create unhappiness among the voters over another's good fortune to gain the voter's votes. At the same time the politician desires to have the same good fortune as the one they are attacking and causing others to dislike. Politicians like Elizabeth Warren, Bernie Sanders, and Alexandria Ocasio-Cortez are the worst offenders. They want to tax the rich. They say they hate the rich—*but they are rich*. They create envy in others against the rich while simultaneously wanting that same good fortune for themselves. The contemporary term for such conduct is "class warfare," or we might say in their case, "intra-class warfare" because they are trying to turn the poor against their own class, but just not against them. As hypocritical politicians, this strife they create is used for their personal gain. In better and more sane times in this country, these hypocrites would be lucky to find employment again.

Within the last 50 years, we have seen politicians become multi-millionaires while in office, which cannot honestly be done on a political salary. Meanwhile, they attack the rich and say they aren't paying their fair share of taxes when in fact the wealthy pay most of the taxes. Nearly half of the country pays no taxes at all. The politicians who make such false claims know they are false and don't care because mentally impaired Americans will never hold them accountable.

If the word "hypocrite" had the cultural power it once had, then many politicians would be forced from office *today*, and, needless to say, we would all be the better for it. The examples of Fetterman, Buttigieg, Walker, etc., are exemplary of the Left talking out of both sides of their mouths. The words and terms describing such conduct appear to have no impact. Psychosis has rendered people indifferent to the consequences of their dissonance.

Systemic psychosis has numbed our nerves, making us dull to the brazen hypocrites that live with and lead us. They exploit it. It truly is a match made in hell, like the two demons from C.S. Lewis' *Screwtape Letters*. I'm here to expose their exploitation so you can be equipped to see through it and reject it. So next, let's take some very poignant and contemporary examples of hypocrisy and consider how, if the word had the impact that it *should*, it would have caused the near-permanent ostracization of the hypocrites and radically transform our government in a positive way.

Hypocrisy on Parade: Exposing Hypocrites for Who They Are

First, the Left says they don't know what a woman is. However, when the Supreme Court overturned *Roe v Wade*, suddenly you can only have an opinion on abortion if you are a *woman*. Wait—who is a woman? Remember, they can't even define it.

Second, let's go back to Justice Ketanji Brown Jackson. Justice Jackson was appointed for two reasons: She was black and a woman. By those standards, any woman of color in America would be qualified as a Supreme Court Justice. The color of skin or one's gender is no qualification for a judge, or anything else, but that is beside the point. We are no longer in Kansas, Dorothy. This is the city of Oz, a world upside down. By the way, the most consistent and brilliant justice on the Supreme Court is Clarence Thomas, a black man who faced the open racism of our current president and then senator Joseph Biden during his confirmation hearings. Go watch the historical video of our hypocrite-in-chief at Thomas' confirmation. As Thomas said, it was a "high-tech lynching." If this had occurred today and Biden were a Republican senator, he would not have lasted a week in office, yet this white, liberal, racist hypocrite is now president.

Legal and intellectual ability wasn't on the list of qualifications for Justice Jackson. Good thing, since she couldn't even define "woman." Of course, they knew *she* was a woman, since the Left appointed her for that very reason. They did so to appeal to a voter group they created in the minds of the public, "women," as if 50% of the population needs to be identified as a separate minority group and victim class under law. They did this nonetheless, conditioning low IQ voters who need to hear a rhetorical dog whistle in order to know what to do and how to think and vote.

Jackson knew exactly the game being played. President Biden knew she was a woman. She knows how to define a woman but would not define it since she was catering to the radical Left. Why? She is supposed to be unbiased. She already knew her whole life was lived in hypocrisy in order to ascend the ladder. Clearly the people are oblivious to contradictions or simply don't care. With the stakes being so high and the consequences so dire, such indifference is again, psychotic.

Third, remember when the Department of Homeland Security attempted to create a "Disinformation Governance Board" to police misinformation and supposedly defend the truth? Then after two-quarters of negative economic growth, the Biden Administration decided to redefine the age-old definition of "recession" overnight in an act of massive misinformation because their political power and fortunes depended on it. Now a recession was not two-quarters of negative growth, but instead whatever they wanted or needed it to be. There were enough mental midgets in the country to accept the hypocrisy. So much for disinformation governance.

Fourth, some of the worst hypocrisy we have witnessed of late came during the COVID, so-called, "pandemic." Politicians across the country embraced a "rules for me but not for thee" approach to dealing with mandates. You had to wear a mask and sit a magical six feet apart in church, but for Speaker Nancy Pelosi it was okay to be seen maskless, rubbing shoulders with Democrat Party donors. You had to cancel your vacation, but many politicians got to take theirs. You had to watch loved ones die alone, but the career criminal George Floyd got a hero's funeral because of his victim status. This is hypocrisy.

In an excellent opinion piece published in the Washington Times, entitled "Progressives' are hypocrites, and they don't care if you know it," Dr. Everett Piper called out more examples of progressive liberal hypocrisy. He astutely claims that "members of the elite class never believed any of their previous posturing about human rights, personal freedom, and the dignity of every human being. Their call for diversity and inclusion was simply sleight-of-hand."[39]

He then goes on to list a few examples, which serve to make my point as well. He records that:

---

39 Everett Piper, "'Progressives' are hypocrites and they don't care if you know it," Washington Times, accessed on October 28, 2022, https://www.washingtontimes.com/news/2018/aug/19/progressives-are-hypocrites-and-they-dont-care-if-/.

Rep. Maxine Waters persists in encouraging politically liberal restaurant owners to refuse to provide service and food to conservative patrons while at the same time the entire leadership of Ms. Waters' party doubles down on its demands that all conservatives should be required, by law, to provide food and service (i.e., bake a cake) for any non-conservative who aligns themself with Ms. Waters' politics and party.

On MSNBC, Candace Owens, a conservative black woman, is lectured about "tone" by Michael Eric Dyson, a liberal black man, who then calls Ms. Owens a "little girl." One must wonder if Mr. Dyson, a sociology professor at Georgetown University, will next be modeling his exemplary "tone" by calling black men who disagree with him "boys."

In California, the land that legislates "tolerance" as its highest good, an advertising company is forced—under "serious threat"—to remove numerous billboards from across the entire Los Angeles area because the billboards showed evangelist and pastor Greg Laurie holding a black book presumed to be a Bible. This threat was all done by those who proudly wave their banners and placards of "love trumps hate," "inclusion," "diversity," and "tolerance."[40]

Fifth, a most glaring and multifaceted example of leftist hypocrisy is when Texas and Florida started bussing and flying illegal immigrants to liberal bastions and sanctuary cities around the country, often directly to the homes of liberal, white elites. The word hypocrisy today is nearly a synonym for, "liberal white men and women." And these liberal types had a melt-down when they had to deal with the illegal migrants.

One of the most exclusive areas for the elite liberal whites in the country is Martha's Vineyard Island off the coast of Massachusetts. They voted 80% for Biden in the 2020 election. When Governor DeSantis of Florida flew 48 Venezuelans to the island the white virtue-signaling frauds

---

40 Piper, "Progressives Are Hypocrites," *Washington Times*.

melted down. They went into crisis mode; they stripped off their robes of self-righteousness and within 48 hours they had their leftist Republican governor transport the Venezuelans off the island to a military base.

If ever you wanted a poster for hypocrisy, it is the actions of Martha's Vineyard. While they supported the very politicians who did nothing to stem the invasion on the southern border where over 8 million illegals have crossed into the border states since Biden became president, Martha's Vineyard's residents wouldn't even accept 48. The true face of racism was seen in the near exclusively white island resort. They were exposed. It's okay for Florida and Texas to absorb millions but Martha's Vineyard won't even take 48 of those they contend have a right to be in this country in the name of compassion. We see how far compassion went with the liberals of Martha's Vineyard, but it is not just endemic to that island, but to liberals and leftists across the country in general. They know they are frauds and the criminals of humanity, but they also know their low information and IQ voters will keep them in power. The vast damage that has been done to people of color by the liberal white community with their false virtue and piety is astounding; but they are the masters of hypocrisy and hide their racism by accusing others. No one has documented that damage and the demagoguery better than one of the greatest intellects of our time, a black man, Dr. Thomas Sowell.

In a normal and functioning country, such conduct and hypocrisy never would have been allowed. It would have been shunned and those participating in it would have lost all influence. Not today. Psychosis has gripped the country and the Right can barely respond to such conduct, since that would require courage, sacrifice, and determination. Most on the Right have "the right stuff" policy-wise, but there are not enough of them who are serving in government that will make the hard choices.

In January 2023, only 20 Republicans stood up to 212 Republicans, holding up Kevin McCarthy's ascendancy to the Speakership without concessions. They were condemned by the other 212 but when one looks at what that 20 stood for and insisted upon, any Republican would and should ask, "why would any GOP lawmaker not support such demands? In fact, why should they ever have been part of a debate as opposed to being part of a sacrosanct list of principles that all Republicans should support? This is not a slight to McCarthy individually, but to the party as a whole on something that was an unnecessarily self-inflicted wound.

These examples are just the tip of the iceberg of the hypocrisy that could be provided, as more and more are created daily because there is no consequence for bad conduct anymore, particularly hypocrisy. In fact, the examples, if all listed, would be encyclopedic. As Dr. Piper puts it, "Welcome to utopia. It's 1984 and all will be 'free,' they tell us—as long as we are ready to give up our freedom."

Given the above facts and examples, why would anyone ever tolerate those kinds of people with power or authority? Why would you ever trust your vote to them again? If you have acted contrary to this evidence and tolerated such conduct via your voting, then you are infected with the psychosis plaguing the populace of this country.

You will pay dearly for it with the loss of your liberty, happiness, property, and at some point, perhaps your life. Life is a serious business, and this country is committing suicide through the psychotic behaviors and conduct coming from those we have allowed to lead us in government, news, and education. How and why did this happen? As goes the church, so goes the nation.

Once upon a time a common moral code kept us united, at peace and prosperous; but the wicked enticed us with heresies, lustful desires, and envy—and dumbed us down in our institutions of higher education with false teachers. We relegated our mental faculties to the perverse in turn for comfort and convenience. Now here we are, in chaos, facing our cultural mortality. We are a lying, thieving, covetous, and adulterous species deserving of the miseries we elect. We love lies and hate the truth.

The Greek word *katechontōn* means suppressors of, or the suppression of, the truth. One of God's greatest hatreds and stored up wrath is targeted against the suppressors of the truth, arguably the oldest and first sin. Nothing is new under the sun, simply different in form. I agree with many pastors today that contend the country is under judgment. The Bible today almost reads like a newspaper of current events.

How The Right Enables Hypocrites

Truth is inconvenient for both Left and Right. As I have argued, the Left hates the truth and actively suppresses it. It is indicative and revealing of their wicked intentions and destructive agendas. They preach freedom, liberty, and tolerance, yet they are the least tolerant. They hate the truth because it stands in the way of their delusional utopian (rather, dystopian) society where they are the elitists in control. The bitter truth is the Left opposes their own humanity. They are self-destructive and do it with an ungodly passion and rage.

They have little if any real skills other than being consumers on the government dole. They have no real concern about anyone other than themselves and their immediate gratification. They are also the masters at virtue signaling designed to justify their hypocritical greed. The undiscerning will fall into the trap of thinking them noble, but then those are the headline readers only. The Left are masters of phony moral indignation, covering up the fact that they are hateful and mean people. Don't believe it? Try expressing a different opinion or disagreeing with them.

This is the ugliness of hypocrisy. As devastating as that word should be to those guilty and justly labeled by it, it just isn't anymore. And they don't even attempt any pretense or pose an ameliorating excuse for it. They rub it in your face and then dare you to do something about it. Today, the Devil looks you in the eyes without any disguise, tells you exactly how you are going to sin, and that you aren't going to do a damn thing about it. As the famous quote goes regarding Commodus from the movie, Gladiator, "He [emperor] will bring them death and they will love him for it." The psychosis in ancient Rome brought down the empire. It is rotting America and bringing it down as well.

On the Right side of the spectrum, any real defense of the truth is lost in word salads. For the most part, the Right sees the facts as they are and knows the truth. However, it is inconvenient to act. It takes guts. Far too many on this side of the spectrum haven't the courage of their convictions. They are cowards. The truth indicts them in their inaction, sloth, and cowardice. They want it both ways. Truth, while they claim to love it, manages to demand nothing of them; their affections seem more of a mere mental assent because they know that if they really loved the truth enough to act, such service would require sacrifice.

Those on the Right work overtime convincing themselves that things are not all that bad. They don't want the inconvenience of actually having to do something about what is contrary to the truth. They are dismissive of the lies and deceit on the Left as just another phase or fad. They spend nothing trying to preserve their freedoms. They spend no time fighting and defending their freedoms and they live in an unnatural state of denial of the obvious and apparent. That's psychosis. It's the Marie Antoinette Syndrome of "Let them eat cake." And yes, they will lose their proverbial heads because of their denial.

The Right would rather lose nobly than win ugly. Such a British trait! As I say elsewhere, they are the masochists of a sadist-to-masochist marriage. The only problem is the sadist eventually ends up killing the masochist.

The hypocrisy on the Right was on full display in the confirmation of Justice Brown Jackson. Three Republican members in the Senate supported her while gaslighting their conservative base. You heard confusing double talk that Jackson was eminently qualified even by those who voted against her. Seriously? She can't define something as basic as a woman, yet three Republican Senators would have us believe that she can define our constitutional rights while others on the Right said she was qualified. No, she was not! This is the hypocrisy of wanting to appear considerate while deceiving the public. The fools on the Right think they will benefit by appearing nice. They never have so far. Good deeds never go unpunished, which is a lesson the Right has never learned but paid for time and again.

In fairness, had Republicans voted against her, Kamala-lobotomized-Harris would have broken the tie, but that doesn't excuse the conduct of the three or the false signaling of others as to virtue and qualification that Jackson did not have. All 50 Democrat senators voted for Jackson. Surprised? Do you think there is any diversity of thought in the Democrat Party? If this doesn't exemplify the rottenness within the country, then you need therapy.

This is hypocrisy, virtue signaling, and a degree of psychosis so Kafkaesque it is otherworldly, demonic, and even life-threatening. It's a march into the gas chambers with barely a whimper. It is fiddling while Rome burns.

Ancient Israel, again and again, became so nationally psychotic in their disobedience to the clear commands of a wrathful God, that the lack of self-correction resulted in multiple invasions and defeats leading to the enslavement of the people. One of the most memorable ones was the Babylonian captivity. Call that a divine judgment or not, the undeniable fact is a society in such chaos and dysfunction will collapse. Whether you heed the historical Biblical approach or just common sense, the end is predictable.

Hypocrisy abounds and it knows no party lines. So how can we deal with them? What does it look like to fight back?

Things to Avoid When Dealing with Hypocrites

Weary of all the consternation and the wringing of hands and speculations plaguing the country, this book was prompted to address what is being missed. You can only listen to someone continuously cry about being wet until you finally yell at them, "Get the hell out of the rain, you idiot." The same holds for dealing with the hypocrites, acolytes, and lemmings of the Left.

If you want to stop getting wet, you need to get out of the rain. So here are a few admonishments, by the way of negative statements, that you can consider NOT doing when dealing with hypocrites and the mass psychosis in the country.

Don't Be Dumb

The massive split in the culture, exacerbated by unchecked hypocrisy, also reveals the danger and consequences of an intentionally dumbed-down society. The Lemmings, the followers, and the cognitively challenged, are easily manipulated. They are the same types and of the same character that praised Christ on his way into Jerusalem wanting him to be king only to scream for him to be crucified days later. Nothing is new under the sun, and there is nothing new about the human character today. Self-reflection is absent. So many people are electively dumb.

These same malleable and manipulatable types are dangerous. They are mindless drones, always wrong but never in doubt. They seem to invite the Left to prey upon them and use them to implement the same age-old policies that destroy cultures and nations. These were the same people who confronted you if you didn't have your mask on. They were and are those who rarely engage in critical thinking. They live to conform, no matter how insane the dictates or mandates. These are the snitches, the indoctrinated children in Orwell's *1984* who reported their parents to the authorities.

Don't be like that. Educate yourselves, question everything, become an expert skeptic, and take responsibility for your own mental autonomy. Don't be dumb. You will be the first to feel the effects, and no one will come to rescue an idiot.

Don't Be a Barbarian

We look back in history and are aghast at the horrors of the past, such as child sacrifice, and wonder how such a barbaric thing could happen. Well, it still is happening. We still have the barbarian demons among us. Laws are being considered in California today that would allow a parent to terminate a child's life after birth or mutilate children in the name of transgenderism. Oppose these monsters. Take action and be angered when you should be angered. Don't be silent. As St. Thomas Aquinas said, not to be angry at such things makes you immoral and, in my own terminology, barbaric.

So, how could this happen? How could such barbarians be allowed into positions of power to even propose such monstrous things? It happened by default. The thinkers (Right) hobbled by ineffective strategies along with a good dose of cowardice allowed the non-thinkers (Left) to ascend to and assume power. The thinkers have now discovered that while they were away on one of their "convenience and comfort vacations" the non-thinkers they left in charge burned down the house. The barbarians aren't just at the gate—they are inside the camp. To be intentionally ignorant of the world around you is "barbaric," since it makes one complicit with the horrors that result from this posture.

Don't Be Naïve

Laziness lies to us. It coaxes you into believing that once you have proverbially "made it" you can now coast the rest of the way through life and leave the worrying and hard work of defending freedom to someone else. Wrong! Success brings greater responsibility and work that cannot be delegated. Freedom is not free, nor is it maintained by remote control. This is how and why our country has devolved into this mass psychosis and spiraling disintegration as the inmates of the asylum are taking control. To think that nothing bad will come of what is happening in the country or result if you do nothing is sinfully naïve.

Nearly 50% of the population in the United States is at least 40 years old and older. They have had enough life experience to understand there has been a marked deterioration in the trajectory of this country while they have been alive. The pace of the decline has resulted in instability and chaos. As with the collapse of the Soviet bloc in the 1990s, the pace at which it occurred was dizzying and people were left without any points of reference. They didn't know how to plan from one day to the next and were clueless as to how it would affect them. Anxiety was and is today at an all-time high, and this produces tyrants as the people will seek out any means and accept any promise to return to order and normalcy.

The confluence in this country of perversity, political lawlessness, indifference to crime, educational indoctrination of children, institutionalized gender dysphoria, corporate collusion with leftist government agendas, and ideologically based violence and retribution has resulted in chaos amongst half the country who have a memory of the way things used to be. This is why there is such instability and anxiety plaguing the nation.

The other half, the 40 and under, lacking in historical and experiential knowledge, are also suffering economically. They are emotionally frenzied, not knowing why things are happening, or are unable to connect the dots due to their ignorance of history. Consequently, they have ignorantly embraced philosophies, theories, and Marxist agendas that they are acting out in a *Lord of the Flies* dystopia or Orwellian insanity which will destroy any promise of future happiness for them. They have belligerent ignorance and will die in the arms of betrayal, all born of the evil that has so deceived them.

A lot of this blame falls upon the previous generation. Yes, we have had wars and even a Civil War, but people took sides then and knew what they believed. Compare that to today where everything from a defined country with borders, a common culture, defined inalienable rights, sacrosanct church, and faith, even down to whether you are male or female and "what is a woman," is being questioned. Many no longer know what they believe or what to believe. Those things which historically have given one a point of reference and a standard around which to order one's life are now all gone. Yes, it is insane and chaotic, but it was predicted, it was planned, and it is all a logical consequence and outcome. The hypocrites were not called to task. They were not shamed off the platform. Rather, they were re-elected.

The chaos and confusion in this country reveals the problem, but what is occurring is not a coincidence, nor a set of mistakes, nor just bad policies. As I've emphasized, it's a psychosis. And the psychosis is compounded by the hypocrisy of so many actors. It has been planned and implemented by corrupt actors in our country.

However, we can fight back by recognizing it, and by refusing to be 1) dumb, 2) barbaric, and 3) naïve.

Hopefully this helps connect some of the dots for the reader. The purpose of laying it all out like this is so that you can, with some mental clarity, know who the bad actors are and how to methodically remove their influence and power, at least from your life, if not the nation. We didn't get here overnight, and we will not recover what we have lost overnight if it isn't already too late. There is no choice but to fight, resist and oppose the wrong and evil of the Left.

As mentioned previously this all has been planned. In some senses, it was drawn up as revealed by Yuri Bezmenov. That's what I look at next.

CHAPTER 6:

Skepticism And Systemic Psychosis

"Blind belief in authority is
the greatest enemy of truth."
Albert Einstein

The white elephant in the room that everyone avoids talking about in these chaotic times is what the end is going to look like. People know that something is wrong. The country can't sustain the chaos. It's being driven along by the hypocrites we just encountered. We are in the prologue. Will this be a capitulation or will someone ignite the revolution, like the first shot at the Battle of Lexington and Concord? If you haven't been listening to the leftist psychos, they have been using the word "revolution" for some time now. That's old news. If it is *new* news to you, then you have not been listening. You have been asleep, because the ship of state hit that iceberg long ago.

The Left has been a practitioner of violence for a long time, not just in this country, but around the world. Their ideology and violence go hand in hand. They are nihilists desperate for a meaning to the life they lack. That is who they are and that is the destruction they will bring. Einstein's quote is so appropriate for today. Truth has suffered because we had a blind belief in authority, an authority which has become totally corrupt. Whenever you find widespread blind belief, you know that a healthy skepticism is absent.

The revolution in this country has been in full swing for the last several decades. You have been taken by the salami method, one slice at a time. Like the frog in the pot, comfortable at first, they slowly raise the temperature to a boil. The critical mass has been reached and is most likely irreversible and uncontrollable. When this happens, even the psychotic and self-righteous Left will be unable to control it. The fog of war, revolution, and societal collapse all have unintended consequences. Those who brought them about, being the least capable and cognitive of society, having only a knack for destruction, will not be able to control the Frankenstein they have created. They too, along with those on the Right, will perish and their descendants will live in misery if they live at all.

The Left rushes us to this breaking point while the Right asks them to simply drive a little slower. The Right lives in denial, hoping that the reality they deny will at some point come to their rescue. Let me be unambiguously clear here. It is my generation, the Baby Boomers, who utterly failed. They allowed into power the corruption that is destroying the country. There is no need to be surprised by what evil does. They do what is natural to them. What is unacceptable is what those who should know better fail to do. And one of those things they should have done is exercise a healthy skepticism, finding the courage to question the narrative and fight against the direction the Left has been taking us.

Let's consider further the consequences of a lack of skepticism, or put another way, a blind faith so many people have placed in our failed leaders resulting from their psychosis, and the damage it is doing in broader American society today.

Consider first the current suffering of millions here in America under record-high inflation and astronomically high fuel costs. President Biden blames Vladimir Putin for energy costs, yet in the year before the Ukraine invasion (while Biden was president) energy costs had already gone up 66%.[41] The lies and the hypocrisy continue to go unchecked

---

41 Max Bower, "Bracing for sticker shock: It's going to cost a whole lot more to heat your home this winter — 60% or more, on average," Daily Hampshire Gazette, accessed on October 28, 2022, https://www.gazettenet.com/Home-heating-costs-expected-to-skyrocket-this-winter-48548049.

and unpunished. In the times of kings and queens the people had no choice, but today they choose their sufferings and bondage. The people in their psychotic and misanthropic ways have earned the problems that beset them. They lacked healthy skepticism and were too lazy to ask the right questions.

Rest assured, the pain is the point. The forced economic tightening and the forced shortages are all intentional so as to create a new reality that the dystopian left believes is necessary to bring about their one-world global communist fever dream where we "own nothing" and are to be happy anyway. Our lack of skepticism has caused us to readily accept anyone's opinion as long as they call themselves an "expert."

Thomas Sowell, a world-renowned economist and leading critical thinker, notes that many of the large-scale disasters and disturbances of our time have been created by "experts." He humorously (and accurately) points out that "In every disaster throughout American history, there always seems to be a man from Harvard in the middle of it." Maybe it's time to stop listening to the experts.

Speaking of experts, particularly the fraudulent ones of which there is no shortage, let's now consider how the climate radicals are trying to pull the wool over the eyes of those who can see through their lie and duct tape the mouth of the skeptics shut.

The Dangerous Lack of Climate "Science" Skepticism

The climate change activists are some of the main drivers of this psychotic hypocrisy today. They have created dangerous and violent zealots. They love displaying their manipulated statistics, suppressing others, and controlling scientific reports by funding (or withholding funding) grants to various scientific projects by pseudo-scientists, many of whom were not experts in the fields in which they ventured false expert opinions.

The purpose of the whole climate charade was not so much the manipulation of an outcome (that is changing climate, which was always impossible) but rather a behavior. It defies reality. It is made from whole cloth, absent empirical data that is genuine, testable, and verifiable by scientific analysis and observation. As previously stated, just look at the past failures and scary doomsday tactics of the scientists of the past. It is baseless speculation that brings great and needless suffering. However, sweet revenge is baked into the cake. The Left is always wrong but never in doubt. They exude a false and stolen competence, but in crisis, they will fail with the rest and not escape.

These climate radicals and their organizations are so hypocritical that they even accept funds from Russian and communist groups who have no intention at all to reduce their pollution. Those groups want this country and our allies to be dependent upon our enemy's raw resources. This gave the Russians the financial means and leverage to fight the West while rejecting the tenants of climate change themselves. For the most part, they were allowed exemptions, as if they ever would have abided by them anyway.

Truly, in this area, there is no psychosis for the Russians, the Chinese, or the others who have negotiated exemptions from climate controls and regulations. They live in reality. They have played the West for the fools that they are. Authoritarians and autocrats will have nothing to do with the fake climate change agenda as it benefits them not to do so and hurts the West. They know the world is not going to end in 12 years. After all, they are the ones who floated that narrative to begin with, knowing the Western psychos on the Left would gobble it up, and they did. Revenge is a dish best served cold, and that is what Europe ate in the 2022 and 2023 winter seasons.

This plays directly into the Russia-Ukrainian War. It was inevitable that Russia would start cutting off the spigot of oil and gas to European nations for their backing of Ukraine. How detached were the Western leaders not to have anticipated this chess move? All the windmills, solar power, and green energy fanatics must have clouded their vision. Their governments gave in to their psychosis and now they will all have to pay inflated prices for natural gas and oil if they can get it. These green psychos were oblivious to the fact that neither Russia nor China had any concern about greenhouse gasses (you know, that CO_2 stuff that crops need to grow). They were not going along with the green program. Well, I guess they were, in the sense that the green they were after was your money.

I cannot help but gloat over the video of President Trump speaking at the U.N., warning Germany of the dangers of their dependence on Russian oil and gas. The sanctimonious German delegates were seen laughing and sneering at the warning. Two years later where are they? We can only hope that they were among those who froze that winter.

Let's take a brief but deeper dive into climate science which along with COVID has the world on edge. Science has become political. It has been hijacked by the Left and turned into a religion. Consequently, science is no longer trusted, which is a good thing in many ways, but why? Because their models, assumptions, and predictions have been, as stated, so miserably wrong for decades. Where were the skeptics? Had they been around and been loud our world would have avoided all the destruction of the last decade.

Climate experts say we have 12 years left to save the world. They have been saying this for decades. The Democrats and the Left (synonymous) have been on board with the threats and scare tactics because it is profitable politically and financially. This is what they do best. Scientists and their benefactors on the Left have missed their predicted doomsday many, many times, but they haven't separated themselves from their conflicts of interests and the money they make from the fear they spread.

One never hears from the scientists about the effect of the earth's wobble, rotation, and tilt; or solar events and volcanic blasts, like the recent 2022 Tonga blast that was the equivalent of 100 atomic bombs and the largest ever recorded. There is so much data out there proving the fraud of the climate fanatics and how erroneous their so-called science is that the courts should be flooded with lawsuits based on fraud.

Dr. Richard Lindzen exposes the fraud and calls it a politicized power play motivated by malice and profit. His interviews, lectures and expertise are compelling and indicative. Everything is centered on what humans are assumed to be doing but never describes how small and negligible it is in comparison to natural forces over which we have zero control. An educated, non-woke, non-psychotic, and skeptical mind would have readily made these inquiries and observations. We must all sacrifice except the elite who preach sacrifice but hypocritically fly around in their private jets for which you helped pay.

If all human activity were to cease tomorrow, honest, non-political scientific studies reveal that the temperature would at best decline by less than one degree. As I have established previously about the Left's love for inexcusable exorbitant extrapolations for political purposes, the abuses and the economic disasters it has wrought in the climate arena has harmed the world irreparably. It has lined the Left's political pockets to continue their abuse. The lies and hypocrisy are astounding, but what's more astounding are the multitudes who fall for the lies every time. The absence of healthy skepticism, which in this instance if given an honest hearing, would have shut down the whole climate fraud overnight. Unfortunately, the people never ask questions or point out inconsistencies because they lack natural skepticism. We need more Missouri people, the famous "Show Me" state.

To make matters worse, China, India, Mexico, and Russia are the largest polluters but have exemptions. Without their participation there is no possible change based on current, so-called scientific models, even if there was the possibility of changing anything. America could shut down, starve, and disappear as a country and there would be no effect on the climate. And that's the goal. America is killing itself with climate fraud. The science hypocrites know this. And this is particularly true with India, China, Russia, and South America being essentially exempted from any remedial measures from which most of carbon emissions arise.

Now are you waking up? What does this have to do with psychosis? Your compliance and eager obedience to that which runs counter to reality is a psychosis. You cannot excuse yourself and say you are unaware as if ignorance is an excuse. You already live with the principle daily that ignorance of the law is no excuse or defense when you break it. And, as many Christians know, in judgment no one will have the excuse that they "didn't know." We are told that knowledge of God is implanted into every human such that there will be no excuses on judgment day. So, disabuse yourself that you have no responsibility to be informed or that you didn't know. It doesn't wash. No one has a right to be stupid. Whether Christian or secular, there are no excuses or escape routes.

For those so concerned about global warming, remember, warmth is life, and cold is death. More die annually of cold than they do heat. Crops don't grow on glaciers. So, if there is a warming then bring it on. People are slowly waking up to the purposeful attempt to mislead them. Hopefully, it will be in time.

And it's not just "climate science" that has been dead wrong. Remember all the fake health scares over the last 50 years? How many thousands of articles have been published about various foods that cause cancer? Essentially anything we eat is bad for us and is going to lead to cancer. Let's review a few of the supposed deadly, disease or cancer-causing things we consume—that is, according to the "science" for which we should have been skeptical, but fortunately many are beginning to ignore the cries of "wolf."

Fats. First, we were told that diets high in fat would lead to heart disease. Twenty years later we were told the evidence does not single out fat or cholesterol as a heart risk factor.

Sugar. We were told that excessive sugar consumption is related to diabetes, then we were told that it is not related to obesity or diabetes. Later we were told that sugary foods were linked to breast cancer only to find out 10 years later there is no link.

Salt. Experts said that too much salt was linked to cardiac disease, then later that too little salt increases cardiac disease. Which one is it?

Vitamins. Vitamin C was said to prevent colds, then they said it doesn't. Some vitamins were said to prevent cancers only to be later reversed, and now we are told that they do not prevent cancer.

Alcohol. First, we knew that in moderation, some alcohol was beneficial. Now, apparently even minute amounts of alcohol can supposedly increase cancer risks.

The people are exhausted. You should be exhausted and tuned out to all the quackery. Billions have been spent while thousands have made fortunes on all the fake scientific claims causing alarm and fear in the people. Yet during COVID we were all told to "follow the science."[42]

Ponder for a moment, if you will, how much more peaceful and happier and wealthier you would be today if you had been a healthy skeptic 20 or 30 years ago and rejected all the fear that was pushed your way to control your choices.

Dr. Lain McGilchrist in an interview with the UnHerd podcast on April 28, 2023, spoke about the difference between science and "scientism," and how scientism is actually a religious system. He noted that

---

42   Much of the supporting material for both the bogus health science and climate science that I reference in this chapter can be found in two lectures: 1) "12 years to Disaster? How Climate Activists Distort the Evidence," by Aaron Brown, and 2) "How Sure Are Climate Scientists, really?" by Neil Halloran. Rest assured, there are scores of similar reports and findings.

science becomes a faith when it says it can answer all our questions. There are so many things in life that are important that science cannot answer or explain to us, like the beauty of a rainbow, a wonderful landscape, or a piece of music. It is illogical, irrational, and unscientific to say that science can answer all our questions. Science is only supposed to reveal things which can be proven to be the case, but it cannot be proven to be the case that science can answer all our questions. Those who argue like this or demand blind allegiance to "the science" are instead pushing *scientism.*

And remember, humans are imperfect. This means scientists are biased. McGilchrist notes science is practiced by humans and humans are flawed. Given the last 100 years of science, we can see just how unsound and wrong it (science) can be. Science favors the moneyed interest that paid for the research. Professional scientists are not only as flawed as the rest of us but frequently in error. This should cause you to have a healthy degree of skepticism.

Get rid of science as your God. It's time to realize that science is not your friend any more than a politician is, because the two are essentially indistinguishable today. Common sense is your friend. Questioning everything and getting a Ph.D. in skepticism will enrich your life, if not save it. After all of the experience the American public has had in false alarms, fake news, and fake science, if you are not a skeptic by now, then you are neurotic and psychotic. You need more than just being a skeptic. Your skepticism needs legs and feet. You need to stop voting for those candidates that propose, push, and pass legislative measures that are impoverishing you and taking away your freedoms.

The climate radicals and the leftist politicians whom they serve want you to sacrifice your life today, the only one you have, for something that is false and unproven; yet you will not see those hypocrites sacrificing anything themselves.

The chess game the autocrats played against the West was well executed. If I were one of those comrades in arms, I would be toasting them for a strategy carried out well. Was it really an evenly matched game? The psychotic idiots in the West versus the realist autocrats in the east.

Russia and China supported these fanatical causes of green energy, anti-fracking and the like with the goal in mind of making the fools who bought the lie, all dependent. What the Russians did is called, "шах и мат" (checkmate). When psychosis renders its target nonfunctional, in this case, America and the West, then they are at the mercy of their enemies. The sanctimonious European and American green groups ended up funding the Russian military's invasion of Ukraine. Now they are paying for it at the gas pump. Sadly, the rest of us are too.

The Deadly Lack of COVID Skepticism

Then we have the coronavirus pandemic. All the scientific studies debunked the efficacy of masks, yet they were mandated. How many lemmings have you seen wearing masks alone in their cars or walking in the park with their dogs? Months after the mandates were withdrawn, I drove past a home in the countryside. There on the porch, alone, was a woman with a mask on. There is a whole and lengthy discussion and analysis that could be had about that, but suffice it to say, she is a useful idiot for the authoritarians. She is one of the non-thinking, cognitively impaired people, blindly obedient, that will vote slave masters into power. This is proof Socrates was correct about the dangers of democracy and those not qualified to engage in the critical exercise of voting.

One positive feature of the fake COVID pandemic was that it exposed those around us that will be happy to vote for socialism and our oppressors. Now we have seen the enemy of freedom. We have seen the face of our national psychosis. To them blind obedience is a virtue and sanctifying. I will discuss the psychology of obsession to obedience later.

This is a big problem and, to make things worse, as Dr. Jordan Peterson once remarked, there is an alarming state of low intelligence in this country. One in ten people have an IQ under 83. This can't be changed no matter how much money you throw at it. How do you control such a mass of people who are cognitively challenged yet are armed with the vote and default to the demagoguery of the Left?

Then there are the restaurant rules. You wear a mask to your table and then remove it. Apparently, the virus can determine that you are sitting down eating so it doesn't disperse. How was mass skepticism used to stop this insanity? It wasn't. We blindly followed the fake science experts.

There are thousands of examples of psychotic thinking and behaviors on this topic alone that defy all logic, rationale, reason, and reality. By now you have heard them all, and it has driven you crazy too, but I would have everyone reflect on who they voted for. Connect the dots. Understand cause and effect. This is cognitive dissonance – this is textbook psychosis.

A humorous cartoon depicted a gentleman with his dog at a veterinarian clinic saying, "If after your dog's third rabies' vaccination he gets rabies you may want to start asking questions." We never ask questions. We get surprised and repeat our mistakes. We have lost our natural and healthy skepticism as our education system has cleansed us of it. There is a clear cognitive disconnect between how the public reacted to the coronavirus pandemic and the mandates. There was no logical implementation of remedial measures. The rules and regulations continued to change daily, and even the scientific data and medical evidence proved it was more about political manipulation and crowd control than it was about dealing with the virus. It was the perfect storm, the perfect crisis for budding authoritarians in this country and for the globalists to experiment as to how far they could push the people into submission. This was all pushed forward with the Left confident they could count on the irrational 25% of the population to support them in whatever they did. Were any of the frauds held accountable? No!

In a lecture Jordan Peterson discussed the correlation and frequency of infectious disease with authoritarian belief. The higher the prevalence of infectious disease, the higher the level of authoritarian political attitudes. There was a surprisingly strong correlation with COVID. One only needs to look at the ultimate effect and end results of policies on the Left to see that the trajectory of each one is totalitarian, whether it be the pandemic or climate. They want total Democrat Party dominance (uniparty) where what is left of the Republican Party is only to give the appearance of some semblance of a democracy (in their definition), but essentially the two-party system is dead. Freedom is dead.

In comparing the liberals with the conservatives, Peterson also notes that conservatives desire borders in many respects, not just physical ones as between nations, but also in our social constructs for the protection of the species. Therein we can see the protective approach of conservatives who desire lines of demarcation to preserve the historical order that has been proven protective. In contrast, today we see once more the uncontrolled and insouciant exploratory nature of the liberal, becoming more recklessly carefree to a state of near anarchy, practically inviting destruction as if there was almost a death wish.

As discussed by Peterson, we have a biological platform upon which our cognitive processes are erected. Given that fundamental reality we can thus see the trajectory of the leftist agenda. They are deconstructing the biological platform with gender confusion and legislating psychosis. The Left's gender agenda is destroying the biological platform so they can destroy the cognitive processes. This paves the way for a compliant population. They are purposefully destroying borders and foundations to create a new human order according to their perverse liking. We will regress into an Elysium caste system where the masses live in a burned-out world and the elites, as in the movie, revolve around the planet in a symbolic heavenly paradise. One must wonder if in fact science fiction (particularly the horror versions) is becoming science reality.

We just lived through one of the greatest criminal frauds in the history of man, COVID and vaccination policies. Thousands deserve to be sentenced to hard labor for life due to the mass loss of life and misery caused by this fraud. One outspoken voice of sanity has been Doctor and Senator Rand Paul. He saw through the lies and fraud from the start. In my discussions with him on the matter, he knows of Dr. Fauci's lies and the damage he did to millions with his power-hungry COVID policies. Fauci is also responsible for the destruction of our economy which continues to cause so much suffering. Sen. Paul finally got Dr. Fauci to admit that 1,800 doctors and scientists were paid approximately $350-400 million in relation to the research and the vaccines which are hurting and even killing otherwise healthy people.[43]

Some of those who have awakened to the fraud will never demand nor vote in such a way as to create the will and means to enforce justice. Here again, the people are acting contrary to what is normal, mentally or physically. When someone becomes harmful to themselves or others they are institutionalized. How do you do that on a national basis? The people either come to their senses or the country collapses into a repressive

---

43 Adam Andrzejewski, "Rand Paul is doing the right thing by asking for transparency in the NIH: Opinion," Courier Journal, accessed on October 28, 2022, https://www.courier-journal.com/story/opinion/2022/06/20/rand-pauls-questioning-dr-faucis-nih-royalty-payments-right/7622469001/.

authoritarian dystopian society. It has happened numerous times before and is happening again in this once great, safe, happy, and free country. Senator Paul understands this.

The pandemic exposed a huge gap in the culture between thinkers and non-thinkers. The thinkers quickly put two and two together and realized that something was rotten in the state of America, and indeed it is. The thinkers quickly surmised that the numbers didn't add up. The numbers were cooked and obviously so. If you look at the global mortality rate in 2020 compared to 2021 there was a negligible difference. So much for the lethality of the virus. If there was a fatality associated with the virus it was fear. Tyrants gain power and stay in power with fear. However, cowardice is a real illness too. Once again, where was the healthy normal skepticism that would have prevented all the destruction?

As the Centers for Disease Control admitted, the number of COVID-related deaths was revised downward and those numbers will continue to be revised down, but the inflated numbers served the purpose of fear and lining the pockets of hospitals, whose reimbursements were greater if a death was listed as COVID related. However, the deaths and long-term effects related to vaccines will continue to rise.

Tyrants control others by fear. They are counting on you to be so afraid that you refuse to stand up for yourself. However, if you punch the bully in the nose, you will stop being bullied. President Trump attempted that, but if anything exemplifies how dangerous the left-leaning psychos are, it was their anti-Trump resistance. They are eaten up with hatred for both Trump and his policies, which, before COVID, had brought this nation to its strongest position in recent history. They will make and are making an example of Trump to dissuade others from attempting policies that enhance individual freedoms as Trump did. You must resist and train yourself to be skeptical. It causes you to think and examine what is being sold to you. As it relates to COVID, you were scammed. The scam was deadly and now the majority of deaths from COVID are of people who were vaccinated. If ever there was a life experience that should have made you primarily and permanently skeptical of everything (most importantly, toward government and science), it would have been the COVID mass fraud.

While the intentional skewing of the number of COVID deaths I consider a criminal fraud, don't look for any prosecutions by a corrupt justice department. The bottom line here is that this was a dress rehearsal for just how far they (the radical leftists and totalitarians) could push and control the public. The Left was rewarded. The public was amazingly compliant. Years of conditioning paid off. The only way to protect yourself is with a healthy dose of skepticism followed by consistent action.

One of the reasons the public was so compliant is that they fear death. This is natural but is a useful control mechanism by the Left. As the churches die in this country, like in Europe and Canada, the people lose hope for the future and life becomes futile. When this life is all there is, fear controls them. For the godless, the "here and now" is all they have. Those who have hope beyond this life live with greater freedom, and don't give in to the kind of fear that allows for tyrants to take control. Those who don't have this perspective have a paralyzing fear, and thus desire to control others (as if this might change the inevitable).

The planned pandemic gave the Left valuable insight as to what they could get away with when the authoritarian dissolution of our constitutional rights is ushered in during the final act of this play. This is what happens to people who lose their natural skepticism, failing to ask questions and push back. At this point, if you aren't skeptical, you aren't thinking for yourself. And everyone must always think for himself, or a tyrannical government will.

CHAPTER 7:

The Political and Social Redlining of America

"I don't delude myself into thinking that anyone in Washington D.C. is there for me."
Waiter, Orlando, FL

The greatness of this country is due, in large measure, to its Christian origins, its constitution, and free-market capitalism. Those pillars are the sanctity of our constitutional rights, including freedom of speech, religion, assembly, and access to the free markets. Undeniably, those pillars have been our societal strength as a country for centuries and the basis of its greatness.

These foundational commitments should be respected and advanced; that is, they would be by any sane populace. But in the Psychotic States of America, they have been under increasing attack for the last several decades with very little effective pushback or defense from those who should know better.

We have seen the unthinkable suppression of our freedom of speech and thought. Who would have believed that what was so sacrosanct for over 200 years would ever need defending? Who could imagine that punitive headline lawsuits would not be flooding the courts for the violations of our sacred rights against those suppressing them? They are the true insurrectionists, not those on January 6, 2021.

Don't miss this point. When the Left wants to divert attention from what they are up to, they accuse and project upon the Right that which they themselves are truly planning or are guilty of. Every accusation of the Left is a confession.

So, when they immediately began speaking about an "insurrection" after January 6, 2021, they accomplished several things. First, they resurrected the term "insurrection" and got the word into the public domain and consciousness. Second, they got the Right to defend the false narrative that the Left created even as the evidence revealed there was no insurrection. To the contrary, the Left was engaged in a surreptitious political scheme to affect the outcome of the 2022 midterm elections while hiding their collusion with the FBI, Twitter, and other social media in actual violation of the First Amendment. Now the video tapes from January 6th have been revealed by the new Republican Speaker of the House, Kevin McCarthy, proving the January 6th committee not only lied but did so in a premeditated way. They manipulated the conclusion and altered the reality of what happened on that date.

Even as we entered 2023 with a new Republican Congress, testimony was already leaking out that the leftists who conducted the sham January 6th hearings in Congress knew it was a lie. The question now is will there be any consequence for those liars who deceived an entire nation? Most likely not. It served the political purpose of the Left for the midterm elections. They needed a diversion. They were so quick to use the term "insurrection" because it was and is on their minds all the time as that is exactly what they are all about, hope for, dream of and ultimately desire. The circumstantial as well as direct evidence is undeniable. Again, remember what a hypocrite is. They are projectionists. They accuse you of what they themselves are guilty.

Upon taking over Twitter, Elon Musk dropped a nuclear bomb on the Left by revealing the collusion between the leftist Democrats with social media, the Justice Department, and the FBI to actively suppress free speech and the Right. That is now out in the light of day and undebatable. That's the stuff that sparks revolutions.

Hundreds of political operatives and politicians should be indicted and jailed for the real insurrection and silent coup that was going on between the Left, our FBI, and Justice Department. January 6th was the diversion from the real crime. This was not just about suppressing ideas; it was the suppression of the truth and a cover-up. The same tactics were used with COVID. Yes, it was and is deadly. We now know the truth about the COVID pandemic, the vaccines, and how truth was suppressed, and many died as a result while others became more powerful and rich. The Left are the incarnation of evil in this world and what is at the core of the rot in America.

Now, a political analysis is not what is intended here but rather a disclosure of facts to stir one's cognitive juices so as to see how they are being manipulated and how psychosis is being induced. Truth, facts, and evidence are so delayed in their disclosure that people forget and never connect the dots to what originally formed an attitude or perception.

It is not difficult to understand what is happening behind the scenes. There is an ongoing and concerted effort to silence all dissent. Another good way to think about how and why the truth is attacked is what I call the "Social Redlining of America."

Redlining: What's Past is Prologue

In the United States, "redlining" is historically associated with an intentionally racist manifestation of the practice. The Legal Information Institute, run by Cornell, explains that:

> Redlining can be defined as a discriminatory practice that consists of the systematic denial of services such as mortgages, insurance loans, and other financial services to residents of certain areas, based on their race or ethnicity. Redlining disregards individual's qualifications and creditworthiness to refuse such services, solely based on the residency of those individuals in minority neighborhoods, which were also quite often deemed "hazardous" or "dangerous."

> Beyond the discriminatory banking practice of excluding certain neighborhoods from financial services, redlining can also reach the withholding of more important and essential services

such as the construction of grocery stores and supermarkets or even the withholding of healthcare services.[44]

The point of the historic, racist redlining in America was to section off portions of the population that were (wrongly and wickedly) considered "undesirable" or "backward" from the rest of society. Again, to be clear, this practice was abhorrent, and I denounce it entirely. There must be individual and corporate responsibility for the least of those in society, and to care for the widow and the orphan, the poor and the disabled. However, much of corporate America has turned into a fascist arm of the state. If our political leaders had the courage to do so, many woke corporations would be threatened with having their corporate charters/licenses revoked and allow the stockholders to be sued as well as the corporate boards of directors for mismanagement. I have requested state legislators to consider legislation and the institution of *ultra vires* actions against companies that exceed the parameters of their charter. For example, if you make Coke then make Coke and shut up. Coca-Cola is an artificial person and has no rights other than what the state governments allow them. After all, the stockholders are given immunity from liability which no one else gets. The laws must be changed as they relate to these mega corporations essentially controlling the government and the governed.

Back to redlining: In general, it is more than just a racist business practice. Another way to understand it is that it was a practice by companies motivated by "the bottom line," which is essential for the performance of the company and its fiduciary responsibility to its shareholders. Financially, businesses had to discriminate between and among investing in either the good, better, or best placement of corporate dollars and resources. For example, you are not going to sell swimsuits in Alaska or ski lifts in Florida. In other words, companies choose to direct resources toward areas they believe will yield the best return on investment. Not so anymore. Look at the Silicon Valley Bank bankruptcy of March 2023 wherein records now reveal that the bank gave $70+ million to the corrupt and Marxist based Black Lives Matter organization. There must be a

---

44 Redlining, Legal Information Institute, accessed on December 12, 2022, https://www.law.cornell.edu/wex/redlining.

personal consequence for the directors and officers. That will not happen with the current corrupt regime in Washington.

While the current national conversation about "systemic racism" (which doesn't exist anymore, if it ever did, the way the term is used today) has brought the history of redlining back into the conversation. The reality is that most people (rightly) assumed redlining was over.

Well, these people were right in the sense that racist redlining is over, but the practice of redlining never died. It just switched its target.

Modern Redlining: An Effort to Remove the Political Undesirables and Deplorables from Society

Hillary Clinton once infamously said that "you could put half of Trump's supporters into what I call the basket of deplorables...now some of those folks, they are irredeemable, but thankfully they are not America."

Before I launch into the redlining topic itself, Clinton's remark deserves some more context because it is explicitly Marxist language. Clinton was a follower of Saul Alinsky, author of the book *Rules for Radicals*. He devoted his life to strategies for undermining America and delivering the country over to authoritarian rule. By the way, Barack Obama was an adherent of Alinsky as well.

In the current cultural environment, we regularly see mobs storm into retail outlets and ransack the stores, stealing everything in sight. Recently, Walgreen stores in California have been raided by mobs stealing items off the shelves as clerks stood by and watched—they did nothing because they know leftist-controlled law enforcement will not prosecute these crimes. Law enforcement leadership has joined forces with an ideological criminal enterprise. If Walgreens stopped placing stores in cities that are perennially governed by District Attorneys who refuse to put criminals and shoplifters in jail, that might be called "redlining," but honestly who could fault such a decision?

Redlining has morphed beyond best business practices and reared its ugly head in a more malignant and deadlier way. Now, instead of unfairly targeting racial minorities, corporations and governments are unfairly and unconstitutionally targeting and redlining political minorities—that is, reality-oriented and reality-believing conservatives, i.e., the Right.

This is seen on the college campus. If you are not a woke, anti-American, anti-capitalist, feminist-supporting, BLM marcher, pro-transgender, and pro-abortion activist, then your views aren't welcome. In fact, *you aren't* welcome. It's reverse redlining—it's drawing a border around a good or service that was once available to all Americans and now claiming that it's only there for the social justice warriors of the world. The Right supports with their tax dollars the colleges and universities that they have a right to access like anyone else. They are being redlined out because of their political beliefs.

Those put out are white, Bible-believing, family-loving, pro-life, and patriotic conservatives. They are drawn outside the lines—the lines of the universities, the corporate jobs, the big promotions, the media, the entertainment industry, you name it.

The reality is that within the newly redlined United States, if you don't fit within certain intersectional parameters, you will not receive access to the goods and services to which you are otherwise entitled. Had this practice broken upon the scene one hundred years ago, the cherry trees around the reflecting pond in D.C. would be decorated with those woke politicians, academics, CEOs, and agency heads twisting in the wind.

Redlining Our Way to Revolution

The social redlining of conservatives in America is well underway. Let's be clear: this is discrimination, exclusion, a form of enslavement all too familiar by the historical party of slavery, the Democrats, now owned by the radical Left. Where does this lead? Nowhere good. In fact, most likely it will lead to a new revolution, to be avoided at all costs, but that requires the Right to fight with the same tenacity, ruthlessness, and intensity as the Left. Ask no quarter and give none. The winning playbook was written over 50 years ago and the Democrats have been using it ever since. The Right is as wrong in its failure to protect our institutions of freedom as the Left is wrong in destroying them.

Again, my contention in this book is that America is suffering from a certain social psychosis. According to the natural law (and Christianity), there is a healthy way of living–in the warp and woof of the normal and natural. Psychosis unravels these threads.

The most committed progressive psychotics oppose these necessary foundations of reason, natural law, and Christianity. They do so to become sovereigns, both over truth and over others, aiming to control and shape "reality" as they see fit. They are leading our culture in a departure from the normative. Their godless embrace of on-demand abortion, their redefinition of marriage, gender, and the rejection of the very real categories of men and women only serve to undermine human dignity and destroy a life worth living. They are destroying the very biological foundation upon which the cognitive is built. They are the new mercenaries.

Many people oppose these misguided and wretched endeavors to play God. The Left sees those who are still committed to common sense and the normative of nature as an existential threat to their dream of permanent political dominance. Therefore, they demand conformity.

I call denying anyone their basic inalienable rights a criminal act (whether legal or moral), and criminals should lose their rights. Where is the justice? Where is the government serving the good of the people and protecting all instead of some? Sadly, it lies in the hands of uninformed, low information, and psychotic voters.

And here is the kicker: if you won't conform, you will have to be removed. You will be redlined out of society. Many won't go easily. And that's where the real threat of revolution is at play. Redlining is just the first step. Ultimately, you will conform, or you will be eliminated. More on that later, but first, let's consider why the woke and the Left are doing this.

Woke Redliners

The "woke" and other proponents of "cancel culture" have decided they must punish people who think differently. This is part of their larger effort to suppress freedom of speech. As Elon Musk recently described this woke culture, it is: "Divisive, exclusionary, and hateful. It gives mean people a shield to be mean and cruel, armored in false virtue."45

The woke are malevolent frauds, and they know it. They are the losers, both according to Peterson and yours truly. That's not just conjecture, it's

---

45 Elon Musk, "FULL INTERVIEW: Elon Musk Sits Down with The Babylon Bee," The Babylon Bee, YouTube, accessed December 12, 2022, https://www.youtube.com/watch?v=jvGnw1sHh9M&t=8s.

a fact. They shut down speech because they cannot win the argument. They are the insurrectionists who have invaded the public square, and if you try to voice your opinion, they will physically harm you.

Ukraine fought back against its invasion with like force (not just words), and the same must be done against the lawless woke. Stand your ground. No, retake your ground, and use whatever countervailing force is necessary. Clearly, words and reason didn't work for Ukraine. Likewise, words and reason will not work for the victims of wokeness in this country. It is time for the pusillanimous Right to wake up.

I would go a step further to define the redlining of our constitutional rights as criminal, an anti-social mindset that given enough power, will kill with impunity. Look at Portland and other cities that burned in 2020. They aren't just woke—they are dangerous.

What we are facing today is the violent anarchist in the image of Lenin, Stalin, Mao, and Pol Pot. They are those who have a resentful and murderous rage stemming from their failure as mentally normative functional human beings. Yes, they are the losers of society, and it was not because someone did something bad to them. No, they made poor choices, did it to themselves, and don't like the consequences of their choices. Today the anarchists have allies in government. The Left in government see the anarchists as useful tools who therefore are given free reign. The woke are the Left's revolution proxy, just like we are at war with Russia via Ukraine as our proxy.

The dictators I mentioned were just human beings. Let's emphasize the word, "just," meaning not in the *justice* sense, but in the *limiting* sense that they were not God; they were and are simple, flawed humans who took what was not theirs. They could have been stopped, but they were not. In the case of all these dictators, they were mentally ill sociopaths. They were also psychopaths with a seized platform, seized power, and an army behind them. However, they didn't get there by themselves. They got there with the assistance of others—the social redliners and the passivity and indolence of those who saw the danger but did nothing to prevent it, i.e., the cowards on the Right. For years these dictators in the making occupied our universities and colleges brainwashing our children while we the people paid them to do so.

Dr. Jordan Peterson has warned that you never trust a resentful person with power. Human horrors have come from humans playing out their resentments against others. All too often the humans that suffer the most are those who place monsters like Hitler and Stalin in power. Yet despite knowing what people like that do once in power, we are doing it all over again. History is repeating itself, or at least rhyming. Dr. Thomas Sowell said, "Marxism is the conceit of rich kids with fancy educations." Today the education they have is not fancy nor worth anything.

The mental misfits of society have coalesced into a woke mob with shared traits. They are godless losers, resentful of a world where they, due to their own bad life decisions, are sidelined. They want to sideline others. They want to burn it all down. They are what they are: psychotic and dangerous. The burned-out buildings in cities around the country today are proof.

It is this group that has hijacked redlining to destroy businesses owned by people that don't share the woke dysphoria to deny you the services and goods that businesses provide and to which the Right is entitled.

They have gone after Hobby Lobby, Chick-fil-A, and My Pillow, to name a few. If they catch wind that you deviate at all from the woke orthodoxy of the moment, they will drum you out of business, out of your job, and out of your political position with arbitrariness, capriciousness, and impunity. They are intolerant and a mentally malignant group who hold much sway due to the lack of moral courage or principled character of those who provide the platforms. This gives the malevolent woke power to inflict damage upon the culture and society, and they do.

In fact, many who are in control of companies that provide that platform have been infected themselves with this disease of the mind, resulting in the redlining of political thought such that if you are not of a socialistic, authoritarian, woke, gender-denying mindset, you are to be canceled. You can be denied goods and services, and even medical care. This is the kind of thing revolutions are built upon because it is so toxic to culture and society that you either kill the spread of this cancer or it will kill you.

International Redliners

A glance at Canada and their China and Castro-loving premier, Justin Trudeau, woke to the extreme, further establishes the point. As soon as COVID-19 gave him an opportunity, would-be dictator Trudeau unapologetically shed any pretense of democratic values. He did so essentially overnight and with authoritarian moves that would make the leaders of China, Russia, Venezuela, and Cuba proud. He crushed the trucker's freedom protest. President Biden, unknown to most, encouraged Trudeau to crush the protests. Gutless to condemn, Trudeau's minority government sided not with freedom of speech or assembly but cowered to the woke psychosis embedded even in the Canadian public through indoctrination and grooming of the citizenry.

Polls indicated that the public was not in favor of the protestors, but it was mainly because of the inconvenience caused. Here we go again: the people are for freedom until it becomes inconvenient. They wanted to keep the goods flowing, their comforts and conveniences in place, and they proved that they would crucify anyone (to hell with their freedoms) if they caused the slightest inconvenience or required any sacrifice. When the public embraces such behavior so detached from reality, they have contracted a mass psychosis. One only need look at Hitler's Third Reich and how ambivalent and complicit most Germans were in the 1930s and 40s. The same is occurring in Canada, Australia, and America. We are on the same course.

The rule of law is blatantly ignored with impunity. Machiavelli is their justification—not in service of the people but in service of themselves. We are seeing this in Soros-backed prosecutors and leftist administrations when the appointed members of the Departments of Justice will not prosecute crimes. They will not enforce the laws to protect the public. They want chaos. They leave you unprotected while trying to confiscate your guns.

This is not just a total abdication of their sworn duties, it is impeachable conduct, if not criminal in and of itself. What kind of a mind is capable of justifying such conduct? A psychotic one detached from reality that desires the chaos that ensues because it provides opportunity.

Speaking of Australia, it is gone! Once a great Western culture, the COVID pandemic and its lockdowns, as well as the enforcement were so Orwellian and Communist, that it would be difficult to differentiate them from the China lockdowns. There was no freedom, no due process, and no exceptions. The Australians were brutal. My personal acquaintances and interviews of those with first-hand accounts were both astounding and verifying. Australian authorities were subhuman, if not inhuman, in their conduct and edicts. As a former penal colony populated by the criminal class and criminal minded, the Australian government, if not the people, have regressed to their ancestral character.

The conduct of these governments is detached from reality. Based on new studies, the excess death rates were the lowest, if not numerically insignificant, in Sweden, a country that did not lockdown during the COVID pandemic. However, they were the highest in Australia, Canada and the US by multiples even after adjusting for population differences. The truth was suppressed; the authoritarians seized the opportunity for a test run, and they won. The people are ripe for enslavement by their own choice.

The church is dead in Australia, Canada, and New Zealand and has been for decades. (The countries are over 65% atheist.) The population is so disconnected and dehumanized at the human level that it has the shallowness of an ink blot. Australia, once thought of as the down-under sanctuary of human freedom and rights, is no more. The radical Left took over there many years ago which began with the decay and death of their church. I won't go into the individual horror stories I was given in interviews with Australians and those who made the mistake of visiting there, but suffice it to say that the government exercised no restraint, and the people were enslaved. I applaud tennis champion Novak Djokovic for not bending the knee to Australian authoritarianism and repressive lockdown rules by dropping out of the Australian Open. He exercised a healthy cognition, resistance, and self-respect in comparison to the Aussies, who benefited nothing from their lockdowns only to find themselves slaves of the state. Americans would do well to follow Djokovic's example.

Back to the Land of the Free—Or Is It?

The same is happening in America. Americans with no religious affiliation or belief skew heavily toward the Left and the Democrat party in their voting according to a recent report from the Associated Press (AP). For example, in the recent U.S. midterm elections, self-identified religious "nones" voted for Democrat House candidates by more than a two-to-one margin (65 percent to 31 percent) over Republicans, according to data from a survey by AP Vote Cast. I repeat, without God there is no order, and without order there is no freedom. So, when I identified and referred to the Left and Democrats as a godless and a hedonistic lot, I was not speaking without the evidence or the facts to back it up.

Dr. Thomas Sowell, disdained by the Left as he is no longer on their "plantation," also said that "The Democrat's (now totally consumed by a radical Left) drive to power is so extreme that they smother their own natural instinct to love and disregard it in others." They are not the political party that most identified them as being in the past.

The people, through their own slothfulness and preference for being the "non-thinking" as Thomas Edison referenced, have lent support to an institution now devoted to their own aggrandizement, hedonism, depravity and warped moral code.

It annoys the governing elite when society doesn't need them. The mental sickness within the Left is that they assuage their need for significance by bathing themselves in power and fake virtue. Yes, it is totally delusional, out of touch with reality, and, you got it, psychotic. However, more importantly, it makes them some of the most dangerous people on earth as they will, without exception, become the totalitarian commissars that will murder with impunity to salvage their power as their policies cause the system to collapse. These are people whose souls are so dark and rotten that the only way they quench the parched desert within is ruling over others with a brutality we have seen throughout man's history, which we repeat again and again. They will redline you and starve you out. History is my proof.

Sowell, in characterizing the actions of the leftist, Marxist, elites, noted the consequences of their actions and their desire to disassemble the family. In other words, they want to destroy the autonomy of the family. He remarked with disdain on Hillary Clinton's claim that it takes a village to raise a child. Humorously, he quipped that "Frankly, it takes a village idiot to believe that."

The Left pays no price when they are wrong. Just as in the 2022 midterms, the conditions in the country were dire, and over 70% of the people believed the country was heading in the wrong direction. Yet they voted the very people back into power (except narrowly in Congress) that were essentially responsible for their suffering. Frankly, the people have not suffered enough, as they are themselves not changing course. Even as the noose of redlining gets tighter, the people suffer but do not change their ways.

The most glaring example of the national rot is what the people did in the 2022 elections in Pennsylvania with the election of Fetterman. I've seen street people better dressed, more presentable, and more articulate than he is. And then you have Arizona, with the election of Katie Hobbs over Kari Lake, where TV interviews established that Hobbs was just as intellectually disabled and incompetent as Fetterman. Truly the people of both states should hang their heads in shame. Both of those races never should have been close.

As for the Right, the alternative they presented to the people in Pennsylvania was breath-taking, not so much in the quality of the candidate but from the infighting and poor strategy that was implemented. Here the Right was being surrounded nationally by the invading authoritarian armies out to kill the votes cast by the Right or anyone they supported. The Right barely noticed them, as they were so engaged in fighting amongst themselves. The Right truly fit the adage of those who were busy rearranging the chairs on the deck of the Titanic.

Social Redlining Will Ultimately Wake Up the Most Dangerous Men; Men Who Want to Be Left Alone

As more and more areas are red-lined and drawn off, and as more and more of the Right are told "you're not welcome here," we see again the true intolerance of the so-called and self-proclaimed tolerant Left.

Make no mistake, they don't just want to be intolerant. The powers that be are rounding up conservatives, the Right, to block them from being able to live productive lives in society or challenge the Left's power. Once they get the "reality seers" into the corral, they will determine who is eligible for the re-education camps. Understand this: If you are not eligible, you are irredeemable. If you are irredeemable, you will be eliminated. Remember Hillary Clinton's talk about the "irredeemable?" That was not a mistake, and that is what Stalin and Mao Zedong did. You will be eliminated unless you fight back. What does it look like when you awaken the man who just wanted to be left alone? It looks like what Alexander Solzhenitsyn, that great Russian dissident and freedom fighter, described in his musings on what will happen when the men who just want to be left alone realize that they are one step away from being put on a train to the gulag.

In *The Gulag Archipelago*, he says:

> The most terrifying force of death comes from the hands of Men who wanted to be left Alone. They try, so very hard, to mind their own business and provide for themselves and those they love. They resist every impulse to fight back, knowing the forced and permanent change of life that will come from it. They know that the moment they fight back, their lives as they have lived them, are over. The moment the Men who wanted to be left alone are forced to fight back, it is a form of suicide. They are literally killing off who they used to be. This is why, when forced to take up violence, these Men who wanted to be left alone, fight with unholy vengeance against those who murdered their former lives. They fight with raw hate, and a drive that cannot be fathomed by those who are merely play-acting at politics and terror. TRUE TERROR will arrive at these people's door, and they will cry, scream, and beg for mercy... but it will fall upon the deaf ears of the Men who just wanted to be left alone.

True terror awaits those who try to redline reality lovers out of America. Conservative Americans, the Right, deserve free, fair and unfettered access to all the public goods and services this country affords. After all, they are the ones who built it, not the incompetent resentful wannabes. Racist redlining was a bad and immoral idea. Ideological redlining is terrible as well. In fact, if you are a black conservative today, you will be redlined as well.

Now that you know what it is, you can keep an eye out for it. Knowing is half the battle. The other half is being willing to fight when you just want to be left alone. It's time to follow the example of Djokovic. Resist and refuse to take the knee.

CHAPTER 8:

How Non-Discernment and Naivete Neutralize The Right

"The stupid neither forgive nor forget; the naïve forgive and forget; the wise forgive but do not forget."

Thomas Szasz

In a 2018 interview Jordan Peterson warned that: "We cannot live with the integration of the past if we are not united consciously with the past. We will be divided internally and socially and that has consequences; some of those can be fatal."[46]

One of the main issues Peterson speaks to regularly is the need for discernment. He encourages young men in particular to discern the truth and orient their lives to it as best they can. He also encourages people to discern natural hierarchies in the world, learn how to operate in them, and see the goodness and inevitability of hierarchy, as opposed to the radical egalitarian Marxists who try to destroy them, inexorably plunging society into chaos.

My heart goes out to the youth of today because they have been mentally abused, misled, lied to, deceived and manipulated by those whose

---

46   Jordan Peterson, "First full documentary on Jordan Peterson," David Fuller, Medium, accessed on December 15, 2022, https://medium.com/rebel-wisdom/first-full-documentary-on-jordan-peterson-70feef5a266f.

only interest is themselves and their pathological ideology. They are the selfish, resentful, and malevolent totalitarians who want to enslave us all but enlisted the youth through indoctrination to be their foot soldiers. The youth today truly have no clue as to what they are doing or what is being done to them. My goal every day, for those I can reach, is to set their minds free of the bondage the Left has placed on them. As the adage of unknown origin goes, "If youth but knew, if age could tell." I would change that to, "What age could tell if youth would listen."

Peterson has railed against what has happened to the youth, and particularly young men, who make up 80% of his audiences – they are the ones starving for his message and the truth. The revolution needs to start with rescuing the minds of our youth to give them a chance at life and not a life of lies and fear.

Marxists cater to envy and preach a false equality which does not exist, has never existed, and never will. Do you really want your neurosurgeon to be your equal, on the same social/economic plane, and as uninformed as you on the subject when he goes to operate on you? If you do, then you deserve the botched surgery you get—if you survive it. Do you really want the pilot of your plane to be equal to you? Not if you desire to arrive at your destination safely, if at all. Do you really want to eradicate all hierarchies, as the Marxists do, except the one from which they control your life? Of course not, but the Left breeds envy, covetousness, and resentment; and wants to penalize those who spend years studying and learning to do things that make life wonderful for the rest of us. For those who do not recall, due to this flawed and false equality (equity) that was imposed by communists upon their people, they couldn't manufacture washers, dryers, cars and much more that would work. They became an international joke.

Furthermore, the disciplines and needs of those in specialized fields require an income to pay for the services they need to make their lives more conducive to providing you with the vital services they can provide you. If you can't discern the importance of this, then you deserve the suffering you will experience when the services and skills you need are no longer available or are provided by those unqualified, but are there in the name of equity or equality. (The two words are often confused and have drastically different meanings and outcomes that you would not like.)

Peterson has been a prophet of common sense in our modern era of insanity. He's right—we must be more discerning.

This brings me to one of my biggest criticisms of the Right regarding their culpability for the general state of psychosis. They are slow to wake up and slow to action. They should know better. A discerning populace perceptive of the consequences of the Left's agenda would not accept what's happened and is happening to America.

Losing Our Discernment

Over the last few decades, many studies and surveys established that the United States is becoming less and less religious. This is having serious consequences. It's clear that along with losing our religion, we are losing our ability to make wise judgments and exercise common sense. This is discussed in greater detail in the chapters on hypocrisy as well as the one on the church.

We have lost our discernment. We know from experience that the Left drowns us in their false piety and virtue, but only operates on the basis of what benefits their position of power, never what is best for the whole or the nation. They have EDD (empathy deficit disorder), where they are incapable of having concern for others outside of what is in their best interests. They will only do that which advances their personal agenda even if it means feigning or exhibiting a false virtue or concern. We cannot count on the Left doing any better and the Right *should* know better.

Sadly, even many leaders on the Right and those who follow them have failed to steel their minds and use discernment. Non-discernment in our social media-driven society is like a virus. It's part of the overall inorganic psychosis. The Right should have been more immune to contracting this virus but was all too often attempting to befriend those who wanted to destroy them and the country.

The loss of discernment has succeeded as a consequence of a planned agenda implemented by grooming, indoctrination, and manipulation (inorganic). This non-discernment is a product of a lack of critical thinking as well. The people today offshore their mental processes and powers of judgment to the "experts," whether that's the government, media, some corporate institution, or authority figure to tell them how and what they should think and do. The government is out there serving their own interests, particularly given the bureaucracy, what is now called the Deep State, because they see themselves as above the people. They expect the people to honor, if not serve them. They see themselves as the angels of society. It is only they that have the truth and ability to rule, or so they think. This is part of the fraternization that I speak about, and produces the dangers of the various agencies within government. They become their own little fraternities, nations, armed and empowered by the central government. From where has all this come?

The loss of discernment comes from 12 years spent sitting in public school classrooms. Many "conservative" parents continue to send their kids to these brainwashing stations, allowing radical secular teachers to drain the natural skepticism and discernment from their minds as a spider drains its prey of life fluids. Whether your children are from conservative or liberal households, they are not being taught life skills. They are not being educated. They are being indoctrinated, which will not earn them a living or pay their bills in the future, or help them navigate the problems life will throw their way.

By the time otherwise conservative youth who have been raised in homes on the Right walk across the stage for graduation, they will have become incapable of understanding cause and effect, deductive reasoning, or following a line of logic. In other words, they've traded their discernment for a drone mentality. It's the kind of stuff found in science fiction movies and dystopian novels, where people are slaves and owe their very existence to the state; but this is not a movie or science fiction—this is real. This is *now*. The Left, in its obsession to create a singularity of thought by wiping out conservative viewpoints, is destroying the children from the families of different viewpoints.

It's not just the kids. The kids are not alright, but neither are the parents. They are worse. Parents on the Right should know better. They have traded discernment for comfort. After all, if you know better, you must act on it, but in the current environment acting can come with a social cost few these days are willing to pay.

This lack of discernment in the population in general can be seen today in policies and practices such as letting boys compete in female sports simply because they claim to be a woman or letting some kids act out being "furries;" that is, pretending that they are cats, dogs or red pandas (I'm not joking). Adults have abrogated their authority and responsibilities. The kids are not the problem. For the most part they will self-correct as they get older, but not the teachers or their Marxist union ideologues; they are hardwired and truly the "irredeemable." They are the real danger, along with some Munchausen-by-proxy parents who allow their children to be subjected to such profane indoctrination.

Justifying pornographic "sex education" materials and books in school libraries, even for elementary grade schoolers, should (itself) be enough to drive the point home. Those who promulgate such policies and think it healthy are wicked and evil. They will ultimately pay an eternal cost, but the children must be protected from these evil doers.

To make the point of the disengagement, lack of discernment of parents, what has been allowed, and how off course the ship of education has sailed, consider that Thomas Sowell noted in the 1960's that sexual disease and teenage pregnancies was insignificant, even declining. However, after the implementation of sex education in the schools, STDs and teenage pregnancies skyrocketed. The evidence should have been enough to shut down what clearly was not working. Instead, the programs became more perverse and expansive. Don't look for help from cowardly legislators who were elected by parents/voters woefully ignorant and undiscerning of what was going on. And what was going on was the planned demoralization and corruption of the nation and its youth.

Fighting this foe is not easy when even those on the Right must be dragged kicking and screaming to do the right thing. For example, when trying to get the legislatures in Indiana, Kansas, and Kentucky (all of whom have super-majority Republican legislatures) to pass legislation that would prohibit pornographic "sex education," they found it difficult to muster the courage to outlaw such practices. This shouldn't have even required debate. This was a self-evident truth. Fortunately, Kentucky has turned the corner and enacted sweeping legislation protecting children and parents from radical teachers and their unions, but this took way longer than it should have. What the Kentucky legislature achieved in their most recent session was bold and encouraging. Hopefully, the other states with like majorities will follow course soon if they haven't by the time this book goes to print.

Proposing and practicing gender transitions as an option for minors who embrace gender dysphoria is yet another example of the complicity of the adults and their lack of discernment by allowing these things to occur. This happens in schools and the parents are not informed. How could a parent not be informed? Are they that detached from the lives of their children? Perhaps we need less fast food, less use of microwaves, and more sit-down meals around the dinner table with family at night.

I mention the microwave because with the introduction of that technology I recall that my family stopped having meals together. The family scattered and went in varying directions. Microwave or not, the question remains, how can you not be involved in your child's life and not know what they are being exposed to at their schools? How can you not know what they are being taught?

In California it is being proposed that children be allowed to obtain abortions and gender transitions without notice to the parents. Where is the outrage and the measures to remove these psychotic administrators from positions of authority? This is child abuse, plain and simple, and has nothing to do with education. Your children are slowly being taken from you.

The Real Costs of Non-Discernment

There are real costs to non-discernment, naivete, and plain stupidity. Consider how we have been funding the war in Ukraine by buying Russian oil. Where is the logic or discernment in shutting down oil production in this country in 2021 when 18 months earlier, we were energy independent? We became dependent again as President Biden shut down America's oil production simply because the radical climate priests demanded ineffective green policies, damn the consequences.

Here are some real stupid policies evidencing what non-discernment has allowed:

Electric vehicles (EVs) do not have zero emissions as they have been marketed. Gas vehicles have a 400-mile range, electric vehicles have a 200-mile range and require you to charge them twice to produce the same mileage as a gas vehicle. The creation and operation of an electric vehicle over its lifetime produces more CO_2 than a gas-powered vehicle by a substantial amount, yet EV's are falsely labeled zero emissions. The rare minerals and mining needed, the construction costs, the toxicity of the batteries, not to mention the electricity to charge them from gas, oil and coal power plants, render the claim that electric vehicles are zero emissions false. Fill up a gas vehicle and you go 400 miles. Charge up an electric vehicle two times and maybe go 400 miles. This is a lack of discernment.

In 2021 a fierce snowstorm stranded automobiles on I-95 overnight. As you would expect, the electric vehicles ran out of power since it takes large quantities of electricity to produce heat from a battery. The gas-powered vehicles stayed warm. That's called learning the hard way. Oh, the electric vehicle users feel good about themselves, as if they are saving the planet (or so they think). That false virtue didn't keep them warm. In fact, it is making things worse, and many are getting rich from the fraud and stupidity.

We ship our manufacturing jobs to China since we would rather pay slave labor rates and then virtue signal against past slavery here rather than provide our own citizens with well-paying jobs.

Opening the borders to a flood of millions of illegal immigrants hasn't worked out well either. Still, many of the displaced workers continue to vote for those who placed them on the unemployment lines and shipped their jobs overseas. The real lack of discernment here is that the culture is being displaced for the purpose of establishing a one-party, permanent ruling elite class. How could anyone miss this? How is this anything but obvious?

Allowing our environmental policies to be set and partially financed by foreign actors who are hostile to our interests is another example. They want to create our dependence on them so they can fund their wars and undermine our government and financial institutions.

To top it all off, after decades of wiping out racism, a new form of racism is being taught to our kids via Critical Race Theory (CRT), which labels the very people that got rid of racism as racists by virtue of their immutable characteristics and the color of their skin. Now we have white liberals saying if you are white, you were born a racist and reparations are needed; or there is systemic racism due to white privilege. I've yet to see any of these sanctimonious white liberals make any personal sacrifices to support the cause they push much less any evidence supporting their claims. They are racial racketeers, making a fortune, with no intention of giving up one penny of their ill-gotten loot. They will make you pay. Who is the fool here? The only evidence is the foreign influence of our enemies offshore who recognized decades ago that stoking racial division in America was a weakness they could exploit, and exploiting it they are. Liberals are essentially misery looking for company. Watch out as they try to work out their sanctification at your expense.

We have also lost our discernment, because if the Right knew its history it would know how they are being gaslighted by the Left. If the Right and Left knew their history, they would know the truth about the relationship of racism to slavery which has been the fuel for false racism claims. As Dr. Thomas Sowell has noted, slavery is one of the oldest institutions in the world. In fact, slavery was not about race until after our Civil War.

Throughout history most slavery occurred within the same race, whites owning whites, blacks owning blacks, and the same with every other ethnicity. In fact, there were more white Europeans enslaved in North Africa than there were Africans enslaved in America. It was Africans who were selling Africans to slave traders and Africans who owned slaves themselves. However, few know this, because it does not fit well with the narrative and agenda of the Left. The fact is they want to tie racism to slavery when history does not reveal this.

Sadly, a lack of discernment has the Right wasting resources and efforts in fighting what was logically and factually incorrect—the false charges of racism. Bill Maher gave the same message about woke stupidity to the chagrin of the Left. When Republicans, conservatives, and the Right need Bill Maher to speak the truth, then they are in bad shape. Maher is saying things the Right should have been saying for a long time and he is saying it in a devastatingly effective way.

Where Have All the Thinkers Gone?

As bizarre as this all appears, there is little outcry or moral indignation by the masses. Yes, there is some outrage amongst the thinkers, but they have lost the lectern and allowed the non-thinkers the foothold they now possess. The thinkers have the money, the numbers, and the power to rectify the decline in the country, but they simply can't seem to roust themselves into action. It is just too inconvenient. There is no other explanation than that we as a nation are suffering from mass psychosis. Yes, it is a repetitive refrain of mine, but never underestimate the power of denial.

In the political vein, I have often commented on the need for the Republican Party to retain a national psychologist due to their apparent and incessant need to be liked by the Left, people who will never like them nor ever agree with them. Maybe this represents a mass co-dependence on the Right. This has been repeated over and over again. It's like playing a losing game of chess against someone and then playing it again with the same losing moves expecting to win. The differences between the Right and Left are too great. The worldviews, moral codes (or lack of one) and adherence to a religious faith are either too different or don't exist. There is no common ground. There are simply some situations where co-existence is not possible. It is time to wake up to this reality. The Left is historically associated with oppression and death, the Right with liberty and life. You cannot reconcile them. It defies the law of noncontradiction, which will tell you that fire and water can't occupy the same space at the same time.

Former Senator John McCain was the sycophant poster child, the perfect example of this kind of Republican. He pandered to the Left and parroted leftist talking points. Consequently, the Left loved him, and he basked in their adoration, but the moment he ran for the presidency it was his deserved *"Et Tu, Brute?"* moment. The knives came out—and he deserved them. He deserved it all, and he did not end well. In a bitter, resentful farewell act, he was the lone vote that saddled us with Obamacare and the government's takeover of medical care.

"Doing" without Discernment = Insanity

Where is the discernment these days? It's gone, because people have forgotten the age-old maxim that if you do the same thing over and over but expect a different result, that is the definition of insanity.

We see this particularly when people say they "hate" what is going on in the country and yet keep voting for the very people that promote the radical and psychotic ideas that they claim to hate. In short, there is no understanding of cause and effect. So, the non-discernment pandemic is affecting both thinkers and non-thinkers. The thinkers (Right) are lazy, addicted to their comforts, and emotionally needy as well as living in denial about the ill motives of the non-thinkers (Left) and the disastrous end to which it will all come. History is your proof.

The non-thinkers (Left) are hell-bent (literally) to destroy society in pursuit of some utopia that can never come to pass and will only yield a nightmarish dystopia. This outcome has been historically proven without exception. Their only skill is that of a con artist, never creating, only deceiving and destroying. They do not and cannot think because their *raison d'etre* in life is themselves. I would reverse Descartes' famous line of "I think therefore I am," and instead, in describing the Left, change it to, "they think not, therefore they are not." They are empty drones. They are the zombies of this age. Remember, nothing comes from nothing, or as said in the well-known Latin phrase, *ex nihilo nihil fit*, out of nothing, nothing is produced. The rot in America keeps believing lies and voting for those who will bring them nothing but death. Those who promise you everything will deliver you nothing. Nearly every policy promoted by the Left has been a disaster. Some on the Left operate in a moral and empirical vacuum – others from a malevolent and totalitarian agenda.

Non-Discernment Disasters

Discernment impairment has its consequences. Consider this: President Obama was mentored by the known and notorious Marxist, Frank Davis. (This was documented by Dr. Paul Kengor in his book *The Communist: Frank Marshall Davis: The Untold Story of Barack Obama's Mentor.*) As a quick aside, how many parents today pick an ideological mentor for their children? Give that some thought. There was an obvious plan in place long ago. This family lived revolution and politics. Nevertheless, Davis was a card-carrying Communist according to Kengor. Obama was raised by Marxists (this is not ad hominem; it is a historical fact)—what do you think that made him? And yet, Americans who should have known better still rushed to elect him to purge themselves of a false guilt. Of course, the media covered up and suppressed much of the facts and truth about this, but the evidence was still out there in the public domain.

Look where we are now, living in the ugly aftershock of that massive act of non-discernment born out of a gas-lighted false guilt thinking that Obama's election will satisfy the Left once and for all and rid us of the false accusations of racism. The opposite happened. Under Obama we experienced greater racial tension and divide, which was always the intended goal.

Today the profuse and false accusations of racism against anyone white with a different opinion from the Left is a slander which should not be given the dignity of any response other than a lawsuit. A discerning person would have detected this deceit in the Obama campaign. Many didn't, and we got fundamentally transformed as a nation by a neo-Marxist. In fact, Obama is still the de facto president, pulling the strings behind the scenes, telling the mentally disabled Biden and his administration what to do.

Consider this: if you can't tell that the flame is hot, you've got a problem. If you can't discern that the hole in your boat is going to cause it to sink, you've got a problem. If you can't tell a Marxist from a constitutionalist, you will no doubt lose your freedoms.

Currently, Americans are in a boat both on fire and taking on water. They deny both realities, and either one is going to kill them. The most current examples are the people who voted for an obviously mentally impaired man as president in 2020, who at 80 has announced his re-election bid for 2024 at which point he will be 82. Anyone could see President Biden wasn't fit for office. Now they overwhelmingly admit it, but millions of people voted for him anyway, and despite the slow-motion collapse of the country, they will vote for him again. This is not just a total lack of discernment, if not cognitive dissonance, but irrationality.

And what has the fallout been? Disaster in Afghanistan, skyrocketing inflation, increased interest rates, rising crime, societal disintegration, recession, a doubling of energy costs, failing banks, and war, all in less than two years.

All of this could have been avoided with a little discernment. Half the country got their just desserts, but the other half got what they didn't deserve and had to eat it all the same. The bottom line is this: If you can't exercise discernment, please just stop voting. This applies to both the Left and Right.

Systemic psychosis in America has many symptoms. The lack of discernment is one of the most serious. The Left doesn't know any better, and that is being too kind, frankly they don't care. However, the Right should. If we are going to come back from the edge of the cliff as a country, we must recover our discernment and rabidly take action with a fierce passion to reverse the damaging policies that have been implemented. Nothing less than our lives depends on it.

Thankfully, some on the Right do seem to know better and act in accordance with their knowledge. Tucker Carlson, the number one talk show host until the leftist cabal had him removed, had one of the most thought-provoking and thoroughly cogent nightly monologues on cable TV. He has one of the clearest grasps on reality and the state of our world today. His ability to speak truth to power is nothing less than spiritually inspired. Carlson discussed the hard-to-comprehend madness seen in the faces and eyes of the radicals protesting and destroying cities and refers to it as "spiritually evil and wicked." It's not too often that you hear media figures resorting to religious or spiritual descriptions in their discourse to describe and explain the incomprehensible. He also says, "something is very wrong, otherworldly," and indeed it is.

We need more thinking and discernment like that if we are to have any hope. We will see if we get them.

Not Discerning the Puppet Masters

There is a "core" to everything. That is the main thrust of this book because much effort and resources have been wasted on fighting the wrong battles. In Christian terms, the core of the problems of this world is evil (manifested in sin) versus good. At the core is Satan.

As mentioned, if you desire to excel in law school and the practice of law you must sift through many extraneous facts and get to the core of the problem before a solution can be reached. Doctors must be able to observe symptoms to get to a diagnosis of the core cause before a treatment can be administered.

Think deeply and think logically for a moment if you will and ask yourself, where is all this chaos coming from? What is causing all the chaos and rot in America? It did not used to be this way. There is a cause and there is a core, and it is not from a puff of smoke, or a virus or the gods on top of Mount Olympus. It comes from other humans. This has been written about before and deserves an investigative analysis that would fill up several other books but there are what I call the "puppet masters" who pull the strings of the puppets. For the most part, you never see the master.

All you see are the puppets. You can love the puppets, or dislike them, or get rid of them and think that you have accomplished something. However, if you get rid of one puppet because they did something you didn't like or did something wrong, another puppet will appear and do the same thing—perhaps even worse. Why? Because there is never any consequence for the Puppet Master, only for the replaceable puppet. All your efforts are in vain because you didn't discern what was at the core or that there even was a core. You didn't take the fight to the Master. You only got rid of his puppet. Remember, if you want to get rid of a weed you take out the root. To kill a snake, you chop off the head, not the tail. For example, The Soros backed district attorneys punish good people and let bad people off. The puppet is the DA. Who is the Master? Surely you can pull this answer together by now. So, what is being done about the Master? Where is the consequence for the Master? There is none, and he will keep on destroying the peace and the country.

With all the examples given thus far and others to come, it should become abundantly obvious that the chaos and rot in America will continue until you discern what is at the core of the problem. Something, some group or someone is at the core, pushing the buttons, making the calls and pulling the strings, and until you realize that and start aiming at the core – aiming at the Master(s) and making them feel the consequences of their conduct, nothing will change. Stop, pause, take a deep breath, think, recall, and connect the dots. Discern that there is a core to the problems that you and this nation face, and you had better identify it and take aim. Understanding cause and effect, the subject of the next chapter, will help you to take the steps proposed and take back control of both your life and this nation.

CHAPTER 9:

The Deadly Absence of Cause and Effect

"Those who cannot remember the past are condemned to repeat it."
George Santayana

Santayana's quote is not only true, but it is the very reason why the Left is so obsessed with cleansing our children of any knowledge of the past and rewriting history to suit their narrative. If they didn't do this, the Left would never be able to get by with the twisted policies and laws they propose today.

Every day we see on display one of the major symptoms of psychosis: the failure to understand cause and effect. This is also referred to as causality, but we will stick with the phrase, "cause and effect," which is defined as "the operation or relationship between a cause and its effect." Decisions have consequences.

Let's say you back your car out of a parking space without looking and hit another car. There is a crash, which is the effect. The cause is your inattention - your reckless behavior. Let's say you were ordered to evacuate your home due to an approaching hurricane, but you decided your family would not leave. Your home is washed away, and a member of your family dies. Your decision, not the hurricane, was the primary cause of death because it was avoidable but for your decision.

Here's a very current example that has disastrously affected the entire country. You voted for Biden. He campaigned on eliminating the use of fossil fuels and forcing you into unaffordable electric cars. Then the domestic production of oil is shut down and your gas prices go up, as do your groceries and everything else; while your income and purchasing power shrink. You get poorer because you voted for it. The cause is your vote, the effect is the suffering you are now experiencing for putting into office a man whose policies bring you and the nation misery.

In response, we buy Russian oil. Then Russia's military gets financing and Ukraine gets invaded. You are horrified and saddened by the mayhem and become so exercised (really manipulated) over it that you want to risk World War III. We send tens of billions of dollars to Ukraine while being $31 trillion in debt ourselves. Inflation hits a forty-year high. You struggle to make ends meet. The cause? Your vote! You got what you voted for.

Now you are waving a little Ukrainian flag in your social media profile and are unhappy. Here is how out of touch most are when it comes to money and why the country will bankrupt, and you will lose everything. Let's put this in perspective using time as a measure.

1 million seconds is 12 days.

1 billion seconds is almost 32 years.

1 trillion seconds is almost 32,000 years.

Our debt of over $31 trillion is equal to 1 million years in time. It's no stretch nor sacrifice to say the Left and Right have lost their minds as well as have the voters, including you! Why didn't you see it coming? You denied the reality that spending what you don't have, or voting for politicians to spend what they and you don't have, will have a consequence. That's psychosis.

Another symptom of this inorganic psychosis is the loss of understanding of the basic principle of cause and effect. To be frank, people deserve the consequences of their votes. Yes, you have been manipulated. After having been manipulated into bad decisions so many times one should know better by now. People should be more discerning and understand there is an effect, a consequence of their actions.

The voter never seems to understand that there are consequences to their vote, even though one of the most often repeated phrases in politics is that "elections have consequences." Many Biden voters will likely not vote for him again; but many will, and they will never learn their lesson. They will never make the connection between the kind of person they vote for and their suffering. Unfortunately, it's not just their suffering – it's the entire country's as well. As the saying goes, "If you don't think, you'll feel," and indeed those who put Biden into office are feeling, as is the rest of the nation.

Few (if any) Biden voters can think of a tangible benefit they have received from their vote in 2020 but they now know their misery. If they were truthful, they would most likely have to tell you they have no idea why they voted for Biden other than some indoctrinated need to cleanse themselves of empty guilt and a desire to feel virtuous. This is not just a partisan observation; it is the sentiment of over 70% of the population. We no longer live in a time where public servants go to Washington to serve the people and make their lives better. Rather, the so-called public servants go to Washington to serve themselves, and they do so lavishly. Biden has done so for over 50 years.

For some, suffering brings knowledge and wisdom. They learn from their mistakes. There are those, like a dog who returns to its vomit, who keep doing the same thing. They keep voting for the Left as if there was some virtue in it, but they suffer for it. It reminds me of the old joke about why the moron kept hitting himself on the head with a hammer. He said, "Because it feels so good when I stop." So much of the electorate are moronic or like the Greek word from which we get moron, *moros,* meaning "dull, stupid, foolish, lacking a grip on reality, or acting as if brainless. Merriam Webster's definition is no kinder but poignantly descriptive.

Every time I ask someone why they voted the way they did, they never cite one fact or cogent reason, but always preface the excuse with, "Well, at the time, I felt like..." They are always learning but never coming to a full knowledge of the truth. The lack of discernment always plays into this as well, since a dumbed-down education is now being combined with political indoctrination. The conduct within this country is such a departure from normative, cogent, and deductive reasoning on such a mass scale that it can only be described as a "mass formation psychosis."

There comes a point when society becomes so mentally dysfunctional that they cease to care about the sufferings they have brought upon themselves and others. Those who still function mentally and know the cause are, to some extent, handcuffed to those who don't function mentally and deserve their suffering. These are the seeds of revolution.

This takes us back to the universal problem of systemic psychosis. This psychosis has been implemented with patience, persistence, and dogged determination by those who have a nefarious and corrupt agenda, and they don't care if they sink the ship of our nation. They think they have their life rafts and are safe from the consequences of the chaos they create. I call these people at the core of the Left the "puppet masters." They're all in, just as long as they bring it down. Yes, it's suicidal and detached from reality. You can just hear those on the Right side of the spectrum using their favorite word: "Why"? Why is this happening? Why are they doing this?

Why have all these awful things happened? Because they were allowed to happen. Not just allowed but encouraged. It happened in broad daylight. There is plenty of blame to go around, but it's important to note the difference between those guilty of the sins of *commission* and those guilty of sins of *omission*. The committed Marxists who control the non-thinkers are guilty of crimes of commission. They are driven by a blind ambition and a delusion of utopia which stems not from an informed mind or concern for their fellow man, but one driven by an evil resentment, rage, and self-loathing. They are obsessed with power. They fake competence and enhance their reputation by ruining others. Cause and effect are ignored or lost upon them.

Then there are those guilty of the crimes of *omission*. They are the "thinkers," but they are too lazy or cowardly to do anything about the problems they can identify. This is contrary to what one would expect, but those who could and should do better sadly often don't. Is there any cure or hope? I would ask those on the Right to look at their checkbooks and calendars to see just how uninvolved and disconnected they have been. Is it too late? The jury is out, but I'm not optimistic if for no other reason than today's technology is in the hands of the Left. For decades, I have warned about a coming time when, on the political graph, the technology line crosses the political line, and whoever is in charge at that point would be empowered to stay in charge in perpetuity. We have recently heard all the warnings about artificial intelligence (AI) and that we need to pause it for 6 months due to the potential dangers to society and mankind. The genie is out of the bottle. It won't stop, but more alarming is that AI is being engineered by the Left and AI is being trained to lie. Freedom will die.

Cause and Effect in Politics

During the 2003 election cycle, the Republican Party in Kentucky was in its ascendancy. For both the gubernatorial race and all the other constitutional statewide offices, it had a great bench of candidates—save for one. In fact, all of the Republican candidates won except for that one. And that one bad candidate would end up being, in part, the undoing of the Republican governor, the first in nearly 40 years.

I'm a big fan of grassroots political organizers, enthusiasts and parallel structures and organizations. Truly, we need them. On occasion you will find one or two that live in an alternate universe. Most profoundly, they misunderstand cause and effect. They have an unbridled passion, fueled with emotion, like the Left, but lacking in experiential knowledge. On this occasion, in 2003 there was a primary for attorney general. Party leadership (not always qualified themselves) was behind a good and qualified candidate whose credentials were right for the job, but a grassroots organization had a dark horse candidate as an outlier, selected with blind passion.

Primaries are very volatile, unpredictable, and it doesn't take much for the unusual to happen since so few show up to vote. In this instance the unusual happened. The grassroots organization rallied behind the outlier candidate. While this organization's principles were basically good, its direction and leadership were blinded by their passions and naivety; and they took no counsel, nor did they do their homework.

Their candidate won. The next morning, I was flooded with calls from the media. Why? It was revealed that the grassroots candidate, now the official Republican nominee in the general election for attorney general, previously had been a judge removed from the bench twice by the Kentucky Supreme Court on disciplinary grounds. Cause (grassroots rally behind unvetted nominee) meets effect (a total disaster and loss in the general election).

For twenty-four hours I huddled with leadership to try and figure out what, if anything, could be done. There was nothing we could do. We were shocked since the opponent on the Democrat side was as wicked and out of touch with Kentucky values as anyone could be. It was devastating to consider that this grassroots organization essentially handed the office over to their nemesis—the one who eventually helped bring down the governor they supported. The leftist AG was there for himself, not the people, filled with loathing and destruction; and destruction he brought.

The grassroots organization had not done their homework, refused to listen, cooperate, or reason, as they were passionate about opposing those who they saw as doctrinally or ideologically impure or establishment. The purists at times have a blindness born of inexperience and will walk into an ambush every time, as they are devoid of battlefield reality. Sometimes the ones who have lost sight of cause and effect are those on the Right.

This blind passion and ideological purism are a danger, and while an exception to the Right, it is endemic and the rule on the Left. Historically, it has proven to be deadly. In this case it cost an election and control of a critical office for justice in Kentucky.

Fools Refuse To Admit that the Stove Is Hot

Once again, nothing is new under the sun. When the Israelites complained in the desert after the Exodus and then refused to go into the Promised Land, God wiped out that generation. He had them wander in the desert for forty years so that generation would die out. Cause (disobedience)—and effect (destruction).

There are some instances where irrationality is so ingrained that it is futile to fight with it. When this occurs, redirect your resources elsewhere. Even if the Left was willing to allow an open conversation, sometimes the hard truth is that you can't reason with fools. For example, if someone keeps touching the hot stove top, even though they are getting burned, they will eventually lose all feeling and use of their hand. In other words, at some point, the warnings don't matter anymore—the deed is done and there is no going back. To mix metaphors, irrational ears are often deaf ones. Many times, there is no cure for irrationality. It just has to die off, like that generation of Hebrews in the desert. We saw this so many times with employee union mentalities who either bankrupted companies or chased them offshore. They left many cities in the rustbelt hollowed out shells of what they once were. There was no reasoning with them. The mentality had become cultural and their identity. They simply had to just die out, and they did.

Thus, in some cases, the irrationality (the inability to understand how cause and effect works) is so deeply embedded that you have to proverbially "nuke it" so to speak and wipe the slate clean. Sadly, that's highly likely where we are in America. A generation becomes a hopeless cause and gets wiped out, and possibly the country with it.

This reminds me of the Great Flood story in Genesis. Everyone drowned except eight, Noah and his family. The world didn't heed the warnings, nor did they understand the cause (wicked sin) and effect (righteous judgment). I'm not preaching here but simply giving anecdotes that, regardless of your religious beliefs, you have most likely heard before. The moral of the story endures, and I trust you know what I mean. Nature will ultimately have its way with the psychos, but unfortunately others as well.

Even on the Right, they never cross that finish line of cause and effect. They never help the public connect the dots, assuming they were capable of doing so themselves in the first place. They are not, but if they were, the Right always misses the boat. The conservative media (as small as it is) will interview someone on the street and ask how they are faring in the poor economy (in this instance just 18 months earlier when it was historically the best), but the media will never ask an interviewee that last and most important question that would connect the dots, close the case and connect the effect to the cause: how did they vote?

Now, on the Left, you would not expect that question, but even on the Right, the question is rarely, if ever, asked. All you hear or see from the masochistic psychos on the Right over and over again is, "Why?" or "This doesn't make sense," or "Why would they do this?" They never ask the correct questions and instead descend into their analytical orgy. They never call it what it is. They wring their hands. They have no plan and have no clue who the enemy is because they believe in a false equivalency.

They don't understand who or what they are fighting. They hit the target but rarely the bullseye.

I have little faith in those who purport to be ready to do the right thing. All too often when the time comes to act, they crank up their excuse machine. Just as the Left has a bottomless pit of excuses and lies for why they must do something for the mythically oppressed 1, 2, or 3% deviant of society, the Right likewise has a bottomless pit of excuses as to why they can't do something to fight what is self-evidently wrong.

The right questions are never asked. Voters never make the connection between how they voted and the consequences of that vote and their suffering. They want sympathy for their present suffering but do not want to be held personally accountable for their role in the suffering.

You must realize this: to sympathize with them is enablement. You are facilitating future bad decisions. Unless there is an understanding of cause and effect, you will continue to have the likes of gray-haired men acting like juveniles. We see this occurring today while they make the same mistakes over and over again. Unfortunately, many who don't deserve the resultant sufferings are tied to those who do. Remember what John Adams said when asked about what kind of government our Republic was? He said that it was, "A government wholly fitting only for a moral people."

Are we still that kind of people? It seems not. To add insult to injury we are also dealing with illiteracy via public education (by design) and a hedonistic, godless culture incapable of rational thought and doomed to repeat the horrors of the past.

As bad as it is, and as dumb as so many of the voters are, guess what? Most knew when they voted as they did, that it was wrong. Deep down, their consciences told them so. Yet, because so many no longer understand cause and effect, they did it anyway. They lived in denial. They tempted fate—and fate delivered. Decisions have consequences.

The motivation for voting as the public did was not based on the desire for good governance, but rather on what they thought was in it for them. They placed a bet on the racehorse based on the name of the horse and not its stats. That would require too much thinking. It was envy, greed, and wanting something for nothing, a handout they didn't deserve, and not caring about the consequences of their indolent ways upon others. They live in denial that anything bad will occur as a result of their decisions or personal corruption. They shun personal responsibility and want the government to take care of them.

It's an ill-minded man who sees the storm coming and refuses to take shelter. Even worse is the man who pulls the rug out from under the feet of his friends, indifferent to the consequences. Half the country did this to the other half in the last elections of 2020 and 2022. Cause: Voting for Biden. Effect: National disaster. Again, this is not just my opinion, as 70+% agree with the scenario that the country is not heading in the right direction, and all the facts and metrics bear it out, yet of that 70%, many were complicit.

Will the psychotic Left ever learn? No! They already know. It's just not in their best career interests. Only profound suffering that forces people to do what is right will bring about effective and productive change. Unfortunately, the rest must suffer as well. At some point the damage will be so irreparable that a return to a normal, healthy, and productive society will be impossible.

Toxic Toleration and the Danger of Fraternalism

Another dangerous feature of the absence of cause and effect is the spread of what I call "toxic toleration." What do I mean by that?

The term toleration comes from the Latin word "*tolerantia.*" It means "to put up with, countenance or suffer, generally refers to the conditional acceptance of or non-interference with beliefs, actions, or practices that one considers being wrong but still 'tolerable' such that they should not be prohibited or constrained" (Stanford Encyclopedia of Philosophy). Don't miss the point of "actions or practices...considered to be wrong." That's like saying you don't believe in child abuse, but a little child abuse you will tolerate. You have just denied someone justice and clearly not at your expense. You have accepted a condition or situation that is totally voluntary and self-evidently wrong. I would say that America has sleepwalked into this toxicity, but the reality is it was born of sloth, indolence, cowardice, laziness, and simply not wanting to be inconvenienced by saying no. It's an immorality from which this country cannot survive. We tolerate what sane people would never tolerate.

The problem is that some beliefs and practices should be prohibited and constrained (such as pedophilia and child mutilation), but we have lost our collective ability to determine which ones fall into this bucket. Our society acts as if there is no limit to tolerance—that people will be forced to tolerate whatever the latest degenerate behavior is marketed as a new protected class. An example of toxic tolerance and its destructive and negative impact is well summarized by Edmund Burke's famous quote, "All that is necessary for the triumph of evil is for good men to do nothing."

Good men have been doing nothing, using "toleration" as an excuse for a long time. It's as if there is some virtue in the toleration of evil. This practice must end in every form. It must start with you, and it must start now. You have a right to be intolerant of wrong and evil. Let no one tell you otherwise. The Left may not like your opinion but why should you care unless you lack autonomy over your own mind and emotions.

Amid the chaos swirling about the country today, this toleration is a subversion of the adage, "live and let live". People wrongly tolerate friends, family, and colleagues being profane in their social life and accept every perversion that comes along because they don't want to be "judgmental." Or maybe they do it because they are compromised and guilty of something themselves. They elect every politician who supports the radical departure from the normative in a detachment from reality. Tolerating what our society has been tolerating over the last couple of decades is as insane as letting a pedophile watch your children—but rest assured, it won't be too long before your toxic tolerance will even allow *that* to be a new protected class with rights as well. What did you think the "+" in "LGBTQ+" stands for anyway? We are making sin a "gender"—that is, a protected status—which I will address more later.

You must stop the psychotic tolerance of socialists, leftists, the profane and the deviant, who are proven monomaniacal and murderous. If you don't know that by now, then you are woefully ignorant and have lived a life devoid of any self-awareness or examination of the world around you. You might be irredeemably irrational, or a useful idiot (as the Marxists would call you). You are, in ignorance, doing their bidding as they extinguish yours and others' rights. Think not yourself to be so wise and righteous in your ignorance and toxic toleration, as there will be a terrible price to pay for those who have practiced deception or turned a blind eye to injustice in the name of tolerance.

We don't tolerate bad behavior or erroneous beliefs in our children. Why do we allow it with our associations or our leaders? Light has nothing in common with darkness, and bad company corrupts good character. So, why soil yourselves with such associations? Many self-identified conservatives or those on the Right are at fault. They have allowed the disease of tolerance to proliferate and in fact, enabled it by turning a cowardly blind eye without any concern for the consequences. The Right, out of selfish ambition, ignored the wrongs and tolerated them, thinking that they will correct the problem once they get into office. They never do. The Right is guilty of paying homage to tolerance, hoping to benefit from a false virtue. They have yet to learn that no good deed goes unpunished, and the Left always delivers on that score. The Right wastes their time, talents, and treasures in pursuit of wooing evil to their side.

Here is the inconsistency. You live as a conservative in your personal life but tolerate the metastasizing liberalization of the world around you as if it will never demand that *you* comply with its beliefs and commitments.

The Right thinks they can, with reason and persuasion, make the enemies of freedom see the light. This is the worn-out excuse for toxic tolerance. It is also the error of equivalency, that is assuming that the maniacal Left, are just like you. No, they are not. They have no tolerance for the Right as does the Right for the Left. It's too late anyway. The chemical reaction has gone too far and has reached critical mass. The conservative/Right took a nap while at the controls of the nuclear reactor. Now they are going to have to give up the lives they enjoyed just to save the basic liberties they squandered. The shepherd has gone away. The wolves have been killing off the sheep, and there is no longer a flock to protect. Too few conservatives, or those on the Right, will write a check, attend a freedom rally, or boycott a woke company. It's just "too hard" to give up all those conveniences, comforts, and pleasures. Judgment is here and conservatives/the Right will now learn the cost of their pusillanimous ways. In the case of Disney, there was a ray of hope in the courageous action of Governor DeSantis to protect the children and he was successful, but don't lose sight of how powerfully he had to fight and how entrenched evil had become before corrective measures were taken.

Another current example of the dire consequences unfolding from the leftist ideology (that is in control) was the unprecedented raid on former President Trump's home. This was all over so-called classified documents, which has been an issue with nearly every past president but resolved with negotiation and settlement. Not so with Trump. The Left wants blood. However, less than six months later, President Biden was caught with thousands of classified documents in several locations from when he was Vice President. Here again is the glaring hypocrisy of the Left. The excuse machine of the Left began manufacturing both excuses and distractions. The duplicitous, hypocritical, and maniacal conduct of the Left today has never known its equal. The Left weaponized the Justice Department and the FBI as its surrogates to implement their dystopia which leads me to the topic of the dangers of fraternalism that has developed within our bureaucracy.

Consider this: What do the drug cartels and gangs, and the mafia have in common that attracts their members? Camaraderie! It's a fraternity! It's a need for a sense of belonging, and feeling that you are part of something.

The FBI, the DOJ, the Department of Education, and the IRS have become insulated fraternities—immune from the rest of us and thinking they are above the law. They are so entrenched and embedded they are without challenge. Not even in Congressional hearings can congressmen and senators get a straight answer when interrogating operatives from these agencies. They have become separate from the rest of us. They live among us but are not part of us. They see themselves differently. And they are armed to the teeth!

The psychotic Left, with the Right looking on, has literally armed all these agencies with munitions. Think about it. Each is like a standing army in and to itself, just like the cartels. The leftist and socialist Democrats have been arming these agencies with guns and munitions while trying to take away yours. In case you don't know, each agency, even the Department of Education, is armed with thousands of guns, ammo, and other weapons to subdue your protest and protestations. Do you really think they care about you or about your rights?

In a rare speech, former Justice Anthony Scalia warned us about our overconfidence in the Bill of Rights and Constitution. Once the deep state and the bureaucracy get so big, the Bill of Rights goes out the window. Even Russia, Cuba, and China have some form of "bill of rights." Go try to exercise them and see how far you get. The only cure here is unification, dedication, and sacrifice of freedom lovers, constitutionalists, and the Right. If they ever regain a majority, job one is to de-fang these out of control and unaccountable agencies. Most likely, even with a majority, the Right will continue to be infected by sloth, denial, and those devoid of any statesmanship.

Again, history shows that over the last 100 years the Left has killed and exterminated over 100,000,000 of those who disagreed with them. The psychosis on the Right let this monster grow up. They lost the advantage where once they could have fought with policy and law in a peaceful manner. Now they are looking at a scenario where revolution, as some on the Left have already discussed, is becoming a reality. It won't be resolved. Having seen this trajectory evolve for decades, I've fought to avoid the revolution and the violence that accompanies it, and I still do. A country infected with mass formation psychosis and the technology that is in the hands of the Left make it impossible to avoid. The Left cannot constrain themselves and the Right will stay in denial until the barrel of the Leftist's gun is literally in their face. The fraternalism that has grown up in these governmental agencies is a real threat and danger to the country and to your freedoms. The effect here will be the loss of your freedoms by uncontrollable agencies. The cause is the abusive delegation of power from elected officials to these governmental agencies.

Think about it. While many who work in the various governmental agencies are good hard-working people who have to take orders from their leadership, it is a fair question to ask, "what kind of person or character wants to be an IRS agent or an FBI agent?" Here's what I mean. Let's take this a step further. Studies have shown that many of those who gravitate to jobs like Emergency Medical Services and the like tend to be codependent personality types. So, we better be asking what types go into these various government agencies armed with weapons? In a leaked job description for the IRS, applicants were asked if they could handle a gun and be able to use deadly force. Seriously! Deadly force for what and on whom? Americans? We have seen the FBI raid the homes of families who are prolife in the middle of the night, frightening children and placing them in harm's way. These are raids with dozens descending upon homes of law-abiding citizens. The agents are on video acting as if they were gestapo agents yelling, screaming and threatening the citizens. So, what is the personality profile of someone like that? Do you want applicants for the IRS, or the Dept. of Education willing to use deadly force upon American citizens?

What's more alarming is that as these groups and agencies grow, they become communities separate from the rest of us. They live amongst us but see themselves as above and better than us. They cease to have a camaraderie or a brotherhood with the rest of the citizens as one nation. This becomes not much different than the psychology we see occurring and binding together the gang members here in America and in Mexico. Throughout the many examples given in this chapter, there is a cause (either an uninformed omission or commission of something) and every time the effect negatively impacts your life, liberty and happiness.

The unelected bureaucratic state ceases to be your equal, but rather they become your interrogators, intimidators, and harassers, denying you your presumption of innocence and due process. Just look at the disgraced Peter Strzok with the FBI and his overt condescending and arrogant attitude exhibited towards those in Congress when he was called in to be questioned about his illegal activities in the agency. As a reminder, he was fired from the FBI, but then reinstated by the Left. Even Senator Schumer (no friend to freedom) has expressed fear of the intelligence agencies, a monster he helped create. Now we know things are way out of control when agencies that are answerable to Congress have Congress fearful.

Back to toxic tolerance. We've killed ourselves as a nation by letting the Left convince us that we need to be tolerant of everything antithetical to human dignity and individual freedoms to the point of toxicity. The Right has allowed agencies to populate and exist as their own autocracy, and as sovereigns. The effect of our excessive toleration is causing our national suicide—if we don't radically and immediately reverse course.

CHAPTER 10:

Our Addiction to Convenience and Comfort

"Throughout history, it has been the inaction of those who could have acted; the indifference of those who should have known better; the silence of the voice of justice when it mattered most; that has made it possible for evil to triumph."

Haile Selassie I

There's a saying from a postapocalyptic novel by G. Michael Hopf, *Those Who Remain*, that expresses a certain cyclical understanding and moral progression of the nature of history. It goes like this: "Hard times create strong men, strong men create good times, good times create weak men, and weak men create hard times." Whether it is entirely true or not, it is certainly a popular cipher for our day and age. Which stage of this cycle do you think America is in now? I'd say weak men are creating hard times. How did we get there?

The good times made weak men. And good men are doing nothing. The Boomer era made weak-minded men; men who, in their mental weakness, would be susceptible to the onset of systemic psychosis. Mind you I am aware of the importance that worldviews play into this but that's a topic for another book.

Men who loved convenience and craved comfort above all else were unable to rouse themselves to defend their minds, bodies, families, and ultimately, their country from the onset of this societally deadly disease. These weak men brought us hard times, as they were content to coast in the good times brought to their generation by the hard men who fought and won World War II.

The progeny of these hard men can barely get off their couches and go vote. Just consider the rise in mail-in voting, born out of that same indolent attitude that created the hard times. They pay no mind to the consequences of such laziness, or ever stop to consider that such a voting arrangement is not only fraught with fraud but banned in many other countries around the world because they know it is unsafe and unreliable. After that planned so-called experiment in 2020, excused by the pandemic, many states banned it; but not until it likely affected the outcome of an election and the resultant economic chaos due to the policies of a Leftist President. People want their comfort and convenience regardless of the cost.

Our Comfort Is Costly

One way that our addiction to convenience and comfort is on display is in our nonchalant attitude towards the massive incursion by the federal government's security state apparatus into our daily lives. Freedom is being sacrificed for a false security and has been for some time. As Benjamin Franklin once said: "Those who would give up essential liberty to purchase a little temporary safety, deserve neither liberty nor safety."

The Patriot Act was the mother of all legislative catastrophes, and it was under the globalist President George W. Bush that this Trojan Horse was brought into the camp. As with COVID, fear drove the narrative. Yes, 9/11 was truly a national tragedy. The enemy that attacked us came from outside our country—radical Islamist terrorists. The Patriot Act was a knee-jerk reaction, but it passed. Now the NSA, CIA, and FBI could spy on law abiding citizens. This was one of the biggest steps forward toward an authoritarian state in the last 50 years.

Now, of course, it was necessary for the United States to take strong action against our overseas enemy, teaching them a lesson about what happens when you attack the United States, but the solution to removing a splinter, relatively speaking, isn't to cut off your hand. It's to pull the splinter out, bandage it and make sure it doesn't happen again. When it came to protecting our own people from collateral damage (i.e., creating a surveillance state) in the counterattack, we were lax. The long-term consequences of such surveillance state actions are rarely considered. This was no exception. I recall Reagan's Assistant Secretary of Defense telling me that this would be a disaster and posed a real risk to our freedoms. Truer words were rarely spoken. How right he was, and the risk and subsequent abuses were the result. Our forefathers warned of trading freedom for security, as did Franklin. Now, the cure has become deadlier than the disease.

The reason we tolerate the ever-expanding surveillance state is that we are easily manipulated by fear and are addicted to comfort. We want to *feel* like we are being taken care of, even if we pay for that pathos with our privacy and our freedom.

One result of this fear is that the government actors can manipulate the news cycles and our social media timeline, disconnecting us further from reality and the truth and acting accordingly. At the end of August 2022, we saw this on clear display when Facebook CEO Mark Zuckerburg admitted that Facebook "killed" the Hunter Biden laptop story at the request of the FBI. After the fact polling revealed that such information would have changed the outcome of the election. But it's too inconvenient to hold, much less expect, our officials to follow the law and respect our rights. Again, the result was the elections of leftists which has brought the nation so much misery. Many of those who voted for the misery would irrationally support the party and leaders again.

People who challenged the legitimacy of the election were derisively called "election deniers." Now the truth is out. The FBI and DOJ are politicized, and the political opposition is now subject to suppression by those in power and by our justice system. Here's the cherry on top of that sundae: those (the Left, the Democrats) who have convinced you that the 2020 elections deniers are wackos and conspiracy theorists (as if such were a bad thing, it's not!) destructive to a Democratic Republic, did exactly the same thing in the 2000, 2004, and 2016 elections. Oh, how quickly people forget.

The Democrats stood up in January in each of these years after those November elections, in Congress during the certification process, and said that the elections were illegitimate. They even attempted to keep the electoral votes from being recognized by various states. It was a full-court press. Hypocrisy? Yes! Did that stop them? No! Did the public recall the hypocrisy on display? No! Clearly, it is too inconvenient and uncomfortable for the public to keep informed, and to drag themselves away from their addictions to their phones and internet to take action to secure the freedoms they are losing. It's as if we have national dementia in addition to our psychosis.

Church Comfort or Church Confrontation

There are few places in life that can lull you into a sense of comfort and complacency more than a bad church. On the other hand, there are many who want to wait on the mountainside for Christ to return, sitting on their hands (either metaphorically or actually) feeling justified in letting the world go to hell. However, the Bible calls us to be on watch, vigilant, and "about our tasks" and our calling until that time comes. Sometimes, that work involves speaking up. So, whether it is through the allure of comfort, or the comfort of apathy, choosing to upset the apple cart at church can be very hard to do. That's what it takes, speaking up, when lies start to slip in and live under the steeple—with all of the people. No, I am not talking about being a divisive spirit, but being one devoted to preserving fidelity to the essential doctrines of the faith particularly at a time when the church already has been compromised.

Having done a stint in seminary, I learned to critically analyze what was being taught from the pulpit. I could no longer sit in church like a zombie and not listen intently to a sermon, with the goal of determining its correct teaching and application before I diligently applied it to my life. If I was going to do something that important, that is, pattern my life according to the teaching, then I was going to be sure that the word and the teaching was being spoken and taught accurately and correctly. Few do that; thus, they lack discernment and fall into error.

After working its way through the culture, wokeness started creeping into the church. That's when I knew the churches in the country were in big trouble. It was decades in the making, but it was clear as to what was happening. Thankfully, my antenna was up so I was going to have none of it. It would have been so much easier, so much more *comfortable*, to just let error go. That's the path that leads to death, not to life. As goes the church, so goes the nation.

In August of 2017 I started hearing some rumblings of social justice (which is a replacement for the gospel and totally heretical) coming from the pulpit of my church. A relative who had attended a Saturday service at my church called and told me to be prepared that when I attended the service on Sunday, I would hear it implied that St. Peter was a racist. Then he said that "If we didn't believe in racism then we were racist." I was incredulous, and my first reaction was that I just wouldn't go to church that Sunday. Then I thought better of it, as I couldn't comment on it to the church leadership if I didn't hear the sermon myself, so I went.

The reports were true. Social justice gospel poured forth from the pulpit that Sunday. Again, the easier thing, the more comfortable thing, would have been to just let it go. Instead, I wrote several strongly worded and well researched letters to the leadership of the church after having the sermon examined by professors at the seminary, who advised that my take on the message was correct and that the minister's representation of Scripture that Sunday was wrong. The church leadership met for nearly an hour over my confrontation and were ultimately dismissive as it was the easy, comfortable, and convenient thing to do.

The moral of this story is two-fold. First, the minister was wrong and handled the word of God incorrectly. Second, it cost me my comfort to speak out, but I did not shy away from the confrontation. Here again I was in the midst of the storm. You can make a difference if you speak up, resist, demand accountability, and call out corruption and incompetence. It might take a while for the fruit to come, but it will if you are diligent. This was neither comfortable nor convenient, but it was the right thing to do. It had an impact, but it took a while for that tree to bear fruit.

All organizations are prone to corruption if not held accountable by people willing to speak up. Speaking up is not the easy way out. Your freedoms are neither convenient nor comfortable. They must be defended every day.

One of the most important things in life is to have a purpose; otherwise life is futile. God and church give that purpose. They also give order and freedom. Without God, men and government become God, and that is and has been at the core of all of the world's atrocities and wars. I knew that the dying church was one of the main issues at the core of the problems in our country today. That is why I didn't tolerate seeing corruption within the church I formerly attended. Committing to a church and its teachings is one of the most important things one can do in life, but its sanctity and fidelity to its purpose will not be maintained with an indifferent congregation.

The Easy Way Out

One of the ways that the mass psychosis perpetuates itself is on the backs of those who know better but refuse to speak out because to do so would be costly, specifically costly to their comfort. The longer they stay quiet, the more damage is done. Totalitarianism is the end stage of this implemented systemic mass formation psychosis. Towards this end we are inching closer every day.

One of the factors that drives our addiction to comfort, which fuels our silence and allows psychosis to grow, is how disconnected we are from the truth. One reason for this is because, as a modern society, we are so removed from subsistence living, and agrarian exposure where the skills of observation, simply noticing reality for what it is, and self-reliance used to be honed at an early age. However, much of that has been lost, as well as any logical and deductive reasoning. Farmers aren't confused about the fact that there are only two genders.

In our present, comfortable existence, we have no idea of the suffering that went on in the lives of people throughout most of history. We are disconnected from the past. Why is that so important you say? Because history repeats itself, particularly the horrors of the past if we do not remember the errors that were made that led to those horrors. These days most suffering is done with cellphones in hand, inside warm dry homes, with hot and cold running water, cars in the garage, healthcare, food to eat, and 24/7 entertainment. Millions are now working from home. It's possible now, like never before, to be about as lazy as you want. You can skip out on work for days and claim that you needed the break for your "mental health." This is our kind of suffering, and it is first-world suffering. And it makes us weak.

How far are we removed from the likes of the rest of the world? How far are we today from the time in England when children were kicked out of their homes at the age of seven because their families couldn't afford them? How far are we from famine or war in the Middle East? How far are we from a reality that if we didn't get up at dawn and work till dark, we went hungry?

Our problems today are indeed "first world." We've lost the connection with reality and truth. Too few have had the grim reaper as a partner, day in and day out, where he got his way if you did not perform up to par each day. Our problems today aren't ones of subsistence living, but the threat of inconvenience and lack of comfort. Our perception of problems has been so warped and detached from an existential reality that we would kill the golden goose if given the chance. In fact, we are. And it's our own country.

The brutality that the Left will bring to society today, compared to the past, will be unlike any in the past, as people are weaker, more gullible, and more naïve today, and will be lambs to the slaughter. They are not like previous generations who had a healthy degree of skepticism and were more apt to take precautions and be more self-sufficient. Society today will either totally capitulate or be massacred, and the Left will convince them and themselves it is a good thing. Don't believe it? Many in the radical climate movement would rather the earth be cleansed of humans. This should call for their institutionalization, but they are not only roaming around free, they are also making policy.

Trading Freedom for Security

There is no doubt that our addiction to comfort is costly. We sit on our couches watching ballgame after ballgame, TV series, movies, etc., knowing the ground is being cut out from under us. Insanely, we justify it because it is just too much effort to get off our rears. You will complain, but you will never write a check to help fight for your freedoms. You will never schedule any time to join an organization for the preservation of your rights or support a candidate loyal to preserving your rights and freedoms.

On the Right side of the spectrum, the comfort and convenience addicted don't write that contribution check because they might not be able to buy that 12th pair of Nikes or take their third vacation of the year. Their calendar is absent of any community group gatherings or meetings to organize and support the rights they claim to cherish because they must chauffeur Johnny to his 3rd ballgame of the week and Sally to her piano and dance lessons. The addiction to our conveniences, our fast-food lifestyle, our Amazon deliveries, and our remote-controlled homes come at a price. That price is the loss of the undisciplined masses' rights, religion, and freedoms.

Some say, "well, if I can keep living as I am, then I don't care; who needs freedom of speech, assembly of religion, or right to bear arms?" These are the people who have been bred and conditioned to care about nothing but themselves and what makes them happy. So, if they can just keep what they have now they're happy to sit back and watch the country die. Well, that is a big "if." You're betting it all on the hope that "if" will not materialize. Because if it does, you will keep none of it. You will lose all you have along with your freedoms and lack any means of protest. Do you think you will like the long lines in the grocery store to get a loaf of bread? Or having your thermostats be set at 80 in the summer and 60 in the winter? Or, likely you will not be allowed to charge your electric car if you have traveled too much. You will mask up and get jabbed with dangerous vaccines whether you like it or not. How do I know? Because most of you reading this already did in 2020!

This is happening every day, both in America and around the world, with the totalitarians setting new precedents and breaking new boundaries. Will there be an invoice for it all? Yes! There will be a price to pay and there is no bankruptcy court that will get you out of it. Once your freedoms are gone there is no getting them back without the supreme sacrifice. The addiction to our comforts and conveniences will eventually cost us everything. The time to show some discipline is now.

CHAPTER 11:

DEI and Your New Digital Masters: A Dangerous Combination

> "All animals are equal, but some
> are equal than others."
>
> **George Orwell**

Dictators, Digital and Otherwise

In 2022 we witnessed freedom-loving truckers in Canada protest for weeks over the vaccine mandates. Prime Minister Trudeau, a petty, Cuba and China-loving dictator, crushed that peaceful protest by having their trucks towed, their pets taken, children separated from parents, and bank accounts frozen (including people who were not part of the protest but merely financial contributors), along with other acts of thuggery. He was roundly condemned by the European Union Parliament (not that they are any paragon of virtue but that speaks to the degree of his unlawfulness); yet despite all his treachery, he remains in power. Since then the Canadian Supreme Court has ruled his actions unconstitutional, but given his admiration for China and Cuba, wouldn't you think this would have led to a massive defeat at the polls on election day? Not when your country has slipped into atheism and the consequences which I will address later. Less than 100 years ago had some-one like Trudeau committed such political crimes he would have been dragged out of office and dealt with as a traitor.

By the way, calling Trudeau a "Castro and China loving" dictator come from statements he has made in the past expressing his admiration for both systems of government. This speaks volumes about the people in Canada and how far they have regressed. Now, I know this book is aimed at America's psychosis, but many times when Canada sneezes we catch a cold. In fact, what we see occurring in California and Canada is just a sneak peek, a preview of what is to come to the rest of the country. Make no mistake, we go from California to Canada, to China in one slippery slide down the communist slope. We may very well have a communist neighbor to our north in the very near future as Canada has essentially done away with freedom of speech, religion and the right to bear arms.

So, what does all this have to do with the theme of this chapter? As the world slips into a global totalitarianism, it doesn't require much mental effort to understand why certain nations around the world want to go fully digital and switch to crypto for currency (cashless). In order for total-itarians to seize power and stay in power they must control every aspect of your lives. If this becomes reality then soon you will have to have "social credit" to engage in any kind of commerce, even buying groceries. If you drive too much, contribute to the wrong causes, use too much electric-ity—your access to food, gas, transportation, and money will be curtailed. You will have no freedom or privacy as to what you do with your money or how you live your life. Today's reality in Canada is shocking.

You have already lost your privacy; you just don't know how much at this point, mainly because you are not on their radar yet. The Left will think of your money as the money that they gave you. After all, they want to control the means of production to decide who gets what. One cannot use enough negative adjectives to describe the malevolent charac-ter of these types. I repeat and remind the reader that these very types are responsible for the deaths of over 100 million in just the last 100 years and the enslavement of over 2 billion. They simply will not let people alone to live their lives as they wish.

In January 2023, the Biden administration announced that it was looking to ban gas stoves and force everyone to be on electric. Just think, when everything becomes electric all the government has to do is throw the switch and you are frozen in the place where you are. They will control if you live or die. Time out! Is it the business of the government to determine these things? That's the first question to ask.

Don't believe me? On September 1, 2022, in the Democrat-controlled state of Colorado, thousands of customers of one electricity provider were complaining as they were locked out of their thermostats during a hot day. The company claims this was because they (the people) had voluntarily joined a certain rewards program, and in doing so agreed to give up some control of their own home's temperature. What idiots! They were rewarded for their stupidity. Never give anyone, much less the government or a corporation control over your life. Either way it shows that the technology is there. What's going to happen when it's *not* voluntary? Here again, freedom was traded for convenience.

You may not be forced to get an actual tattoo of 666 on your forehead or hand, but metaphorically, you will. It is already here. If you lack discernment as to the technological danger that is here, if you don't know your history, if you are addicted to your comforts and conveniences, or if you just don't care, then you will deserve the oppression that is clearly coming. Just as ignorance of the law is no defense, ignorance as to the dangers confronting your freedoms is no excuse.

From facial recognition to the digital currency that will monitor everything you spend and what you buy, government-controlled third parties will have the power to stop you from engaging in the public square simply based on whether they like your lifestyle or beliefs. And that decision maker will be ideologically aligned with the same envious, resentful, and cognitively challenged psychopaths that are seizing power from you now.

As a quick aside, remember—technology will not be our savior, it will be our guillotine. AI now has the power to know what you think, like, believe, purchase, and how you are likely to act. It's worth asking yourself, if man can do this to man, then why can't God do even more? Why can't the God of creation know your thoughts, deeds, and sins, and keep them recorded for the day of judgment? Some have argued that nothing in existence, not even God, could keep track of everyone. If our man-made thinking machines can do it, surely the God who made the man who makes the machines can too. And He will. So, who do you want as *your* god, man or God? If the creators of AI are worried and asking for a pause in the development of AI, then you better be too.

The surveillance abilities that technology has provided to government agencies has led to the abuses that are accumulating. The My Pillow Guy, Mike Lindell, had his phone seized by the FBI in a drive-thru restaurant. Truth be known, it was because he was a Trump supporter. The conduct of the FBI of late has enraged many, but it should be no surprise. It never should have been allowed to go this far. Sure, lawsuits will fly, but by the time the inefficient and ineffective courts and the Supreme Court rule upon the unconstitutionality of the FBI and other governmental agencies' actions, the damage will have been done and the issue moot. As the adage goes, "Justice delayed is justice denied."

For the most part, we elected these dangerous and malevolent people. We gave the sadists the power to inflict pain on us. As R.C. Sproul once said at a conference in response to an inane question that related to problems facing the church today, "What's wrong with you people?" He was trying to wake them out of their mental stupor as to the bad things that were happening within Christendom and the Church. Sproul, as discussed elsewhere, spoke to the irrationality of people. Sadly, mass atrocities occur because the people were oblivious and naïve to the evil being planned.

Diversity, Equity, and Inclusion (DEI) is Coming for You

The digital front is a real battle. However, we have other fronts we must fight in this war against psychosis. One of the biggest consequences from the psychosis is and has been the acceptance of "Diversity, Equity, and Inclusion" as a core commitment of the media, universities, and major corporations. To accept DEI is to relinquish your mental sovereignty and willingly cheer the advancing tyranny and control over our lives.

One way to think about DEI is that it's the professional, corporate manifestation of Black Lives Matter mixed in with an LGBTQ pride parade. As the Left is so adept at doing, they deceive you with words and terms. They deceitfully use terms that seem benign but are a deadly cancer. They are the adults that take candy from babies. They find it so easy to get you to buy into their narrative, every time. They play upon your good nature because they know the meaning you attach to words and terms, but the Left has its own dictionary and will implement their policies based on their definitions, not yours. You vote on the basis of one interpretation, and they enact laws and regulations based upon another that they knew you would never agree with had you known. Yes, you were fooled because you were ignorant of the character and agenda of the people you were electing. The chaos and the discomfort you are experiencing today is ultimately your fault.

On the whole, DEI is a combination of certain commitments to hiring and promotions by organizations and entities. It's tricky because as we have talked about earlier, DEI is a clear manifestation of the corruption of language under Marxism and systemic psychosis. Who wouldn't want "diversity, equity, and inclusion"? Well, you won't once you know what it really means, and how the terms are defined and implemented.

On its face, DEI is the ostensible commitment by an institution to ensure that they are not practicing "unconscious bias" against minorities—ethnic, sexual, and otherwise—in their business practices. Here your government becomes your psychiatrist. You will most likely have an incompetent, if not malevolent, woke HR department manager making biased and subjective decisions as to what is in your mind or in your heart, and all to your detriment. Woke corporations are paying billions to companies who advise and help implement the most perverse policies, all based on fraudulent narratives born of a pathological ideology that the Right allowed to slip into the public conversation.

So, what does DEI even mean? The truth is far more sinister, but had you been paying attention you would know.

On the website, New Discourses, which is run in part by my friend Dr. James Lindsay, he defined it like this:

> The Diversity, Equity, and Inclusion industry under Woke Marxism is easy to understand. Equity is a rebranding of Socialism: an administered economy that makes outcomes equal. Diversity and Inclusion are tools used to install political officers and to censor and remove dissidents, respectively. In other words, the

Woke Marxist DEI industry is a racket designed to install commissars for its ideology.[47]

That's right, DEI is just another tool in the toolbox of the Marxists. It
is radical social engineering in the business world and workforce while it
presents itself in nice-sounding language and an easy acronym. It's nothing more than a slow-motion revolution and the practice of reverse racism against white men by other corrupt liberal white men and women.

In another entry at The New Discourses, Lindsey explains the "diversity" part of DEI:

> We think "diversity" means people with diverse backgrounds,
> but the Critical Theory twists this definition into a very specific
> interpretation. Specifically, in Critical Social Justice, "Diversity"
> means something like "people with 'diverse' ethnic origins who all
> have the same Woke political understanding of the 'social posi-
> tions' they inhabit and the world in which those have context.'"[48]

Lindsay goes on to warn that:

> It must be understood, this is the utter poison of the "sys-
> temic racism" approach: it actually stops us from being able to
> solve real problems. By treating everyone as avatars of "intersect-
> ing" socially constructed identity groups, we can't identify real
> problems (like wealth inequality, which is highly socially and pro-
> fessionally determinant) and make poor policy. To Theory, poor
> policy is fine, though, because people who use Theory get to just
> blame "systemic racism" for their own failures. It wasn't the The-
> ory that failed but the "white supremacy" in the system that made
> it fail, thus we need more of it. Because "systemic racism" is ordi-
> nary and permanent and present in all interactions and situa-
> tions—this being yet another tenet of Critical Race Theory—it's

47 New Discourses, "DEI Explained," New Discourses, accessed December 15, 2022, https://
newdiscourses.com/2022/04/dei-explained-new-discourses-bullets-ep-1/
48 James Lindsay, "The Diversity Delusion," New Discourses, accessed December 15, 2022,
https://newdiscourses.com/2020/06/diversity-delusion/.

always possible to make this argument. *Always*. Thus, Theory's own failures in application are proof that Theory is right, so says Theory, anyway.

In conclusion, it's of incredible importance at this moment in history to understand that "Diversity," "Inclusion," and "Equity," as described in the Critical sense, truly aren't what they seem to be, and it's therefore rather appropriate to order the three words in this nonstandard way and apply the acronym "DIE" to their program. These words have real meanings, of course, and can, when rightly understood and rightly applied, lead to real improvements. As they are being served up to us by these DIE consultants, however, rooted in Critical Theory as they are, they are an unethical scam that will bring us nothing but heavy costs.[49]

Lindsay is right again. The heavy costs of DEI are already upon us, because DEI is affirmative action on steroids.

Harvard University was sued for discriminating against whites and Asians in their admission process. The Supreme Court ruled against the university, but don't expect much if any change since the DEI agents will frustrate the court's ruling.

Such discriminatory action is driven by DEI commitments. If this is happening at Harvard, you can be guaranteed it is also happening in your local businesses. In fact, local business leaders have complained to me that it is occurring, and it's both costly and terrible, but they don't know how to confront it. The real issue here is cowardice. You will rarely find the strong and the brave in the corporate world anymore. They lack the insight to see how corporate America is being used to implement authoritarianism and the destruction of a free people. Why? They are too focused on the 30 pieces of silver (the corporate bottom-line) to be concerned about the ethics of selling out their country.

---

49   Lindsay, "The Diversity Delusion."

What Is So Wrong with Privilege?

One of the main aims of DEI is to flatten all natural distinctions and what they pejoratively refer to as privilege. So, we must ask: How did the word privilege become a bad word? I bet you never stopped to think about that. You just gobbled it down and accepted the narrative with nether a thought.

Privilege is a word that comes from the Latin word, *privilegium,* meaning a law or benefit for a person or group beyond what others don't have. NBA players born with the genetics to grow 6 to 7 feet tall can play basketball and earn millions. They are privileged. Good for them. My neurosurgeon who operated on my neck and saved my life has an intellectual brilliance and natural ability that provides him with the privilege to live better than 99% of the populace. Good for him.

The pilots who fly me across the country safely at 500 mph at 37,000 feet make well into the 6 figures of income. Good for them. I'm happy for them, and have not the slightest bit of resentment. I want them to be better than me. They need to be better than me, particularly in those areas. I do not begrudge them the privileges that come with those skills that benefit me as well.

Whether it is a nuclear power plant operator, my doctor, CPA, or attorney, all of whom are privileged in skill and the resultant income that allows them privileges to afford things most cannot, I'm happy for them and want them to be happy. Society reaps the benefits.

To become a lawyer, I went through years of education. Then I suffered through several years struggling as a young attorney trying to make ends meet while building a practice. I deferred gratification while others were living it up. I now enjoy privileges most don't. And with that privilege I've created companies, employed thousands, created charitable foundations, and worked pro bono for those who couldn't afford my services. That is all because I enjoy privileges that others don't because of my efforts, merit, and skills.

So, once again, who made the word privilege a bad word? The resentful, the envious, the covetous, the haters, the losers, and those who made bad choices and want others to pay for it. They sound like Marx as previously described in the book, don't they? He lived off everyone else and justified it with a warped and evil philosophy and economic theory. He gave losers like himself an ideology to hide behind.

Privilege is not a bad word. In today's vernacular it is used by the Left to label those possessing something as if they don't deserve it and should be hated for it. Apologize for nothing. You must powerfully push back against those who would deprive you of what is yours. Treat them as the thieves they are.

Dr. Thomas Sowell recounts a story where he was once asked by a Jewish man why the Jews are so persecuted and hated, and how it could be stopped. Sowell prefaced his story by telling of all the oppressed people around the world, the Asians, Armenians, Jews, etc. Our world history is filled with the persecuted. African Americans have not suffered to the degree of others around the world, but why all the hate? Why the persecution?

Sowell answered the Jewish man's question and told him that to stop the persecution, just, "fail." Yes, he told him all they needed to do was simply start failing. Now, that sounds odd, but think about it. The Jews have been a very industrious people and they succeed. The Asians come over to America and apply themselves, and within a few years they have their own businesses, are successful and are hated. Success draws hatred. It's the sin of envy and resentment that I have been talking about throughout this book, and they have devised the scheme of DEI as a means of taking from you or denying you what is yours.

As previously stated, the liberal, the Left, are a dangerous, violent, and resentful people (something Jordan Peterson has noted as well). They have seized control and are implementing a totalitarian psychosis, but don't feel the victim. This has been self-selected by the people. Who did you vote for? Essentially, who did you hire to protect you? If they are not doing the job then fire them and start paying attention.

Granted, there are those who by no fault of their own are suffering and down on their luck or born of low intellect and can do no better. Don't ever, ever expect those who use the unfortunate as a prop to advance themselves with a showing of false virtue to sacrifice anything other than empty words. They are a godless, hedonistic, resentful, narcissistic, hypocritical, incompetent, envious, and hateful group who haven't the competence nor the heart to care for anything or anyone but themselves while faking a virtue they don't have. Again, it's worth repeating,

Elon Musk is famous for saying about them: "Wokeness gives people a shield to be mean and cruel, armored in false virtue."

So, back to privilege. Privilege is a good thing, particularly when those who have it are governed by a righteous moral code and use that privilege to benefit others. Those on the Left who whine and feign virtue, or those on the Right whose checkbooks show no contribution to the causes they say they support, are the fakes, frauds, and dregs of society.

My housekeeper, my garbage collector, my lawn-care guy, the waiters who serve me in the restaurants I frequent, will most likely never do what I do or have what I do because they either don't have the ability or have no desire for my kind of work. That's okay. They are valued and they are needed and have often received my services without charge. I have more meaningful conversations with them at times than with any leftist who lives in an alternate universe. Frankly, those who do what would be considered the most menial jobs in life are essential and important, as they provide a valuable service that allows me and others to function as efficiently as we do so we can serve thousands of others to make their lives better. We meet on the plain of glorious humanity. I care for them, and they care for me. I can do what I do because they do what they do. There is no shame in your labors. There is every shame in envy, but that is the Left's staple diet.

The Left suffers from the guilt of their own fraud and need to feel as if they have some virtue by targeting those they define as oppressors in order to be seen as the savior of those they define as the oppressed. Their blackened souls are only quenched and relieved by lording over you their self-importance, condescension, and their oppression. Yes, it's sick, but that is who we have allowed into the halls of government and other institutions. As for me, I'd rather have a beer with my gardener, who has more genuine virtue, than I would a five-course meal with a self-righteous limousine leftist.

My privilege has not deprived anyone of anything. In fact, I will compare my charitable giving, and the use I have made of my privilege, to any leftist, any day. In fact, my privilege has provided employment for many. Those on the Left who are filled with hate and resentment (who keep Asians out of Harvard and are closeted antisemites), want to destroy any unity or relationship between the classes or races. There is nothing wrong with classes, they will always exist, and must exist if humanity is to continue functioning. Some will be great mathematicians, some brain surgeons, others will be inventors, and this is good. It will never change and should never change. The Left wants to make everyone poor so no one can help anyone. The only acceptable helper is the inept government.

The Left judges harshly. If they were judged by the same standards they judge others, particularly those whom have privilege who they resent and envy, those necessary for the advancement of society, the Left would never see the light of day, as they have caused so much division and misery in this country and world. They are divisive people and have made enemies of people who would otherwise be allies and get along. It's not the earned privilege of those who have worked hard, but the unearned stolen privilege the Left has seized that is destroying America.

While there have been some nonmalignant liberals with whom I have been able to have productive dialogue, most of the white liberals (bleeding hearts who want access to your checkbook) are resentful and hateful in all ways. They hate anyone who has abilities they haven't or anyone who has benefitted from hard work the Left could never discipline themselves to do. They are the ones who have made privilege a dirty word. They have created class warfare. They have created divisions and suspicions among people and created discontent to advance themselves and to create purpose in their otherwise purposeless lives. It's time to make these people on the Left the servants of my housekeeper, my gardener, and others in the services industry, for they have more character and common sense than those degenerate, liberal white male and female reprobates who destroy rather than create.

Here is one by-product of the dissention the Left has sown between the sexes. If women didn't vote, no liberal or Democrat since John Kennedy would have won the presidency. Carter, Clinton, Obama, and now Biden won because of the female vote, and all of those presidencies have been disasters, destroying many lives because the women fell prey for the touchy, feely and deceitful emotional messaging of those candidates who played upon not just a woman's emotions, but sowing discord between the sexes by making women a victim class and segregating the sexes.

If anyone attempts to shame you for "privilege," take it as your invitation to address the assault with a withering delegitimizing and humiliating condemnation that strips the Left of their pretense and false virtue. Again, don't be fooled, DEI is a tool to punish your skills, talents, and privilege you earned.

So, What's Wrong with Phobia?

Speaking of linguistic trickery and false virtue, somehow, we have let the idea of endless "phobias" be weaponized against conservatives on the Right. What's wrong with phobia? Well, it depends upon how you define it or apply it. In today's world, the cabal of prevaricators have seized the glossary and either redefined words or misapplied them.

We all know that there are healthy, life-protecting fears. For example, you don't jump into deep water if you don't know how to swim. You don't walk the dark streets of a crime infested neighborhood at night alone (or even with someone). You don't smoke cigarettes, whether you have a family history of cancer or not, for fear that you might.

In each of those examples there is the fear of drowning, murder, or cancer. These are healthy fears. No one is going to label you a "cancer-phobe." Yes, there is the possibility, remote or not, that those outcomes may not occur, but the fear that they could happen causes you to act in a way to diminish the possibility they will happen. This is a healthy precaution. This is life preserving. This is also known as *wisdom*, that is, living in such a way as to prosper. It is living in reality and responding to reality in such a way as to increase the likelihood of a beneficial result for you and your life and likewise society.

Now, we know that the Left engages in linguist sabotage by either making up words, changing their definitions, or misapplying them. That is the dirty hidden secret of DEI. It's sophistry and deceit. Nevertheless, since the point of this section is "phobia," let's look at its definition, the foundation of which is "fear."

Phobia is generally defined (from Merriam-Webster) as "exaggerated fear of...or intolerance or aversion to something or group, or an irrational fear." On the other hand, a lack of normal fear can be extreme. In some cases, a disease known as Urbach-Wiethe syndrome can be present, which is when an individual's brain cannot process fear in an appropriate manner, such that someone will stick their hand down into a pit of poisonous snakes without a care.

Today, the psychotic Left has misappropriated the word "phobia" in such a reckless way that they border on being like those with Urbach-Wiethe disease. They throw caution to the wind and demean and try to delegitimize others who oppose their corrupt agendas. For example, if you agree with nature, truth, rationality, and yes, science and biology, that there are two genders male and female, they will say that you are "transphobic." Or if you don't believe that men can become women, knowing the belief to be a mental disorder, and it is, then you are also, you guessed it—transphobic. If you oppose the homosexual agenda, that has expanded way beyond the freedom they wanted (which was never absent), beyond what they do in the bedroom and into teaching children that it is normative when it is the abnormal or technically a deviance from the normal, the Left will call you "homophobic." The implication is that you want to do harm and have no right to your opinions. The DEI enforcers are there to cancel you and they will do so by labeling you as phobic.

So, we see that the word phobic has been affixed to words for political purposes and as a means of discrediting those who do not agree with the Left's agenda. The Left delegitimizes you, and it is their way of removing you from the public square where, based on their malevolent attitudes, they never should have been allowed in the first place.

Well, let's set the record straight. Phobia is not illegal. You have every right to dislike or be afraid of certain things or agendas or have a phobia, especially toward things that are unhealthy, abnormal, or could cause harm. And most importantly not all phobias are irrational, nor can all fears or concerns be characterized as a phobia. Moreover, your beliefs, values, morals or opinions should never be accosted as phobias as a means of excluding you from the public square. If accused with the pejorative term, and it is almost always absent any proof or empirical evidence, then it's time to fight back. Metaphorically, you don't just push back, you must utterly defeat them, as it is clear that's the Left's intent for you. Their intent is to ban you from any discussion.

So, the bottom line is there is nothing wrong with the word phobia, or having a phobia, legally or otherwise, and any time the Left uses or applies the word phobia it historically has been wrong and slanderous. If you are transphobic, good for you, that's your right. By the way, there is no such thing as "transgendered" anyway. It's one or the other. There is gender-dysphoria, a mental condition, but physically you are either male or female. If homophobic, again, depending on definition and application, then that is your right—*never apologize* and push back hard such that they won't cross that bridge again with you or anyone else. You gave them tolerance, and now they want to obliterate you. That was always the gameplan; it is their nature and character.

Frankly, I'm idiot-phobic, i.e., I have a rational fear of idiots, particularly those running the country, and of our schools and universities. I'm pedophilia-phobic and would never trust one of them anywhere near a child. While it's currently enshrined in law as a crime now, the Left is heading in the direction of legitimizing that as well. I'm phobic over the nihilistic, authoritarian, malevolent reprobates who would enslave us all and deny us our inalienable rights and freedoms. We need more phobias like that in the rotten states of America. We need another "red-scare" like we had back in the 50s and 60s.

Next time you are accused of a phobia, you now know what to do. You fight back with the plethora of adjectives, not pronouns, that the dictionary gives you that succinctly describe these godless, hedonistic, freedom-hating slanderers. There! I've given you a few fitting adjectives and there are plenty more where they came from. This isn't for the purposes of calling names, but rather for rightly labeling your opponents and exposing their conduct, their character and agenda in a relevant way. The use and repetition of such labels is important to define these sociopathic actors to protect yourself and family.

The truth is that the Left has already given you all the empirical evidence you need to back up your adjectives of who and what they are. So never allow or permit the Left's linguistic appropriation of words, such as "phobia" or "privilege," as previously discussed, to go unchallenged, shamed, and excoriated. Above all else, never apologize or explain. Go immediately on the attack. Call them what they are: incompetent, crass, malevolent, liars and slanderers. Remind any listener who the accusers are. Know their background and educate the listener as to the accuser's character, their failures and lack of knowledge. Take back the dictionary—starting with "phobia."

This section could not be summarized any better than by Proverbs 1:7: "The fear of the Lord is the beginning of knowledge, but fools despise wisdom and instruction." In an interview, Jordan Peterson was asked how he has been able to be so courageous to speak out as he has regarding the chaos and insanity in the world. Peterson referenced the scripture verse above but also added that he has learned to fear the right things.

We live in a generation of depraved fools that wrongly have been given control of the levers of power and governance. In Matthew (ESV) 10:28, "And do not fear those who kill the body but cannot kill the soul. Rather fear him who can destroy both soul and body in hell." That's God, and He will have the final word.

If you follow the morals of the Left today, then the one who will pass judgment upon you is also the one who can and will kill body and soul in hell, the God of the universe. As Peterson said, he has the right kind of fear, and you better have the right kind of fear as well. That starts with everything that God hates, which is everything you find in the agenda of the Left. As already established in this book, the Left and the Democrat Party of today have nothing in common with Christianity, or any other major religion for that matter.

Digital Masters and DEI Combine to Rule as Psychotic Princes

Having identified some of the tools of the Left, like mislabeled phobias, we must come back to what is happening with DEI. The ideology of DEI is going to combine with the digitized world and bring DEI from the workplace into your very own home.

The social credit monitors might penalize you if they think you somehow practiced non-inclusive behaviors. If they don't like the way you look, they will concoct a false diagnosis of you being privileged, phobic, racist by virtue of your skin color, or a plethora of other fake subjective conclusions they don't like and penalize you and cancel you from the marketplace.

You might be locked out of your bank account for 24 hours because they think you were rude to a member of some special class of minorities deserving "equitable" treatment.

Do you see where this is going? Millions are cooperating with the DEI and digital regimes even now and easily accept terms such as privilege and phobias. They try to alter behaviors that never needed altering. Again, this is insane, and this is psychosis. If we are going to have any chance at living free in America again, we must cure this psychosis and get back to the truth. We must recover a world where Martin Luther King Jr.'s dream had come true. Where all people "live in a nation where they will not be judged by the color of their skin but by the content of their character." Or, might I add, presumed to be guilty of thoughts in violation of another's beliefs, which would not in any case be violative of any law, even if they were offensive to another.

Let's let people be judged by the fruit of their lives, not the deceit of their lips. Or, how about just being left alone to live their lives as they see fit without requiring others' participation or approval.

DEI is the opposite of this dream. It's the Marxist-infected nightmare version. And it will weaponize the digital future if we don't stop it. Sounds crazy, right? Welcome to the nation's systemic psychosis.

CHAPTER 12:

Lies and Envy Have No Rights

"The point of modern propaganda is not only to misinform or push an agenda it is to exhaust your critical thinking so as to annihilate truth."

Garry Kasparov

Psychos from the Fall

The first sin in the world was a lie. It was the first effort at inducing a detachment from reality, i.e., an inorganic psychosis (intentionally brought about by the Devil himself). It was an effort to detach the created from the Creator, and by extension, from reality itself. This is the fundamental root of all psychosis. The Serpent deceived Eve, twisting God's good command, and caused her to question the truth that she knew. Adam failed to intervene, and as the sad story goes, they both disobeyed God. In their disobedience they brought death into the world, thus the "fall of mankind." This "original sin" gave birth to envy, murder, covetousness, greed, resentment, and all kinds of other evils.

Argue with the analogy, theology, or the text if you want, but either way you're living with the consequences, like it or not. The root of sin, or if you will, let's just say, "wrong," is found in a lie—a distortion of reality. Truth corresponds with reality and reality with the truth, and that is important to recognize. Whether you accept the Biblical model or not, the lie is meant to hide and conceal the truth. It's meant to get you to act in ways you would not otherwise.

Of course, you know this from personal experience because when you lie, and we all have, you know that your purpose and motive is to distort reality. However, so many don't seem to get it when it is done to them. Today the world hates and suppresses the truth and embraces lies because the truth speaks to the folly of their lives. They are detached from reality, and such detachment is not only irrational but psychotic. The media is a lie by any other name. The government lies. Politicians lie. The truth is both stranger than fiction and rarer than gold.

Rationality is built into our being whether we choose to exercise it or not. Everyone understands the realities of the world. As I said earlier, we are, by nature, conservative in our daily lives. If we get cut, we put a Band-Aid on the wound. If we get sick, we go to the doctor, and when the doctor asks you what is wrong, you will tell him the truth as you want to be healed and get well. After all, your hypocritical self knows that the lie will not heal you, only the truth will. We only like the truth when we think it is beneficial to us, so we are honest with the doctor because otherwise there are immediate and unpleasant consequences.

Understanding cause and effect leads to reason and reason works on cause and effect and as such leads to rationality, except for the 25% who seem to have made chaos their ethos. To understand who you are really dealing with (an irrational or rational person), let's summarize it this way. If you believe in the truth, can see it and recognize it, then you are in the domain of light and can be discerning. If you readily believe in lies, particularly after being presented with the truth, you belong to the domain of darkness. Just as a doctor cannot heal a lie, if you live a lie, which is what a departure from reality is, then you are living in a state of psychosis and will not prosper in this life, and for sure not the one to come. Living in the delusion and lie of a utopia is destroying society. It's a lie and psychotic.

It is folly to live a lie. We see this folly being lived out in a bold and unapologetic way today in the most profound way ever known to man given our technology and the beast to come, that is artificial intelligence (AI). I like the quote from the poet, Thomas Gray, who said, "Where ignorance is bliss, it is folly to be wise."

This is the great danger of our times. So many prefer blind bliss. I recall Jack Nicholson's famous movie quote from "A Few Good Men," "You can't handle the truth!" And clearly, those who intentionally live in a self-imposed ignorance and state of irrationality can't handle the truth. The Left is not only living in a lie but is imposing it upon the rest of society. This makes the Left a truly miserable lot that you want nothing to do with. So be warned: The Left is misery looking for company. Those who are wise are a threat to those who live in an ignorant bliss. It's the psychosis we live in and are governed by today.

Truth lovers, those in touch with reality, and those living with a moral code and an active conscience, find themselves hated and reviled by the Left because they live lives full of meaning. Here are some pertinent contemporary examples of the cesspool of lies we live with which are destroying our nation and the lives we love.

Politicians Trick You, Or Do They? Either Way, You Pay for It

There is a provision in the law called, "detrimental reliance." In abbreviated form, the idea is that if you rely on another's promise, or representation to act in a certain way or do a certain thing you would not do otherwise, and act to your detriment based upon the false representation, you have a right to recover your damages resulting from the deception (mainly in contractual situations). You can sue the deceiver (fraud), avoid contractual terms and/or be compensated. This is generally based on the promissory estoppel doctrine. Not to get in the weeds of legalese, suffice it to say that the point here is that an erroneous reliance, one caused by deceit and resulting in harm, can be recoverable. It can also go both ways. That is, even if you were led astray by the fraud and deception of another, your own negligence and inexcusable ignorance may result in an outcome that you are ultimately responsible for. Again, we find ourselves back to the old term, *Caveat Emptor* (let the buyer beware).

Too bad that recovery of actual damages cannot be had in the same way against the woke politicians, media, and corporate America, who deceive so many daily. For the damage they cause to millions there must be more accountability, particularly for politicians, other than just being voted out of office. Don't count on that happening anytime soon.

It's illegal to lie before Congress (yet they lie everyday), and it's illegal to lie to the FBI (and sometimes even if you don't, they will treat you like you did—just ask Michael Flynn). If the media lies in print (even though they do daily) they are subject to being sued for libel. Even so, as the laws are written, it is nearly an impossible hurdle to jump when it comes to proving this in court. If the government lies or causes harm, you must get permission to sue them. The problem of lies and deceit is a central theme in fallen humanity and all the distress and chaos in which we live. The laws have been constructed in such a way today to allow them (the media, politicians, etc.) to lie with impunity. It's almost as if we have given lies First Amendment rights and freedoms. They lie with impunity because they know that they essentially have immunity and can get by with it. Why? The public tolerates it.

The astounding news coming out of the Twitter revelations reveal the active and coordinated suppression of fact and opinion by woke personnel pushing their leftist agenda. Justice can't come quickly enough against those who participated in it. However, what good would it do as long as people keep electing corrupt politicians, district attorneys, judges, etc., who suppress the truth?

As Mark Twain has been attributed to saying, "A lie can travel halfway around the world before the truth puts on its shoes."

To be clear, under the First Amendment protection of freedom of speech and expression, individuals are allowed to say all kinds of obnoxious, rude, offensive, and crazy things, but a lie is a much different thing. The moral code we once lived by kept discussion within bounds. We wanted those in power to be accountable to the people and subject to scrutiny no matter how blunt and severe the language, but again, the moral code kept things in proper bounds. If you lied there were consequences, not the least of which was your reputation. The lie hates the truth as the truth is and always has been offensive. Our forefathers created the right to free speech, even obnoxious speech, to prevent the suppression of the truth even when it was uncomfortable and inconvenient.

Protections were built into the law against the abuse of free speech until today. Now speech is canceled, not in protection of the truth, but its suppression to protect the lie. The Left has seized nearly all control of the media, judiciary, and social media. We have seen the Left lie with impunity as there is no longer any consequence for doing so. Speech is no longer free, and truth no longer has a platform.

The Russian-Collusion Hoax was the perfect example where the lie was used to sway an election while the Left attempted to shut down free speech and suppress the truth to keep the lie from being exposed prior to the 2016 and 2020 elections. Again, there have been no consequences for the liars, only the reward of power.

That kind of lie is a slanderous attempt to subvert public opinion against another. It's an attempt to destroy someone's reputation on a claim that isn't based on facts. And that's what I have in mind here: the massive lies that pose real and legitimate harm to individuals and society. These are lies leading to mass governmental action as we saw in the pandemic and the lockdowns.

The truth is now coming out about the lies and fraud surrounding the COVID pandemic as well as the vaccines, but only after irreparable damage and a mass loss of life. When the populace is infected with a mass psychosis rendering them unlikely to hold their elected officials accountable, there is not much hope.

This deception runs deeper still in the American system. Consider how many politicians enter office poor and leave rich. Socialist Senator Bernie Sanders has been in government service for decades, so how in the world did he become a multimillionaire with several houses? Even worse, consider Nancy Pelosi. She's been in Congress for 35 years and has somehow amassed a net worth approximating $300 million (these are the same people that tell you they hate rich people and want to impose higher taxes). You don't become a multi-millionaire on a Congressional salary, but lies and deception have made this possible.

The American voter is not blameless. They have forgotten about "*caveat emptor*" as earlier stated. This Latin term, once well known by most people in the past, has been forgotten. The buyer does have responsibility. Put more bluntly, buyers have the responsibility not to be stupid. Responsibility is a hated word, in our day and age. It is always someone else's fault. Like the comedian Flip Wilson joked: "The devil made me do it."

When the lie becomes so obvious, and should be outright rejected, many fall for it anyway, or choose selective ignorance or (more likely) stupidity, and if you do, the consequences are on you.

In all these scenarios, there is both a perpetrator and a victim. The perpetrator is wrong no matter what. With the victim, it can be another case altogether. "If you want to keep your doctor, you can." Remember that? President Obama promised that during the push for Obamacare, the government takeover of our healthcare system. That was a lie. He was the perpetrator. The deceiver-in-Chief. The facts were abundant that what Obama was proposing was a lie, yet he was re-elected. Shame on the victim.

The victim-voter knew better (or should have known better). Maybe it was greed or wanting something for nothing, another hand-out. It was another entitlement that had to come out of another's pocket. The numbers and statistics, as they related to the healthcare plan, were false and the advocates of it knew them to be. They were not real. The facts as to the flaw and fraud in the plan were obvious and readily available to all. There were no victims here, just the fools who ignored the truth. It was a psychotic populace who wanted something for nothing, who wanted someone else to care for them, throwing caution to the wind, ignoring reality in their delusion.

Here the detachment from reality becomes more than just inorganic, as it has an evil intent and element tied to it, an evil agenda. The agenda was this: If you can control the public's health you can control most other aspects of their lives and gradually enslave them and remove their constitutional rights. That was Obama's "fundamental transformation." You caved to temptation. The Left knew it as a step toward positioning themselves in power permanently.

Let's take another example. President Biden ran for president three times. Due to scandal, particularly plagiarism and pathological lying, he had to pull out of previous runs for office. People forget and don't know their history. If you were to pull up the news clips of Sam Donaldson, an ABC news anchor of several decades ago, he eviscerated Biden with the truth resulting in Biden having to pull out of the race as he should have, never to return. Unfortunately, that didn't happen. Why? He knew the people would forget. And they did. Also, in the meantime the people grew more callous to moral corruption and insensitive and indifferent to lies as they became morally debased themselves, and the lie was becoming socially acceptable.

All of Biden's information was publicly available. He historically has been known by most all his colleagues as a pathological liar. With almost 50 years in Washington D.C., the public had no excuse not knowing that fact either. Today's victim-voters of Biden's policies suffer from psychosis. Many knew him to be a liar from all his years in Washington, yet voted for him anyway. Now they are reaping the consequences as are the rest of us. Herein the victim is as much at fault as the perpetrator.

Thus, we find ourselves in an environment where those who are fooling others—lying to them, deceiving them—are getting away with it and the ones being fooled are indifferent and not doing anything about it. Here is the marriage between the sadist and the masochist. Lying has become institutionalized.

It seems as if the "Lie" reigns supreme in our psychotic culture. It is almost as if the lie has "rights." Lies have no rights—there is no right to deceive someone, or to continue in deception yourself. Until you, the victim, say enough is enough and start voting accordingly, this disaster will continue to unfold to the detriment of you and the country.

A good-ole-boy Democrat became governor in Kentucky in 1995. By just his physical appearance, empty words, and history alone, you knew he was for sale. He was the typical good-ole-boy hypocrite, professing his virtuous belief in all the things that tickle our ears to keep us from scrutinizing what was being sold and who was selling it.

People fall for the empty promises of politicians year after year. As Carl Jung once quipped, "Those who promise everything are sure to fulfill nothing." How psychotic is it to repeat these mistakes every election season?

Well into that leftist Democrat governor's term, a scandal broke out. It was a quiet, low simmer scandal at the start. It was based on an insinuation that there had been an illicit affair, sexual favors given, and later retribution committed by the governor. It didn't get much press at first, but then one fateful day a client walked into my office for some legal help. As our discussions rambled, he (knowing I was in Republican leadership) informed me that he was the advisor for the lady that was being harassed by the governor. I asked him what he meant. He informed me that the governor was manipulating her with government funds, granting them or withholding them from her business in turn for sex. When she stopped the affair, he cut off the funding to her business, which funds she was legally entitled.

Well, this was no longer going to be a quiet affair. I was indignant that this virtue signaling hypocrite was out there bloviating about women's rights, the gender wage gap, etc., you know, that whole charcuterie board of false narratives and made-up problems that the Left wants to fix, all while sexually harassing a woman in secret.

At first, I knew that as chairman I could not, would not, and did not assist or get into the middle of that legal mess. She was going to have to hire a separate counsel, which she did. As things evolved, my client's relationship with advising that woman entrepreneur became more problematic. As I was helping the client on his separate legal matters, he would fill me in on all the inside details, including the threats and the settlement offers being made to his client. Yes, I even knew the dollar amounts that were offered, but hidden from the public.

It was just like the Epstein scandals that pulled in so many famous people, from Prince Andrew to others. Of course, we are still waiting for the truth to be released about Bill Clinton and his relationship with Epstein. Also, we await the truth that is being suppressed about Epstein's death, and the suppression that is coming from both sides, but nevertheless, in Kentucky I saw firsthand at our state level how this old sin, the game of corruption and cover-up, played out. And, it was not just Kentucky, it was being played out in every state across the nation in one form or another. Wherever there is a concentration of power, money and opportunity, liars and corruption will abound.

I will leave a lot of the salacious details out but suffice it to say there was intense communication between me and a reporter who had contacted me on the matter involving the governor. I was able to provide the information he needed to get past the lies and obstruction coming from the highest levels. The reporter did a particularly good job of investigative journalism and reporting regardless of the politics involved (which is nearly non-existent today), and he ended up winning one of the most prestigious awards in journalism for his work. The search for truth and exposing corruption was the primary goal in spite of the politics or the consequences. Personally, I was disgusted as there are so many urgent needs of the people and so much time was being wasted due to this one governor's lies and corruption.

Machiavelli, Lies, and the "Nice" Guys

I approach Machiavelli from two different perspectives, both which help us understand how the widespread lies are being weaponized against the "nice guys." First, Machiavelli was misunderstood—he wasn't lusting for power, he was trying to keep the "nice" guy(s) in power, that is, leaders who wanted to help the people. The second way I refer to Machiavelli is how the Left has appropriated his principles, ones that he meant for the good guys to use against the bad guys, but that the bad guys are now using to further consolidate their own positions of power against the good guys.

So, what is at the core of Machiavelli's philosophy of politics? One lecture from The School of Life explains it well:

> Machiavelli was a 16th-century Florentine political thinker with powerful advice for nice people who don't get very far. His thought pivots around a central, uncomfortable observation: that the 'wicked' tend to win. And they do so because they have a huge advantage over the 'good': they are willing to act with the darkest ingenuity and cunning to further their cause. They are not held back by those rigid opponents of change: principles. They will be prepared to outright lie, twist facts, threaten, become violent. They will also, when the situation demands it, know how to seductively deceive, use charm and honeyed words, bedazzle, and distract. And in this way, they conquer the world.[50]

The point here is that Machiavelli was warning the "nice" guys about how to spot and counter the "seductive deception"—the lies—of the immoral power-seekers who refuse to be constrained by any principles.

---

50 "Machiavelli's Advice for Nice Guys," The School of Life, Youtube.com, accessed on March 23, 2023, https://www.youtube.com/watch?v=GTQlnmWCPgA.

What's happening though is that the nice guys haven't learned, and the bad guys are using Machiavelli like a playbook.

Today the truth is suppressed by the media and the press because they are now all part of an ideological cabal. As has been said, across the world, and particularly of western democracies, "we live in turn-key tyrannies." It's happening in America as democracies almost always begin to devolve into tyranny. The Left has discovered that and wants to be in control. In our out-of-control bureaucratic state, we are totalitarian-ready. The Left wants permanent power and rule which cannot be maintained with a free people.

I have discussed how the Right needs to fight with the same tools the Left uses, as they are effective given the state of the electorate. Like Machiavelli observed, the wicked usually win since they are willing to employ whatever device and cunning to further their agenda. They are not constrained by principles or moral codes. They will lie, deceive, manipulate the facts, and even resort to violence. They will also deceive where necessary, charm when beneficial, and employ distraction from not only who they are but what their goals are. We see this in full, naked display on the Left as it destroys the country. They are the rot in America.

Now I know this will rub some Christians the wrong way, but Christ never expected or condoned his followers to be fools or become martyrs as if such was an elective. Yes, you will be persecuted, but don't be surprised by it. And you certainly don't need to encourage it. After all, this would run counter to Proverbs in the Old Testament from which Christ taught. Too few Christians today know what it means to be a Christian, and even fewer are in the pulpits.

Machiavelli weighed the dichotomy between the ruthless and the so-called "nice" people. He liked the "nice" people's approach but realized that it simply did not work in the real world. The ruthless saw nice people as weak, did not respect them, and simply slaughtered the "nice" people who wanted to come together and reason on any issue or conflict. Proverbs warns about reasoning or arguing with fools as they will only harm you.

Bringing it forward to today, we have the Right attempting to reason with the Left, the Republicans with the Democrats. Clearly, the "nice" guys, the life, liberty, and happiness crowd, are delusional, detached from the reality of who and what the Left really is. The Left follows no moral code remotely resembling the teaching of any major religion today, much less Christianity. The "nice" guys have been losing for an awfully long time. They certainly aren't coaches for any sports team, for a coach today is lucky to maintain his job after just one losing season. These political coaches on the Right have been losing for decades. Their opposition couldn't have a better loyal opposition, to steal the term from our British kin. Have you ever known the Right to gain any ground? It's a perpetual slow slide into a totalitarian dystopia.

Machiavelli wrote the book, *The Prince,* to help the ruling class who tried to be nice not to finish last and not to be overly devoted to acting nicely. Today, one never observes the Left acting nicely. They are filled with empty words and false virtue, but vitriol for those who disagree with them. The Right acts out with obsequiousness to their own demise emanating from cowardice and fear of not being liked. Their formula for maintaining good PR and effectiveness does not work, yet they keep repeating the same mistakes over and over.

The Right has a counterproductive obsession of acting nicely and Machiavelli saw its origins in Christianity. However, so many Christians have erred and been led down the proverbial primrose path by unqualified pastors. They have a very sissified image of Jesus, to borrow a term from Dr. Voddie Baucham. I deal with this in my upcoming book being hammered out now titled, *The Jesus to Come is not the Jesus that Was.* If you see him on his second coming, you're toast. Enough of that for now. Suffice it to say I love the Christians who are of the "cross-the-Jordan" or the "Gideon 300" type, devoted types that have their doctrinal hats on correctly and live accordingly.

Nevertheless, there is so much wrong with the approach of the Right that it is enough to drive one crazy. They are, for the most part, liberty lovers who want the government out of your lives, but they have a guaranteed failing game plan, and it never seems to fail to disappoint. Machiavelli's book was not about how to be a nice guy, but how to be effective. The Right must start employing the tactics of the Left. The nice guys must finally get Machiavellian.

I hate judgments and decisions based on emotion, but the reality is that is what appeals to a dumbed-down populace today. If that is what it takes to get the peoples' attention to save them, then employ it. You must play the game as it stands, not in some idealistic, "this is the way it is *supposed* to be played" manner.

As the old adage goes, the path to hell is paved with good intentions. Too often, the Right seems content to lose while consoling themselves with their pious feelings. There is no prize for those who come in second place. There are winners and then there are the losers; and in this game of life, politics, and governance, this is as serious as life and death. The Right doesn't need to invent a new game plan. It already exists, and the Left has been using it for decades. As Albert Einstein reportedly said, "There are three great forces in the world; stupidity, fear and greed." We have all three right now—in spades. The Left is using them to take control of society while the Right refuses to do what it takes to counter them.

One thing that has worked so well for the Left is lying to create fear and then weaponizing the fear to achieve their ends. As Joanna Bourke said in her book, *Fear: A Cultural History*, "It is created with promises to eradicate it." The Left creates a problem, a crisis, or a discriminated group and then appoints themselves as the savior. I recall how President Jimmy Carter was famous for becoming the hero of his own crises. It was exhausting but then again, the Right was not only blind as to what was going on but impotent to do anything about it.

Carter had so ravaged the economy with double digit inflation, double digit unemployment, and double-digit interest rates that, as a young man wanting my own home, I (and millions of others) was unable to afford the interest rates. By God's grace, Carter's ineptness caught up with him when our embassy staff were taken hostage by the very Iranian radicals Carter allowed to overthrow the Shah of Iran (who was a friend of America).

As a result, Carter lost in a landslide to Reagan. The world knew serious people were back in control and the hostages were released upon Reagan's inauguration. The radical Islamists were actually afraid of Reagan. The point in this snippet of history is that if you don't exercise autonomy over your own mind, you will be victimized by the lies and fear the Left uses, allowing them to become the savior of the problems they create.

The one freedom we have under our control is our psychological freedom. We realize that the state can control our physical bodies but not our will or mind to think for ourselves. If we stop being lazy and exercise our mental and moral autonomy, we will deprive the Left of their most essential tool of control. As the Academy of Ideas put it in a presentation, we must become truly *autonomous*. *Auto* means "self," and *nomos* means "rule of law," that is "self-rule." Let no man rule over your mind and wherever possible, your physical being.

I contend that there can be no greater freedom than that between your ears. Be free there, and you are truly free. And you will be mentally healthy. There is no room in that space between your ears for any other than God and you, in that order. Keep it that way. This is one of the surest ways to avoid the manipulation of lies. Let no one take you hostage with the threat of unfriending you, or canceling you, or with the threats of withdrawing approval or affection. If they do that then be rid of them. If you maintain the freedom between your ears, they can never enslave you. To do this, you must learn to recognize and reject their lies.

Lies Don't Have Rights—But They Do Have Consequences

Lies don't have rights—but they do have consequences, and bad ones too. When you have been the victim of a lie, you want justice, and that's understandable. However, too often many want justice when they give no justice themselves. There are legitimate victims of the many lies of systemic psychosis, and they deserve justice, and want to see punishment of the perpetrator. Too often the ones that cry for justice the loudest are the last ones to give it.

I recall an experience my attorney grandfather had in trying a case wherein a woman stored her fur coat in cold storage. In the "good old days," it was customary for those who could afford such luxuries that upon the approach of warm weather, they would store their fur in cold storage so the fur would not be damaged by moths. In this case, the lady had lost 50 pounds over the summer. When she went to retrieve her fur coat in the fall from cold storage, it would not fit as it was too small. It fit when she took it to storage and before she lost weight, but now it was too small despite the weight loss. There were only two scenarios. Either the storage company gave her the wrong coat, or they stripped some pelts from the coat.

The woman sued the storage company, but the case was lost. When discussing the case afterwards one of the jurors revealed that one adamant woman juror on the jury decided that if she couldn't afford a fur coat then the lady plaintiff didn't deserve one either. She influenced others. Justice was denied.

Imagine if the envious woman juror had been wronged similarly. She would be the first to complain and demand justice. Yet when she had the opportunity to do justice, she denied it out of greed, envy, and resentment. She was then, as so many on the Left are today, a bitter, resentful person and more often than not, it is because of the poor choices in life they have made, and they will deny you justice. We see this playing out daily today with leftist District Attorneys punishing the victims of crime while letting the criminals go free.

How Envy Weaponizes Lies

Envy can be defined as a "desire to have a quality, possession, or other attribute belonging to someone else."

At its most basic level, envy is hatred. This is the sin of envy. It is a resentful characteristic that we see too often in most of the Antifa members, the radical Left, and the socialists and liberals of today. I know there are many descriptive terms for these people, but consider them all peas in the same pod. It's a distinction without a difference. They want what someone else has or they just don't want you to have what you have. They will lie to enact policies to get it and they will penalize others to accomplish their goals, goals born of deep-seated envy, covetousness, and resentment. They are the true haters.

I started with discussing the "lie" in this chapter, but it's important to realize that the "lie" is weaponized in the service of envy. It's a mutually destructive but symbiotic relationship.

People first lie to themselves, telling themselves that they deserve something they don't have. They lie to themselves that what others have is unfair and should be taken away. Just consider how the communists and all their offspring talk about "taxing the rich." Then the people act upon leftist lies and elect politicians who then, with the force of the laws they pass, and ultimately at the end of the barrel of a gun, take from you what they want.

They create victim classes and then feign concern for them when they have none, but they just wanted a pretext to engage in unlawful and criminal conduct and theft. They virtue signal to fool you and assuage their guilt. They have no empirical evidence to support their claims or positions. There is no reality to their protestations. They live in an alternate universe, not the real world. There is a total detachment from reality. Like Marx, they want to live off the backs of other's labors.

So lies breed envy. Envy weaponizes lies. And then together, they lead people into believing what belongs to someone else is really theirs. Envy doesn't leave them there—it pushes them to take action based on the lies.

All Opinions Are Not Equal

The English author Douglas Adams once said that "All opinions are not equal. Some are a very great deal more robust, sophisticated, and well supported in logic and argument than others." This is obviously true. Opinions can be handcuffed to a lie. Opinions can be *the lie*. As Plato was reported to have said, "Opinions are worthless." He goes on to say, "True opinions are a fine thing and do all sorts of good so long as they stay in their place, but they will not stay long. They run away from a man's mind, so they are not worth much until you tether them by working out the reason. Once they are tied down, they become knowledgeable and are stable." In other words, opinions must be tied to facts and the truth, or they are ultimately irrelevant and dangerous. The Left is long on opinion devoid of fact, ergo the reason they suppress freedom of speech. They cannot win the argument or debate otherwise.

In our modern world, we have given a platform to those who don't have any business broadcasting their untethered opinions. As Harlan Ellison said, "You are not entitled to your opinion. You are entitled to your informed opinion. No one is entitled to be ignorant."

Yet that is exactly what we are suffering from today. We have regressed as a civilization. We have the "entitled ignorant" in charge, manipulating the masses who already have been conditioned and groomed into a life of idiocy that reflexively does the will of their manipulators, the elite prevaricators.

Most of the masses greatly overestimate how informed they really are. They are drunk on comfort, convenience, and amusement, and they think that watching 45 minutes of CNN will sober them up to the real world. It won't. They have lost the ability to engage in critical thinking. Thomas Edison famously said, "5% of the people think, 10% think they think, and 85% would rather die than think."

Had even 15% of the people really thought CNN would not even exist. We have a nation of trained non thinkers giving their opinion on everything under the sun. Some of them even do it from the White House Press podium. And many are educated that way by design; after all, it is too difficult to enslave a smart person. Smart people question everything as everyone should in today's world.

Try convincing someone who has been conned that they have been conned or lied to. They will resist you. Or better yet, "You cannot argue someone out of something that they were argued into." You will get stiff resistance, and a prideful, if not angry or even violent reaction, as if you are an invading force coming to take something away from them. They cling to their ignorance or lies because they have based their lives on a lie. As the adage goes, "ignorance is bliss." It is effortless, lazy, and mindless love. They will, with all pseudo-authority, try to enforce their baseless opinions upon you. As Mark Twain said, "it's easier to fool people than to convince them that they have been fooled."

Just look at that climate change radical, child activist Greta Thunberg of Sweden. At the age of 15 she started lecturing the world and demanding the implementation of policies that would cause Western economic collapse with talking points that she parrots, and of which she has no investigative, studied, or applied knowledge herself.

She was a little precocious girl (child actor) that the powers on the Left thought would be a good idea to put onto the stage to lecture and influence the rest of us with fact-less emotion. Her opinions are senseless and worthless, yet the unknown farmer in Iowa whose only platform is the town diner has more sense than a young girl who has been given a worldwide stage to spew nonsense. She's done nothing in her life on her own, absent the marionette strings that manage her. Hers is strictly a shameful, emotional, uninformed appeal for the rest of the world to commit suicide.

Historically, the Left always has been dangerously reckless, and such is the case with the messaging from Thunberg. The opinions are fact-less and implemented with lies foisted upon the gullible populace. The results of accepting these kinds of policies and lies have had disastrous results. In 2022 the people of Sri Lanka were facing starvation and overthrew that government in mass protests and demonstrations because of that government's implementation of green policies so they could receive good scoring on the ESG, Climate scoring models. Most recently the same happened in the Netherlands in 2023 where the government was ousted because of the disaster and chaos created by the lies of climate change and the policies implemented by the leftist government. The climate radicals will cause instability around the globe and revolts and revolution because of the climate lies and fraud. This fraud and the climate hoax are bringing chaos and death.

Herein lies the psychosis, and it is at both ends of the spectrum. It's the useful idiots, as the communists call them, such as Greta and those who adore her on the one hand. On the other hand, there are those who have better sense but do little to challenge the fraud on display because of its social cost and inconvenience. It is shameful how they abused and used this young woman as a tool to appeal to the emotions of adolescent adults who once again act on emotion and not cognition.

Clearly, what we have here is not mere benign differences of opinions, but malignant ideologies that are destructive—and no one has the "right" to pour acid on the foundations of civilization under the banner of their "personal (uniformed) opinion." Once again, all opinions are not equal, and you don't have a right to an opinion devoid of truth or fact and driven by psychopathic ideologies historically proven to be deadly.

Evil, its lies, and envy need to be put out of business, not tolerated. Toleration in America has become deadly. I call it "toxic toleration." It's the killer of truth, normalcy, and freedom. It is the justification for cowardice. Reality will ultimately reign, but only after a massive loss of life.

Government Lies and Their Friends Who Tell Them

As Senator and Doctor, Rand Paul said in a recent hearing regarding the proposed "disinformation department" within the Department of Homeland Security, "the United States Government is actually the greatest purveyor of disinformation in the world." Government bureaucrats, politicians, businessmen, and, perhaps most importantly, the media, who actively suppress the truth, have taken lying to a new art form. People lose fortunes, businesses fail, and employees lose their jobs as a result. People lose their lives because they believed in lies.

The COVID-19 "vaccine" is a perfect example of the deadliness of lies and believing them. Far from preventing the spread of COVID-19, it has made those who were "double-vaccinated and boosted" more suscep-tible to future viral mutations. It has now been disclosed that it was all a lie, and that the vaccine never was able to prevent transmission or pre-vent you from getting the virus. The president lied (no surprise), and it is recorded for all to see. You fell for it. What you did in your compliance is give the Left everything they wanted. It was a trial run to see just how far they could push and suppress the public. Now they know.

The vaccine prevents nothing, saves no one, and kills others, all the while making pharmaceutical companies and their directors and stock-holders rich. It was a lie that caused it all. People bought the lie. They got the jab. And there is now nothing more for them to do but pray it doesn't injure them in the long run. There is increasing concern in the medical community that there will be long term cardiac and other organ function problems from this enforced experimental vaccine. How could all this happen, you ask? I will answer that with another question rarely asked by the Right. Who did you vote for?

One of the most concise analyses of the pandemic and of the chaos engulfing the world today was given by Dr. Aseem Malhotra, a leading Cardiologist in England who did commercials for the government pro-moting vaccination. His father ended up taking the vaccine and died, which changed Dr. Malhotra's worldview. Delving into the darkness swirling around the pandemic, the vaccine, and investigating medical findings that were being suppressed, he found that after two doses of the vaccine there were increased markers of inflammation linked to cardio-vascular disease. The leap was astounding. Your risk rose from 11% to 25%. The findings were not published since they feared losing funding from the pharmaceutical industry.

He said, "this is the downstream effect. My hypothesis is that there is a psychopathic entity that has had an increased and unchecked power over our lives over the last three decades, and this must be tackled at the root; with regulations over these companies, data must be published, and politicians should not be taking campaign contributions from these companies."[51]

We must, at all costs, maintain our individual autonomy, our personal sovereignty. Rudyard Kipling famously contended that; "No price is too high to pay for the privilege of owning yourself." Why would anyone give that up to psychosis, or to the likes of the merchants of death, the Left.

Yes, more and more people are seeing this same psychopathy. This same psychosis is being implemented by corporate CEOs, corporate board rooms, and big tech. It's as if demons from hell snatched humans from positions of corporate power and supplanted them with malevolent sub-human, demonically influenced humanoids. There is no justification for the decisions being made in boardrooms around the country and they cannot be described as anything but constitutionally criminal. The lie reigns supreme.

They are morally bankrupt, and that is being kind since that would imply that, at one time, they had morals. Such abuses of individual constitutional rights, as what we see now, deserve criminal prosecution. All corporate money must be immediately banned from all political campaigns and NGOs must be banned when their agendas are counter-constitutional and undermining of our governmental institutions and particularly our inalienable rights.

In 2021, President Biden said from the White House that if you get the vaccine, you will not get COVID. He got the vaccine and the boosters and, yes, he got COVID. It is way past time for you to read up on Biden's history. You will discover that he has been a pathological liar all his life. Your ignorance has cost you dearly from your health, your income, your standard of living and your retirement savings. What you don't know can and will harm, if not kill you.

Lies have brought death from the Garden of Eden until now. It's high time we locked the lies up and held the liars accountable. Realistically, that won't happen, but if we can end some of the lies from those in government and enforce consequences, then we can unwind the envy. If we can restore truth, we can restore peace and contentment in a country in chaos.

---

51 Aseem Malhotra, "Tucker Carlson interviews Dr Aseem Malhotra on the corruption of medicine by Big Pharma," Tucker Carlson Today, YouTube, accessed December 15, 2022, https://www.youtube.com/watch?app=desktop&v=w3MPnBpfrRk.

We have a long way to go. We can start by taking personal responsibility, looking the lies in the face, and saying: "You're not welcome here." That will be a tall order because it will necessarily begin with how you live your lives, vote, and the companies you patronize. The most promising event I have seen of late is the mass boycott against Bud Lite for partnering with Dylan Mulvaney, a man pretending to be a woman in a most disgusting and profane way. The boycott was massive, costing the company billions of dollars and forcing them to fire some of their marketing people. This is needed on a mass scale. Frankly, it would only take several big companies to bankrupt before all of corporate America gets the message to get out of politics and social engineering and get back to their main business purpose.

We are where we are in this country because we voted for lies and liars and then re-elected them. We start by living in truth and stop lying to ourselves. Bring order to your mind. Be informed, brutally and confrontationally delegitimize the purveyors of lies, the Left, and humiliate them as they do when they demean the Right.

We counter the lies that breed envy and the envy that weaponizes the lies with a hefty dose of the only reliable vaccine for this ailment: Truth. Start with yourself. Know the truth, give justice to others, and you will be far down the road to recovering from systemic psychosis.

CHAPTER 13:

Sin Becomes a Gender

"Haven't you read...that at the beginning the Creator
'made them male and female.'"

Jesus

Both religious and secular people tend to refer to "wrongs" and "moral failings" (regardless of how and why you define morals), as "sin." It seems to be a catchall for conduct that is bad for society or mankind. Thank God that our human nature forces upon us some degree of normative and life-preserving conduct to the chagrin of many on the Left who want to remake nature in their image.

Most people recognize the necessity of limits on human behavior, and most of us would consider actions that occur outside of these limits to be dangerous and wrong. However, for some it seems there are no bounds to depravity. More than a few of these "some" have increasingly migrated into positions of power and authority across our country, mostly by default. They merely filled a vacuum. Evil loves a vacuum. Using their positions of power, these dehumanizing degenerates work to legitimize their degeneracy. Day by day, the boundary of what historically has been understood to be normative and beneficial behavior is shrinking, and the circle of toxic tolerance for what is wrong and perverse is expanding.

This is why Romans 1:28-29 (NIV) tells us that: "Furthermore, just as they did not think it worthwhile to retain the knowledge of God, so God gave them over to a depraved mind, so that they do what ought not to be done. They have become filled with every kind of wickedness, evil, greed and depravity."

Remember, as stated earlier, a depraved mind is a nonfunctioning mind, and those who are or have become depraved will deliver themselves into the hands of their enemy. Unfortunately, as a country we will all be collectively pulled into the bondage of the Left's selection.

The Nature of Law and Mankind's Immorality

In the religious sense and context, a sin is an immoral act considered to be a transgression against divine law, an act regarded as a serious offense of commission or omission. Each culture has its interpretation of what it means to sin. Sins are generally considered actions, thoughts, or words that are immoral, selfish, shameful, or harmful. Sin can also be a deviation from a cultural norm. These natural moral constraints existing from the beginning of time are in place to protect society from destructive aberrations or deviations that occur, whether physical or mental.

The Left presumes themselves wiser than the collective experiential knowledge of all of past humanity, yet they have nothing to show for it but failure in all they endeavor. Is there any wonder why they despise history and revise its inconvenient truths? Today, that kind of conduct has thrown the world into chaos, but then when has the Left, when in control, not done that?

Our systemic psychosis has undone established normative and protective constraints. Psychosis has redrawn the previously accepted moral boundaries. Now, the prevailing idea in the country today is there is no norm, no natural law, at all. This is the reason why chaos is now so prevalent. Tucker Carlson has so aptly given some definition to the illness and chaos so prevalent in the country. He says it seems "other-worldly," something "spiritual" and not in a good way.

The deviance runs counter to all major religions today. It is in a class by itself and seemingly not of this world as it is totally perverse and incomprehensible. It's as if Sauron from *The Lord of the Rings* sent his Orcs into all our major institutions, demanding homage to the leftist hive-mind and occupying all decision-making. All the horrors of past unaccountable and deviant governments are about to be repeated.

Deviance is probably the best description in the contemporary sense. In our dysfunction, our world seems to be sacrificing itself in honor of Gaia, the goddess of chaos, and in contemporary terms, "the climate." In the world, and particularly in the West, the Left psychotics have a problem with reality. You see reality prevents them from easily achieving their delusional goals of a utopia that has never existed and never will. While many of the deviants are in control, they can't quite yet make their dystopian dreams work because there are still too many normative thinking people, and the irredeemable on the Right are in their way. The Left will never stop trying, and there is not much time remaining to stop the Left's march to destruction.

Embodied Sin

The Left's top priority, and the Democrat Party that they captured, cleansed of all moderates and conservatives, can be summed up today in three words: sex, sex, sex. That's why they've come for your children because the irredeemable adults are in the way. Paganism has become a pandemic and children are on their menu.

What the deviants have managed to destroy are the historical boundaries of sexual morality and conduct. This is nothing less than remarkable. They have turned what historically and normatively has been seen as sin and/or a mental dysfunction, into a *gender*. They have taken some of the wildest claims about human nature, sexual reality, and deviant desires and managed to embody them into the LGBTQ+ and transgender movement. What would otherwise land someone in the insane asylum now gets them on the front page of Vanity Fair or New York Magazine. Historically, all revolutions and the decline of many countries begin with a sexual revolution, which in America's case started in the late 1940s and blossomed in the 1960s.

How so? Because we reflexively, without seeming to even give it a second thought, anointed the concept of *gender identity* as essentially a newfound human right. This is a trap. Those who assent to this are either delusional, groomed, or, more likely, covering over or trying to justify their own sexual deviance and guilt. Either way, society will not survive this deviance.

What the Bible and the other major world religions would call sin—homosexuality, transgenderism, and pedophilia, etc.—the Left has managed to turn into something prohibitively unquestionable.

Here's a challenge for you: There is nothing in the Democratic platform that unites it with any of the major religions of the world. I dislike having to refer to the Democrats in a way that sounds so partisan, but they and the Left are now synonymous and indistinguishable. The old leadership of the Democrat Party allowed this. They got rid of all differing viewpoints, conservatives, and moderates within the party. Being an equal-opportunity criticizer myself, I have given the Republicans a fair share of criticism as well. I often refer to them as the "stupid party," particularly when it comes to developing winning strategies. They always seem to manage to lose the chess match after putting their opponent in check. The Right is the champion at losing the culture wars, defending the normative, and preserving human dignity.

The Left has been long at work devising schemes to turn the world upside down. They do so by turning people inside out. You once said no one would be that crazy. Well, they are, and they are here at your doorstep.

It all started back in the 1940s with Alfred Kinsey. I helped work on a book exposing his fraudulent science called *Kinsey, Crimes and Consequences* with Dr. Judith Reisman, Col. Ron Ray, and his wife Eunice. This book exposed the fraud. The evidence was so profound and overwhelming that it is too extensive to even begin talking about it here, but suffice it to say, it was the foundation the Left wanted for eliminating all governance and controls over sexual behavior. As predicted, pedophilia is now being added to the alphabet mafia list of sexual entitlements, and is now known as MAP (minor attracted people). Your children will no longer be safe from predators. To make matters worse, I bet many of you, or friends of yours, voted for those who countenanced this move. Making matters worse, the government (through the educational agencies) now contend that your children don't belong to you. How convenient for the pedophile agenda.

The Left's War on the Family

One of the main and current symptoms of psychosis I define in our current environment is support for child mutilation, euphemistically called abortion (today we color the truth, and the reality of what atrocities really are, so we use scientific terms to feel good about it). This goes hand in hand with disrespect for life and family. Disrespect for life in one area will not stay in that area. It is and will come for you. When it does, you will have no defense, because you laid the foundation for euthanasia fifty years ago. In 2021 Canada euthanized 10,000 people. It's coming your way here in America.

Fundamental to life on this earth is procreation and the protection of life. Nothing is more basic than this. As the election season approached in 2022, it was this most profound issue that the Democrat Party and the Left focused on most intently. It was most telling and frightening.

One morning as I lay in my hotel bed awakening to the news (which I don't recommend, as it is not a good start to the day) the propagandists talked about how the Democrats were shifting their message to abortion as opposed to the economy they crashed.

This shift in emphasis is profound. It speaks in such a fundamental way to just how mentally ill, how psychotic, such a large portion of our population has become. How so? Well, the glory of a woman is to conceive life and to give birth. From time immemorial the protection of women, particularly pregnant women, was paramount. The life within the womb and the child to come after were of primary importance and took precedence over all else—as it should.

As I listened to the new strategy of the Democrats to appeal to the lesser in all of us, particularly those who wanted to avoid the consequences of their actions (choice) even to the point of death, two things became immediately apparent.

First, consider how unnatural it is for a woman to want to destroy life, particularly the life within her, life that only she can produce. It makes her unique among the species. Now, psychos are telling us that all you must do is tap your ruby slippers together three times and you, as a man, can be a woman and give life, too. Most know this to be not just absurd but a mental illness. No one suffering from such severe dysphoria is capable of functioning in a way that results in good judgment, or in a way that prospers life, society, relationships, and culture. Something more insidious is at work here, and it is not in the best interest of women at all. Women caught up in the feminist movement—yet again—have been deceived, just like in the Garden when Eve gave up her glory for a lie. The human physical foundation is being destroyed so the mental one can be altered next. Now that "men can have babies," women are not so special, are they? The agenda is so clear, yet the people are so blind.

Second, and equally profound, is how so many women reflexively fall into this trap of thumping their chests and yelling, "I am a woman, hear me roar!" They so quickly buy into the same old deceit they bought in the Garden of Eden. They were easily deceived then and now with the commonality that their sin destroys life. The rallying cry is "pro-choice," as if she hadn't already made that choice. If a woman is pregnant, she made a choice, and now she wants someone else to pay the price with their life. Women are being marginalized through an equality they wouldn't want if they only knew what it really meant and what they were giving up to gain it.

Oh, do you hear the screams of, "How cruel it is to women subjected to rape and incest." Well, as usual the Left always go for the deviant and extreme extrapolations, meaning they go for what deviates from the norm. Just as transgender makes up only 1.6% of the population, at most, the Left does the same with the abortion argument. They take what is extremely rare, that is pregnancy from rape (less than a fraction of 1%), or what is deviant from the norm, and attempt to make it the norm and then force the normative of society to live according to their deviations. Essentially, they want to make all of society deviant and to depart from reality and truth.

The Left would have you believe that there have been over 65 million pregnancies that have been the result of rape or incest. They turn the world upside down and inside out since chaos creates an opportunity for them to seize power while the people are in a state of confusion. All the Left needs is enough time to set in place enough rules, regulations, and politicized enforcers armed to the teeth to keep them in power. They become the monarchs over a dystopian ruined world. Why should they care? They are on top.

As an aside, our borders are flooded by illegal migrants. Leftist Senator Chuck Schumer claims that these migrants are needed since we don't have enough workers. This was a predicted response years ago, but oddly enough there is a correlation between the alleged shortage of workers and the number of potential workers who were aborted. Think about it. Over 65,000,000 workers, Americans, were aborted in the last 50 years. Now we are replacing those workers and our culture with illegal immigrants. Now we see how monstrous the Left is: they will lie, kill, and destroy to seize and maintain power. They care nothing about what they profess to value, or the consequences since it is only a means to an end, a selfish and self-serving end, and it doesn't matter to them that they are dehumanizing their fellow man in pursuit of their power.

Many women who are keen to the deception are rightfully outraged that Democrats would think them so shallow as to buy into this appeal and vote against their family's interests, as if the only thing that mattered is themselves, and to hell with the country into which their children are born and husbands live. Most women would never consider baby mutilation, but even some of them have been conned into believing they need this "right," oblivious as to the real agenda of the Left. The price they will pay some day is the government deciding that only they can raise your children correctly, and women will have their children taken from them.

The Left appeals to the lesser nature of our character in that they, like the serpent in the garden, ask, "Did God really say that?" They question your basic instincts and lure you into believing that you are being deprived of something "good," that is, "the right to kill something you *think* you don't want." Just ask Tim Tebow's mother.

The Left desperately appeals to evil, enticing women to vote against not just the protection of life and their humanity, but the opportunity to improve their immediate economic situation, for themselves, their families, and the country. Like I said, it always boils down to something sex-related for the Left in their obsessive march toward total power.

Making a Crisis Mountain Out a Gender Molehill on Purpose

Taking something as deviant as transgenderism and making it an unquestionably legitimate category was and is their intent. And you need to know why: Because the chaos they create brings an abundance of opportunity for them to seize the permanent control they desire.

Rahm Emmanuel, Clinton's chief of staff once remarked, "Never let a crisis go to waste." This is straight out of Saul Alinsky's playbook, *Rules for Radicals* (and remember, both Hillary Clinton and Barack Obama were followers and admirers of Alinsky). Yes, there is a core cause for the chaos in our world and country. You simply have not been paying attention, and neither have some of our leaders on the Right. They only need you to be their fool long enough to vote for them.

Just as sexual orientation was turned into a civil and constitutional right along with marriage, now gender identity is being pitched as the cure for any type of mental disorder, dysfunction, deviance, or sin. Once it becomes a gender, it is a protected class and untouchable or non-condemnable. The anarchical Left plunged headfirst into societal chaos. Any time they get questioned, they reach inside their bag of tricks and pull out the worn-out but effective technique of linguistic "redefinition."

The message? If it's wrong, aberrant, reprehensible, immoral, shameful, or harmful behavior, and you want to do it *anyway*, just rename it. This is classic paganism. The Left awaits you with open arms. Today, we name it yet another "gender" and you are good to go. Just add it to the near 100 genders some fools say exist. I'm sure they have room for one more.

What a great sleight of hand to fool the Right. The Right will resort to shouting (ineffectively) things like "That's insane!" or "That's crazy!" Or they will, in frustration, reflexively ask "Why?" or lose the argument in a recitation and barrage of facts, all true but of no effect.

An article by Liel Leibovitz, editor at large for the Tablet, cited a prominent Columbia University Climate Scientist who refused to debate climate science and did so saying: "Once you put established facts about the world up for argument, you've already lost." The Right insanely places "established fact" upon the altar every time to reargue it. This requires the established facts to be re-proven to a deviant and psychotic group who will accept no truths regardless of how self-evident they are.

Meanwhile, the Right is missing the fact that the sexual chaos caused by the Left is a strategic move. It's another liberal/leftist move on the chessboard leading to a "checkmate" of the Right. Instead of looking for rationale and answers, the Right should immediately go on the attack on multiple fronts to discredit the Left and expose their deviancy and shame, forcing them off the platform, using Machiavelli's rules for nice guys.

The Right erroneously made the Left their equal, gave them moral equivalency, and placed them on the platform. The camel's head was allowed into the tent and now the tent is gone. The culture is lost. This is another losing strategy of the psychotic Right. They do not know how to combat the evil of the Left.

Emotion Trumps Reason

Of course, emotion should never prevail over fact. They are not equivalent. However sinful and wrongful, it often does prevail. That is a reality we must contend with. Thus, the Right should answer back with a likewise emotional appeal as do the leftist Democrats. For as wrong as the Left's message is, it is winning the day because its delivery mechanism is "emotion." Remember, that is what works in a lazy dumbed-down society. Those who are "fact" oriented rightfully reject emotional appeals and prefer the facts. However, for the sake of the nation, one must appeal to the irrational emotions of low information voters if the war is going to be won.

It's time for the Right to stop acting like patricians. Take off your sissy white gloves and fight back like real men and women. If you are where you should be theologically, doctrinally, and spiritually, then you would know from whence the gender chaos stems. Those who preach toleration want nothing of the sort. They want obliteration. They are so crafty because the harvest is so plentiful and the message so easy to sell.

Culture now says there are something like 100 different genders. Do you know what that means? It means 98 different ways to sin, because only two of those are real. The Left is legislating the protection of sin. Now it seems that each sin has its own gender, and we have been conditioned and groomed to be silent, accepting, and tolerant, as we turn over the throne of power to the deviant psychotics. The Left has destroyed the Ten Commandments, but not the consequences of ignoring them. If this is judgment, it's a judgment upon those who should know better but lacked the moral courage to do anything about it. To be clear, that's pretty much many of those who might be reading this book. It's time to stop letting every new sin under the sun pretend it's a protected class or status, like a gender.

In the past, God used the wicked to invade and capture the Jews and take them into captivity for their sins of sloth, neglect, idolatry, and indifference. If God still deals with nations like this, and He does, how could anyone argue that America isn't overdue for judgment, if it is not already experiencing it. Look at the map of the world over the last 50 years and see how many changes there have been. Many nations no longer exist. Others are new. There is no history of, or guarantee for any nation's perpetual existence, particularly America's.

So, while you and your pastor (if you even have one that is truly qualified) were asleep, the Left psychos disguised sin as gender and are in the process of guaranteeing its protected status. Sin is being legalized, and in the very near future if you preach against sin, you will be jailed (as is already true in Canada). And you never connected the dots nor called it what it was. Judgment is now being poured out at both ends of the spectrum.

Gender Engineering

If you didn't know any better, you might think half the United States was transgender. After all, it's all that anyone seems to talk about anymore. Most commercials and movies include large overrepresentations of "sexual minorities." A recent Pew Research Center survey found that only 1.6% of U.S. adults are transgender or nonbinary." That's right—only 1.6% of the population is transgender or nonbinary. And that is by some accounts exaggerated. Many have noticed over the last few years that there is much overrepresentation in our commercials of all sorts, as if society and all ethnicities have been placed in a blender, erasing cultural identity and the richness that diverse cultures bring. There is an extraordinary campaign of manipulation and indoctrination of society by a leftist elite to restructure society in their warped image through the media. The Left always cooks the numbers. They grossly extrapolate to create a new (pseudo) reality, one to their liking that will keep them permanently in power.

Movies even get in on the action, like The Aeronauts. In the movie they portray the historical feat as having been accomplished by a man and woman. In actual history, there was no woman involved. The main point here is not so much the skin color or gender of the actor, but the indoctrination and manipulation of the public and a failure of accurate portrayals and representations of life. The media panders to groups that create victims and distort reality. Do you think there is an agenda at play here?

In a survey reported during Jesse Watters' "Prime Time Report" on Fox News, only 3% of the population identified as gay or lesbian. However, when the public was surveyed as to what percentage of the population they thought were gay, the response was nearly 30%, and some surveys placed it higher. The people have been gaslighted into believing that it is normal simply by virtue of the assumed high percentages. Just think how it would impact the public's voting patterns on various issues if they thought that what landed on their back was not a buzzard but a mosquito.

Study after study and survey after survey has shown that those identifying as gay are in the upper tiers of income in this country, and the discrimination complained about was not supported by facts or by their expensive lifestyles. The public also had outrageous assumptions about transgenderism and other groups, 10 to 20 times what actually exists.

Another study by Gallup from 2019 also shows that Americans vastly overestimate how much of the population is homosexual. According to their research, "U.S. adults estimate that nearly one in four Americans (23.6%) are gay or lesbian. Gallup has previously found that Americans have greatly overestimated the gay population of the US, recording similar average estimates of 24.6% in 2011 and 23.2% in 2015. In each of the three polls in which Gallup asked this question, a majority of Americans estimated this population to be 20% or greater."

The reality? Americans estimate [wrongly] that the proportion of gay people in the U.S. was more than five times Gallup's more encompassing 2017 survey, which showed that only 4.5% of Americans are LGBTQ, based on respondents' self-identification as being lesbian, gay, bisexual or transgender.

That might even be too high. Some data indicate that the overall number of Americans who are truly living LGBTQ lifestyles is less than 3%. However, they have turned our country upside down.

So why the focus on this? Because it is driving the agenda in this country. Personally, I could care less what you do with each other or with others as long as it is not with children. That's between you and God. All was well until the alphabet mafia was no longer satisfied to "live and let live." Once they got the camel's head in the tent, they were going to push their lifestyle upon you and make you like it and conform to it. It was never benign. It was never about discrimination or fairness. It was never about rights. They rub their sexual orientation in your face and demand you celebrate it. The agenda was part of a bigger plan.

When 95% of America wakes up in the morning and looks themselves in the mirror, the first thing that comes into their minds is not, "I'm straight" or "I'm of color." We see a person in that mirror and think about how to order our lives that day. The deviant portion of society wants you to think otherwise. They want your identity to be front and center in your mind. How psychotic is that? Is that kind of thinking going to help you with your job or the plethora of issues you must face in a day's time just to maintain your life, a life which is, by its nature, difficult for everyone already?

Now, I have associated with, done business with, and represented nearly every ethnicity and group under the sun (not as an activist). Identity markers are never discussed, are irrelevant, and unnecessary to the business at hand. That is the way it should be, but not so for the radicals. The leftists and the Democrat platform embrace the furthest extremes, as there is a perceived opportunity there for them to gain power by having disparate groups identify as a color or ethnicity as opposed to just being a person, a citizen. The LGBTQ+ community isn't really a group to "represent," but rather to use as the rungs of a ladder on their way to the top.

So, sin became a gender—and then it lied to everyone about how much of a giant it was. Turns out it's more like a mouse casting a massive shadow on the wall. It's time to turn the lights up so we can see this population for what it really is and get away from the proposed deviant policies that do not improve anyone's life, but rather are destructive. I would be remiss not to point out, since this book is about getting to the core, that many who struggle with a sexual identity don't identify with the radical agendas being pushed. They have been taken hostage by the real deviants, the real criminals, the real megalomaniacs in this life, and it is those who have created false narratives in their obsession for power. Don't waste your time on the hostages; focus all your wrath upon those who benefit from the chaos they have created. You will find most of them in D.C. and on the coast.

The normative just want to be left alone, but that is not in the nature of the radical Left. The alphabet mafia cannot and will not ever achieve the legitimacy they desire (however that is defined) any more than I will be the next man on the moon. They apparently think the way to do it is to legislate a forced acceptance of that which we all know is fake. You cannot make anyone like you or love you, whether gay or straight. Life is short, so get on with it and let others get on with theirs. Pretending that something is or isn't what it actually *is* is also psychotic.

As part of the inorganic psychosis, we are being asked to deny the laws of nature and not to believe our own eyes. The militant combatants on the Left are throwing stun grenades labeled "ze/zir" to keep society off balance so it's easier for them to come in and reorganize it as they see fit. The truth is that they fear the masses. The masses are a threat to the elite, so the elite finance the reprogramming of society to accept authoritarianism wherein the elite will always be in charge. And they do this in part by making it impossible to question things like the LGBTQ narrative all while blowing its actual size far out of proportion.

Virtue Triumphs Over Madness. Or Does It?

As John Adams once said, our government was meant only for a virtuous and moral people. Virtue is a way of behaving that brings social and cultural stability to society. Virtue is grounded in the truth, not gender madness. Instability and chaos are needed for a leftist takeover, not stability and reason, because they know that their ideas never work nor are accepted by the public apart from deception. That's why they took the sickest sins and degeneracy they could dream up and demanded they get protected status.

In the last few decades, the Left realized that they could not get their agenda through the legislatures, so they sought to take social action instead. They radicalized the courts and brought about judicial tyranny, essentially enacting legislation through the courts by judicial fiat. This is exactly what happened with the *Obergefell* decision that legalized homosexual marriage (which is a mirage).

That is why all the gloves came off over the recent Supreme Court nominations during the time Trump was in office. Hillary Clinton was supposed to make the court solidly leftist and destroy the constitution without the need for a Constitutional Convention. When she shockingly lost, the Left had to destroy President Trump. They just couldn't do it quick enough. And don't think some on the Right weren't complicit.

At one time the Federal Courts, the Supreme Court, and courts in general were thought to be occupied by good, unbiased jurists that would interpret and apply the law as written regardless of their personal feelings. We now know that is not the case in most situations. Cases of substantial impact on people's rights are decided not according to the law, but according to a judge's worldview or political stance. This is the result of the polarization of the country, but what else would you expect from a morally rudderless society? Most of President Biden's judicial picks have been minorities and their political persuasion radically left. None of the selections, white or black, are based on their legal qualifications. Justice Jackson, the one that cannot define what a woman is, is the prime example.

The church is barely around in a meaningful way to be of any help as it used to be. It was at one time the moral rudder and kept everyone in check – the people, the government, and the courts. When your judges were sitting in the pew next to you on Sunday morning – or your senator or representative were there, you knew you were all on the same battle-field and plain of humanity.

Think what you will about Trump, but the truth is he saved the Republic and bought some time for the people to get their act together and figure out what the Left was about to do. For all his shortcomings, Trump brought a certain virtue to the Presidency, despite your indoctri-nated and groomed views of the man. This virtue was the brave act of telling the truth, as blunt and inarticulate as it may have been. As the farmers say, sometimes to get the stubborn donkey's attention you must hit it over the head with the 2x4.

As much as Republicans like losing, Trump screwed up the game for them too. Just as only Nixon could have gone to China, only Trump could have beaten Hillary Clinton. I believe this is a fact that the Right and Republicans have a difficult time accepting, so one must ask, who is on the side of the people?

Trump told the truth about the absurdities of things like transgen-der madness and intersectionality. Specifically, he addressed the issue of how the present Marxists weaponize both gender and race together. He called out the riots of the summer of 2020 after George Floyd's death. Those were real riots. Now you are being gaslit again about the January 6 so-called "riots or insurrection." Just like gender nonsense, what you have been told about January 6 is a fabrication and desperation on the Left. As with the Russian dossier, it was proven a hoax. The Left knew it would be proven false, but that didn't matter, as the irreparable damage they desired already would have been done to the President and you would quickly forget what went on as usual.

Remember, only one side of the story was presented by the January 6 committee, and it too has been proven wrong. Again, that doesn't matter. They just needed to fool you long enough to get you to vote the way they wanted you to and to put them back in power. Once there, the Left would bury the evidence, never to see the light of day.

I bring up the events of January 6 because it is eerily like gender madness. The Left has blown it way out of proportion to make Americans think something happened that didn't happen – just as they exaggerate transgender and homosexual representation numbers way out of proportion. Now the Left is stoking and trying to instigate violence so they can have a pretext to lock you down again.

Cicero said that "Virtue is its own reward." However, it is not true in our psychotic states of America. Here, lying gets the top prize—and the worst offenders are the progeny of the sexual revolution that just keep on devouring their own, legislating sin and turning it into a gender as if doing so legitimizes it.

If we have any hope of stopping it, the time for truth and virtue to be exercised is now.

CHAPTER 14:

The Church's Complicity

"A preacher must be both soldier and shepherd. He must nourish, defend, and teach; he must have teeth in his mouth, and be able to bite and fight."
Martin Luther

Woke Church, Wrong Church

C.S. Lewis once said that "Of all bad men, religious bad men are the worst."

Unfortunately, the church has not been immune to the mental regression of psychosis we are experiencing in the world today. If there is any truth left in this world, it should be in the church and coming from the church, but for over a generation the seminaries have become infected, both Catholic and Protestant. As the culture decayed and the populace had their cognitive processes re-wired, making them incapable of rational and logical thought, corrective directions and clear warnings were not heard from the pulpits across America.

This is not a "which came first, the chicken or the egg" predicament. Because the church failed to monitor and discipline itself, the country lost its rudder, its voice of reason, truth, and sanity. Those in the leadership of the church failed to see the heretical Marxist-backed insurgency coming into the seminaries and pulpits. It should have excised this malignant tumor immediately upon detection. Figuring this out did not take a lot of sophisticated analysis. The Marxist agenda was no big secret, as established by many communist defectors like Yuri Bezmenov, a former KGB agent who told us what was going on – as if we really needed to be told. The church was a primary target as also revealed by David Horowitz. Then don't forget the fraud of Alfred Kinsey. It was all out in the open for all to see and the Right and the church were clearly asleep.

Far too many seminaries have fallen into real or soft liberalism. Too many evangelical leaders and organizations allowed heretics to take the helm. Subsequently, they began pumping out graduates and future pastors who were adulterous to and didn't believe in the core principles of the faith they were called to preach and apply. I have often said there will be more self-proclaimed priests, ministers, and pastors in hell than not.

The main stabilizing force in the country for centuries was the church and now that is rapidly fading away. If the culture looks to the church for "good news" and the church no longer preaches the "good news," then it has nothing to offer. What a disconnect.

The 20th century saw the consequences of what some call the "death of God." Good men and women sat by while this occurred. You know, the "nice" people that Machiavelli referred to. They attempted to reason with wicked people. You cannot. There is no such coexistence between the two. Unfortunately, good tolerates evil, but evil cannot tolerate good, and evil's primary goal is to eradicate good. It is an amazing phenomenon how and why good cannot come to grips with and understand this basic principle.

The German philosopher Nietzsche considered the agony, suffering, and misery of a godless world when others were blind to the terrible consequences, and he saw in advance the fate of the emerging generation. Such is what we are experiencing now. In the last 30 years we have seen a 2,000% increase in paganism in the country. This is what occurs when the church leaves a vacuum, and it has. This is what happens with infidelity to the doctrines of the faith, i.e., the Bible.

Life without God is an absurdity since God *is* life, and without God there is no life. Truly, it is impossible to live a life with meaning if there is no future, no afterlife. Life in such an instance is a cruel joke and renders everything we do futile. There is no value to anything we do, as it will be lost in the wash of time. What we do today has value because of tomorrow. If there is no tomorrow it doesn't matter what we do today, if anything. The same applies to life itself. Why live another day if there is no meaning to it absent the life to come, our eternal tomorrow?

The crisis of "meaning" we are experiencing today manifests in the chaos and the orchestrated decline of religion in America. The Left, the godless hedonists who side with the atheistic Marxists, have worked long and hard to wipe out all vestiges of religion from our schools and the public square. As the history of the last 100 years clearly reveals, the Right and the church have been complicit, as most didn't fight back with the fervor of the Left to protect that which they claimed. So much for their faith.

The radical and violent Left exhibits and testifies to a life without a metaphysical foundation. They have no connection to their past. Everything is disjointed and lacks meaning. Yes, such a life would make a heathen rage, and rage they do.

The liberal infections of the past are having disastrous consequences, but the inaction, indolence, and lack of faith of the Right has placed their world in chaos, and they are paying dearly. Too many profess a faith they do not possess. They are deluded, and falsely assured.

As previously stated, without God there is no order and without order there is no freedom, but as a corollary to the symptoms of an atheist nation is a nation plagued with mental illness, and that nation will make government and/or science their god. Man will degenerate into nihilism, self-loathing, and as a characteristic of those on the Left, finally result in totalitarianism.

Everywhere that religion and Christianity have faded from the center of society, chaos, meaninglessness, suppression of freedom, and totalitarianism arises. Our cities have become the cathedrals of atheists who, in their resultant mental illness borne of a meaningless life, despite their claims of not believing in God, have adopted climate change as their substitute religion. Carl Jung refers to this as an "urban neurosis." No wonder 2 million people (about the population of Nebraska) have moved out of the cities between 2020 and 2022.

A Warning About Pastors Who Shouldn't Be in the Pulpit

At a conference years ago, Dr. R.C. Sproul (one of the greatest theological minds of our time), in answer to a question involving the problems in the church, said, "I doubt that more than five percent of those in the pulpit today are qualified to be there." Amen to that. Sadly, most pastors are as ignorant as their congregations regarding what is happening in the culture and society. They are defanged, helpless to give their sermons any application that would help their members fight against cultural compromise because they are blind to the evil that has crept into the church.

The Pope is a perfect example of how those who claim to follow Christianity have traded their faith for another religion entirely; he is now more concerned about climate change than the teachings of Jesus Christ. He's clearly not Pope John Paul II. Or we could look at Joel Osteen and his prosperity gospel, or protestant seminary presidents and publishers who have collapsed in the face of the culture, adopting social justice as a substitute for the gospel and true Christian faith.

What's the solution? We need better pastors who are faithful, educated, informed, and willing to confront the evil times in which we live. For example, 80-year-old pastor Dr. John MacArthur stood his ground against one of the most evil and morally debased people in the country, Governor Gavin Newsom of California.

The church has even shied away from confronting the evil in the country, whether it be from institutions or the government. They lost the battle on sodomy and gay marriage. They lost the battle on child mutilation (abortion) 50 years ago, as they were asleep at the wheel before the issue first went to the Supreme Court.

Why were they asleep? Frankly, because many true pastors had been influenced by or replaced by cloaked Marxist wolves, whether they knew that was what they were or not. The cultural Marxists, on their "long march through the institutions," explicitly targeted the seminaries, and infiltrated them. This has been a documented fact for decades and yet the erosion was allowed unabated.

So where did this problem in the church come from? One day, when I was talking with my mentor, Colonel Ronald Ray, he said something that I will never forget. He told about a time when he was on the dais at an event sitting next to David Horowitz. This was after Horowitz disavowed communism. Horowitz was once an avowed and active communist, and very well known. Col. Ray, in a side discussion with Horowitz, was talking about his military background and remarked that, being a military man, he was worried about the infiltration of communism within the country and the military. As an aside, he said, "I guess you will be going after the churches next." To Ray's surprise, Horowitz said, "Oh, we got to them first." Well, it really doesn't take much study or thought to figure that out, but it should be alarming to everyone today. The Marxists got to the churches, and everything else followed suit.

James Lindsay helps document this in his podcast on "Paulo Freire and the Marxist Transformation of the Church." Lindsay notes Freire's explanation of how Marxists see "churches as educational platforms that can be utilized in the same way as schools to raise Marxist consciousness. The model is simple: capture the colleges of education and seminaries and you get the teachers and the pastors, and once you have them you get the students and the laity."

So as the Marxists supplanted faithful ministers, they were then able to start placing "pastors" in the pulpits who didn't believe in the fundamentals of the Christian faith. One must ask: Why go into ministry if you don't even believe what you are preaching? The answer? Imposing their warped worldview upon a weakened church. If the seminaries had been more interested in fidelity to their faith than tuition dollars, the heretics would have been expelled immediately.

We also saw this with the "Resolution 9" controversy at the Southern Baptist Convention (SBC) a few years back. Tom Ascol, President of Founders Ministries, explained it like this:

> Over the last several months evangelical Christians have been forced to think about Marxist concepts that, heretofore, were foreign to them. Due in large part to the infamous "Resolution 9" that was adopted by the 2019 Southern Baptist Convention (SBC), language identifying those concepts, if not the proper understanding of them, has become somewhat familiar to evangelicals. After all, the title of the SBC's Resolution 9 is "On Critical Race Theory and Intersectionality." The Resolutions Committee strongly rejected any critique of their resolution by

the messengers present. They also dismissed my attempt to offer an amendment to it that would have made the resolution more explicitly theological and added warnings about the Marxist origins of the ideologies being promoted.[52]

Resolution 9 was a trojan horse, smuggling in ungodly worldly philosophies like Marxism further and further into the church. Ascol goes on to warn that "CRT (along with every other Marxist ideology) cannot be reconciled with what the Bible teaches about sin and salvation. First, to view all relationships in terms of power dynamics requires that people be seen in terms of the powerful (privileged, oppressors) and the powerless (marginalized, oppressed)."

This must be rejected. Churches need to be up in arms, shepherds need to be driving away the wolves, and pastors need to be warning their members not to let any of this into the church—not even a tiny bit.

Those who promoted Resolution 9 did so in an artful parliamentarian maneuver lacking transparency and honesty. While I am not Southern Baptist, I watched the actions surrounding the Resolution 9 and the parliamentarian gamesmanship played out on stage to ignorant attendees, clueless as to what they were going to vote on. Most were the blindly obedient type, and the Resolution passed.

In my viewpoint and experience as a player on the courts of parliamentary procedure and maneuvering, it was crass politics at its worst lacking anything divine or spiritual. Shame on them, but shame on the naivety of the pastors that let the wolves in. I believe such naivety to be a sin, particularly if you don the robe and you take to the pulpit. If you do, you damn well better be prepared, informed, and correct—or damned you will be. Such ignorance is inexcusable as is naivety.

There is so much selective naivety in the pews today as well as the pulpits, which I call the "Ostrich Syndrome." They feel comfort in their self-imposed blindness and bury their heads in the sand because they simply haven't the emotional capacity to deal with reality. They are just

---

52   Tom Ascol,, Critical Race Theory, Intersectionality, and the Gospel, Founders Ministries, February 2020 https://founders.org/articles/critical-race-theory-intersectionality-and-the-gospel/

going to leave it all to Jesus, ignoring their responsibilities in this life and the persecution predicted for the Christianity they profess. They wrap themselves up in their "Jesus flag," cleansing themselves of any responsibility. They find a false self-righteousness in their ignorance and excuse their indolence with a horrible, erroneous and sissified image of Christ.

Much of the persecution, some of which is promised, is a consequence of the church and Christians' own inaction, but they will blindly accept it as undeserved and think themselves even more righteous because of it and the persecution to come. Truly, some suffering comes from evil, through or by others, or neutral circumstances, or our own sin, but they will never accept the fact that it is a consequence of their own sloth.

Sproul was right—too many men in pulpits have no business being there. Let me give you a very stark example of why.

Kinsey and the Corruption of the Church

In the 1940s, when the foundations of the 1960s sexual revolution took root via the work of Alfred Kinsey, the church was woefully negligent and absent. As previously mentioned, I assisted in the work on the book, *Kinsey, Crimes, and Consequences*. We researched the fraudulent, so-called science that was paraded around in Alfred Kinsey's book, *Sexuality in the Human Male*. Kinsey's book was riddled with false statistics. On one of the pages, it listed the famous "Table 34" wherein Kinsey noted the experiments done on children as young as 5 months old to see if they could have a sexual response.

Hopefully, this didn't go over your head. Hopefully, you just stopped and asked yourself, isn't this against the law to do to children? If you did, you're correct, and even more so back then. These were admitted felonies. Sexual abuse was perpetrated upon children only a few months old. Yet Kinsey was praised as the man of the year and on the covers of Time Magazine. Everyone loved Kinsey. He should have been indicted and jailed for his complicity or sanctioning, if not abusing, children along with his team of fake researchers.

What is the relevance here? I'll answer that with a question. Where was the church? Where was the moral outrage? The church let all of this go. And now we have Kinsey-esque logic infiltrating our entire culture. Not all was well in Denmark, nor is it in America today. It is a disease of the mind. Maybe it's a sleeping sickness; otherwise it is psychosis and there is nothing normative in these omissions or commissions when they run so counter to the functioning of a healthy, normative society. It is so counter to reality.

And to be clear, Kinsey laid the philosophical groundwork for the radical gender ideology that we see today. It's just one short step from Kinsey to Lia Thomas, to Vanderbilt's pediatric transgender clinic, the alphabet mafia, and then, ultimately, the normalization of pedophilia. May all the curses of Psalm 109 fall upon these deviants. If you harm a child, there simply should be no room for you in this world.

Religious Trauma and the Rise of False Churches

The problem isn't just unqualified pastors and silent churches. It's deeper than that. As I have said, as goes the church so goes the nation. As stated, the church was infiltrated long ago. So, I want to alert Christians that churches practicing fidelity to doctrine are on the verge of effectively being outlawed. How? Follow me closely here: There is a new creation on the horizon called, "religious trauma." This will become a new "cause of action" to arise in the courts. Insurance companies will refuse to give coverage in these cases and judgments will be handed down, bankrupting the churches.

This will be brought about via "tort" cases. The issue of religious trauma will become a new cause of action. The goal will be to try to show how someone was injured emotionally or suffered emotional harm through the conviction of their sins. You saw the cousin of this in some US states and Canada where they outlawed "conversion therapy." Wake up! The whole mission of the church is to preach the good news and *convert* the lost. This deserves repeating for those who seem okay with banning conversion therapy. It is the precedent upon which religious trauma will advance to shut down the churches. The church's role is to convict people of their sin and convert them to a righteous life and way of living. How could anyone miss this connection? The main role of the church, religion, and faith is conversion.

The entire effort underway now will be to tighten the screws on the churches to get them to stop teaching the Bible. The category of "religious harm" will be so broad that anything that is said confronting someone in their sin or challenging their self-esteem will be deemed "harmful." Gospel preaching will be viewed as a "micro-aggression." If anyone inside the church gets upset, the church will get sued and run out of existence. Yes, that is who these people are and what their ultimate goal is. Remember, there is no co-existence with evil, but toxic tolerance has allowed the disease to spread.

Many of those originally responsible for the onset of this decay have already passed to their hellish reward, but there are enemies within the church today collaborating with the Left to bring about a new false church that will not preach nor provide a way of salvation, but instead preach a false gospel to anesthetize and ease your path to hell. That is what social justice was meant to do: to replace the gospel. So many touchy, feely, and woefully uninformed pastors are clueless in their embrace of social justice.

I left a church of 32 years because in a woke moment of appeasing the culture the pastor essentially inferred that Peter was a racist. I condemned the sermon and, armed with the opinions of two theologians from the seminary, I confronted two spiritually airbrushed elders. The theology and facts were on my side. In fact, I had more theological qualifications than those elders from an educational standpoint, but they nevertheless refused the truth and said we would just have to agree to disagree. No! That doesn't work for me. I'm not going to make nice with those on such grave error.

When I can't trust what comes out of the pastor's mouth, I'm gone. I hesitated not one second. The fact that I had spent 32 years invested in that church was of no concern, and I wasted no time in fleeing the "City of Destruction" as did Christian in the second best-selling book of all time, next to the Bible, *Pilgrim's Progress*. The moment the meeting was over I walked out the door kicking the dust from my proverbial sandals. I never looked back. The church in America today has a massive infection of naive and woke pastors and elders. God help them regain their sight.

Churches, Country, and Trauma

In a book review by Dr. Linda Jeffrey of Adam Wyatt's *Biblical Patriotism: An Evangelical Alternative to Nationalism*, she discloses not only his bad company (the birds that he flocks with, so to speak) but exposes the fallacy of his thesis. It seems clear that he is in league with the global cabal of the faithless and false.

Jeffrey notes that there have been three generations of "deliberate ignorance" foisted on American children. They have been taught in an education system where American history, civics, etc., have been ignored or twisted and the social sciences exalted. American Founders are now painted, for an ignorant generation, as gold grabbers, slave masters, and oppressors. Most of the Right knew this was going on all along and did essentially nothing other than pay the wages of those who were mentally abusing their children with this fraud. Jeffrey's claim of this intentional dumbing down of children over the last three generations is consistent with the testimony of KGB defector Yuri Bezmenov given back in the 1980s.

As in the countries that were overthrown by communists, the U.S. permitted the riotous summer of 2020 with statues of those who sacrificed their lives for our liberties being torn down. The psycho Right bellyached but did nothing. They didn't match aggression with aggression or fight fire with fire. Had they done so the cowards on the Left would have folded the tent, as that is their character. All the Right essentially responded with was indignation and said, "That's insane," or "That's crazy," and tried to give everyone a history lesson, as if just spouting off an opinion or facts from the comfort of their living room (and censored by the media) was going to have any impact. The Left essentially wins by default.

Jeffrey continues by noting that for three generations communism was whitewashed to young minds, and that capitalism, the very system that was paying their tuition, was dubbed oppressive. Our "fine" teachers and administrators and educational institutions labored to hide the millions who were murdered under communist regimes. Do you see an agenda at work yet?

Progressives see the Bible as a roadblock to their anti-God agenda. Historical revisionism and ignorance have allowed movements bent on deconstructing America and weakening our Bible-based code. It was the Bible's morality that brought stability and trust into our governmental institutions. When conservative Christians and moms at school board meetings are labeled a danger to America, you know the country has descended into chaos and deliberate ignorance. Consider how Samuel Perry, Russell Moore, Beth Moore, and their ilk weaponized the term

"Christian Nationalism," and then condemned it, all from speculation and unverified studies—you know, the kind you make up to self-validate your pre-drawn conclusion to fit a narrative and agenda. So now that they have this term, which is really a neologism, they place people into that description, and who might they be? Conservative Christians.

Let me digress for just a moment, because this is germane to what is happening in the churches and to society at large. The Left con you with linguistics and makes up new words, which is what a neologism is. Technically, a neologism is a newly coined word or expression (mostly by the Left today) to describe something unproven. It is a means of creating a false narrative and draws people into a trap, much like the spider draws the fly into its web.

The Right has what would appear to be a genetic flaw in that they incessantly accept the false narratives from the Left and then legitimize them by arguing with the false narratives instead of rejecting them entirely. They axiomatically accept the Left's framing as if it has some equivalency or credence, and they attempt to disprove the false narrative itself instead of rejecting it and all their made-up words. It is not that the Left is so smart, it's just that they are more cunning and shrewd. Again, as it has been said, when you put established facts up for debate, you have already lost the argument. The Right is famous for this. They give the Left so many additional bites of the apple that none is left.

It's much like going up to someone who knows nothing about football and saying, "let's play a game, and here are the rules; when you have the ball you start at the end of the field, but when I get the ball, I start at the 50-yard line." The Right gets suckered into this trap every time. As stated previously, the Right erroneously grants the Left equivalency. Good has nothing in common with evil nor light with darkness. The Right erroneously gives the Left a platform every time and always argues from a point of disadvantage.

Ok, back to the review of Jeffrey. Again, according to Jeffrey, Wyatt argues that for conservative Christians, "The flag is a source of idolatry." They argue that loyalty to America is idolatry. Seeing America as God's chosen nation is sinful. God uses all nations for his will. I guess that would be North Korea, China, Cuba, etc., even though they are the result of unchecked evil and godlessness. While everything is ordained by

God, don't forget that judgment is in the mix as well. It would be interesting to know if Wyatt celebrated Thanksgiving.

As Jeffrey further notes, Wyatt edges closer to an agenda of keeping Christianity inside the building and your Bible and principles out of American institutions. Most notable is the organization with which he and others are associated whose mission is to discover the under-recognized truth about how religious doctrine can lead to trauma responses in the brain and body.

Now, as an attorney, I can tell you that what they are trying to do is set up a separate and new "cause of action," i.e., basis for a legal "complaint" upon which lawsuits will be based to destroy the church. I'd like to see them try this with Islam or Judaism (but that won't happen). All the focus is on Christianity. Finally, as Dr. Jeffreys notes, millions of dollars will be awarded by judges who have been educated and advised by the new priest class of psychology.

Well, we can't have that. They can't tolerate Bible-believing Christians who serve the real Jesus. No, they want to talk about the Jesus that they have made in their image, and a Jesus that can only be taught and heard within the hermetically sealed doors of a liberal church. If anyone inside gets upset, the church gets sued and run out of existence. Yes, that is who these people are. They should be excommunicated and considered and declared anathema, thus removing them from the stage. It's time people of the faith exercise some discernment for what is coming down the pipe next.

Woke Church, Weak Church, Gone Church

R.C. Sproul also spoke another great truth when he said: "The greatest weakness of the church today is the servants of God looking over their shoulders for the approval of men." This plays a big role in the wokeness of the church today in appealing to a depraved culture. The church has lost its center due to those in leadership who Sproul also said are unqualified to be there. A woke church is a weak church. And a weak church will be a dead church in this current climate of psychosis.

Nehemiah, the wall builder, was a good example of a faithful pastor who stood strong against the cultural forces and pressures of his day. Instead of worrying about accommodating the pagans, Nehemiah focused on the reforms needed among his own people. The paganism

Nehemiah feared was not just the paganism of the pagans, it was also the paganism of his own people. The paganism outside the camp posed a threat, yes, but what threatened Israel so much more was the paganism within the camp. So, he built both a wall to protect his people from the outside evils and worked with Ezra to purge the evils from within their midst. This is what shepherds today must do as well.

In closing this chapter, consider how even non-churchmen are waking up to the spiritual battle, and putting so many pastors to shame. As Tucker Carlson alluded to in several of his monologues, at the root of all this chaos is God. It's about God. There is an evident spiritual component to what is going on in this country and the world. Yes, Denmark was rotten, decaying, and collapsing, as is America, and it comes from a core common cause everyone is missing.

Eighty percent of all religious persecution in the world today is committed against Christians. Christianity is the target, and the world order is doing everything to destroy it without looking like they are. Complex subterfuge is created to hide what is really going on. To the discerning, it is truly self-evident. To a shepherd who is shepherding correctly, it should be truly self-evident to them as well. As our forefathers said in the preamble of the Constitution: "We hold these truths to be self-evident, that all men are created equal, that they are endowed by their Creator with certain inalienable Rights, that among these are Life, Liberty and the pursuit of Happiness."

We are those who must acknowledge our Creator. When we don't, we go mad. What an interesting term, truths that are "self-evident." Well, they aren't anymore because the psychos were given a platform to spew the poisonous lie that truth is relative and that there is no ultimate truth or that truth is situational, and if you try to hold to the truth, you are roundly criticized as hateful, bigoted, or racist. Be bold! As Rev. Charles Spurgeon was quoted saying, "Bold hearted men are always called mean spirited by cowards."

Fire your personal "PR" department and care not what bad and evil people call you. Real men are feared by weak men. Again, be bold. Tucker Carlson has seen this and remarked upon it. The question, then, is why can't the church?

A Caution for the Unchurched Christian

Before I leave this chapter on the complicity of the church, this should not and does not serve as an excuse to be unchurched. If you are one of those who haven't darkened the door of a church in months or years and then think yourself justified because of wokeness in the church, then you're just as much a part of the problem as those who with intent contaminated the church in the first place. Virtuous as you may feel on the political issues of the day, and professing as much as you may about your faith, your words are empty and so is your soul if you are an absentee from church. Virtue will not get you inside the pearly gates. So, while many may adopt and accept the premise of this book, particularly as it relates to the church's complicity, if you're unchurched then your destiny is likely the same as those on the Left.

So, "get thee to a nunn'ry" as Hamlet said to Ophelia, but essentially, find a church. Know your scripture, become an active and participating member, and hold those behind the pulpit and in the eldership accountable. As I alluded to earlier, I left a church, but only after they would not correct a heretical message. I immediately went looking for another church, as I was not going to be among the churchless and pretending to be my own God, or my own church. That is not how it works, and I have no desire to join the Left in their destiny.

PART THREE

CHAPTER 15:

Stop Asking Why and Start Fighting Back

> "The only thing necessary for the triumph of evil is for good men to do nothing."
> **Attributed to Edmund Burke**

The most irritating question uttered by those on the Right and particularly in conservative media, is "Why?" They are always asking "Why do the woke leftist psychotics act and think as they do?" It is a frustrating display of non-critical thinking. No, these are not rhetorical questions the Right raises. If they were, it is wasted on a public that for the most part cannot connect the dots and hasn't the intellect to do so. The election of President Biden and Senator Fetterman is proof enough. The opportunity is lost when such questions are asked, particularly when they are not answered. It makes the speaker, the reporter, or the talking head look uninformed.

My question back to the Right psychos is, "what do you mean, why?" After all this time, destruction and decay in the country, the Right is still asking why. You mean you don't know who and what you are dealing with by this time?

It's astounding. The Right and this nation are in a life and death battle for their life, liberty, property, and happiness and they don't know who or what they are fighting; an enemy attempting to take it all away.

No wonder there is something rotten in the state of America. The Right is fighting a war but has not identified the enemy, much less declared an enemy. The Right, in assuming the Left is a moral equivalent, has surrendered the high ground.

So, this chapter is focused on what it takes to put a stop to a losing prosecution of this battle for the heart and soul of this nation. Far too often the Right would rather lose nobly than win ugly. However, you can't win a fight until you know who and what you are fighting. It's time for that to change. Freedom is at stake. In fact, it's more than just about freedom, it's humanity that is at stake.

If you are still asking why, then you are not fighting. If you are not fighting for your rights, you will only get to cry for what you have lost. Either stand or bow. I prefer to stand and fight. As for me, I will never provide the Left with the "food of fear," since their kind has been the deadliest in history and the fertile ground for tyranny. It's time to demand that the Right cease their navel-gazing and wondering why. If you don't know why by now, then you can't fight, and if you can't fight then you're in the way. Get out of the way so those who do know why and those who can fight can do so.

Why Do They Keep Asking Why?

The first thing that comes to my mind is those chosen to fight for what is right are either compromised and use the "why" as a delay, or they are cowards who are only in it for whatever perks they can get while they can, or they are truly that stupid and need to be replaced. The lack of discernment of the generic conservative/Right is astounding. They look at the destruction, chaos, and dystopia created by the Left and expect to reason with them. They expect logic from them. They expect rationality. These are unrealistic expectations. When combined with the general laziness and indifference the Right has exhibited in the face of an existential threat, one would have to attribute that to a psychosis of the conservative/Right as well.

Even when the Right has had unchallenged power, they display pusillanimous behavior. When the Left is in power, they act quickly and decisively on their agenda, even though it is in reckless disregard of the consequences. They do this despite their incompetence and the evil of their ways. They are part of an "ineptocracy," for sure, but they waste no time in their destruction.

As Morgan Philpot put it, ineptocracy is "a system of government where the least capable to lead are elected by the least capable of producing, and where the members of society least likely to sustain themselves or succeed are rewarded with goods and services paid for by the confiscated wealth of a diminishing number of producers."

This system has sway in Republican politics as well, and it results in leaders who don't know what time it is much less what the real threat is. On the Right, that's part of why they keep asking "why" instead of canceling the Left as the Left has been doing to the Right with little resistance.

Democracy As an Onramp to Socialism

Another reason for the Right's continued confusion is that they hold to a false moral equivalency with the Left. Let's be clear: the Left is not morally equivalent. They are devoid of a moral code except for the situational moral du jour they create from day to day. So, why would you ever disgrace yourself sharing the same platform with them, which in doing so only elevates them to a status they do not deserve? It only serves to confuse the ignorant masses further. To repeat, there is nothing the Left has in common with any major religion in the world today, and neither does the platform of the Democrat Party.

Given that caveat, let's discuss yet another example of how the Left manipulates the chaos, confusion, and language to create more "whys" on the Right. Recently the Left appropriated the word "Democracy." What do they really mean when they use it?

The term Democracy does not mean the same thing to the Left that many think it means. Oh, fear not, the Left knows exactly what you think "democracy" means, and they will have none of it, at least in the way they know you define it. They won't define it to you because you won't like it, but you will fall for it and automatically assume that you're on the same page and speak the same language. You do not and you are not on the same page as the Left.

One of Greece's greatest accomplishments and contributions to the world was philosophy and democracy. Socrates, seen as a father of philosophy, was rightly very skeptical of democracy and gave many warnings about it. In Book Six of *The Republic*, Plato describes a conversation between Socrates and Adeimantus wherein Socrates was trying to alert Adeimantus to the flaws of democracy. Socrates analogized a ship being set to sea and asked Adeimantus, "who would you want to decide who should steer the ship? Just anyone or someone experienced in seafaring?" Adeimantus said he would want the most capable. Socrates replied, "Then why would you leave the decision of who would guide a country to just anyone?" He said voting in an election is a weighty responsibility and a skill, not just random intuition. And, like any skill, it must be taught systematically.

Socrates argued that letting the citizen, just by virtue of being a citizen, vote without an education would be like letting them steer a ship in the midst of a storm. Do you now see the correlation with the schools of today indoctrinating children as opposed to educating them?

Socrates learned first-hand the dangers of democracy. He was brought up on trumped-up charges of corrupting the youth of Athens. A jury of 500 Athenians judged the case and by the margin of 280/220, some say a 52%/48% split, Socrates was found guilty and sentenced to death by hemlock, a poison that would stop his heart. Oh, if only we had that kind of charge or indictment that could be implemented in today's America for the corruption of our youth.

Socrates was not in favor of only a narrow elite being able to vote, but rather those who thought rationally and deeply. He believed in an intellectual democracy as opposed to one by birthright. Socrates feared, as did other Greeks, that voting detached from wisdom would lead to demagoguery. We have given the vote to everyone disconnected to wisdom. All our elections today are filled with demagoguery, lies, and deceit without shame.[53] The Greeks knew how easy it was for those seeking election to exploit our desires for easy answers. Their experience was the erosion of freedom. Can there be any doubt considering the elections of Mayor Lori Lightfoot of Chicago or the newly elected mayor Brandon Johnson? Both are extreme leftists (Marxists) who have left the city a hellscape,

---

53 "Why Socrates Hated Democracy," The School of Life, YouTube, November 28, 2016, https://www.youtube.com/watch?v=fLJBzhcSWTk&vl=en.

now being the murder capital of the country. Or, consider Sen. John Fetterman of Pennsylvania. The list could go on and on. I tend to agree with Jesse Watters of Prime Time on Fox News, that if the people are that stupid to elect such reprobates, time and time again, then let them suffer. They clearly are choosing the chains of their bondage and pain.

Consequently, we have elected many idiots and few intellects. We end up cycling from one crisis to another as there are enough mercenaries, narcissists, and con men in government to advance their own agendas indifferent to the disaster that will befall the country and the world, for they care only for themselves. The most poignant example of what happens with fools electing fools is in Ukraine, where well over 500,000 have died because of the decisions of Biden, Zelensky, and Putin. These are all flawed, corrupt boys playing in an adult world. Hold on, there are more to blame than just them. It's the American people who voted into office a man bent on war while voting out of office a man who kept us out of war. If not today, then at some point you will pay a price for that decision, but likely never associate it with how you voted.

To be clear, direct democracy is a dangerous and deadly form of government. While communism and socialism have proven to be the most failed and deadly, it makes the democracy of idiots even worse as they enable the likes of communism to proliferate.

Let's explain the danger of democracy with a simple illustration. Let's say there are two men and one woman on a deserted island; the two men take a vote as to whether the woman gets raped. You already know the outcome, unless the men have a moral code, which in today's America is unlikely, but of course if they did the issue would never come to a vote, much less be considered. Nevertheless, the woman gets raped. I know that it is visually repulsive, but it is a searing example to awaken the sleepy mind as to the horrors of democracy and what it is not.

You are being fooled again by the Left. It's happening now. How, you ask? You think democracy is freedom and the protection of your rights, and you just love hearing the Left talk about their efforts to preserve and protect democracy. "Oh, what a noble cause," you say. What you don't know is their definition. Frankly, you should already know by the legislation they have proposed or enacted. It is anything but freedom and protection of your liberties and rights. Today the leftist District Attorneys prosecute the victims and free the criminals. That's democracy as the Left defines it.

While you are being gaslighted by the Left about "democracy," they are moving swiftly to flood the nation with illegal immigrants who do not share our culture or know and respect the constitutional freedoms we use and enjoy without question. They will vote in a permanent national party run by the Democrats which we know are controlled by the socialists. Here the ignorant perpetuate the corrupt by defaulting to the Left's demagoguery. The illegal immigrants fled the corruption they voted for within their countries of origin, and will do the same here. The Left knows this. As the saying goes, "You can vote your way into socialism, but you have to shoot your way out of it." In this case the illegals, instead of shooting their way out, are escaping it, but with them they bring the same voting habits and patterns that destroyed their countries. That's the danger of this "democracy"—it won't stay a democracy. Embedded in democracy are the seeds of its destruction, the seeds of tyranny. You are getting metaphorically raped—or will be.

Instead of the illegal immigrants shooting their way-out of the socialism they helped create and support, today's illegal immigrants are fleeing the countries they helped destroy with uninformed votes, supporting demagogues who, like the Left today, promise something for nothing. Since they had no guns to shoot with, they fled. Fortunately for them, they had a country to flee to, the US. Americans will have no such country to flee to. This is the last best hope in this world for freedom, and it is about to end.

Another example is the 93% of the Black population who are totally sold out to the socialist leftist Democrats and have been for over half a century. They are given the same empty promises every election cycle, end up empty-handed, yet do it all again in the next election. Some have broken out of that mold, such as Dr. Ben Carson, Justice Clarence Thomas, Dr. Thomas Sowell, Candice Owens, Larry Elder, Tony Dungy, Walter Williams, Allen West, Lt. Gov. Winsome Sears, Charles Payne, Vernon Robinson, and many others. As incongruent as it is for Blacks to keep voting for leftist Democrats, they do so out of a cultural identity. Ask them where they stand on certain issues and often you will get a conservative answer totally at odds with those they helped to elect. When asked to explain, they don't and can't. The Left has destroyed black families and has caused them to live as a "color" as opposed to being people. It's that identity that keeps Blacks on the Left's urban plantation.

The education factor is monumental in whether a democracy is healthy or horrendous. Education in America is a disaster brought to you by the Left you elected. As stated, democracy inherently carries within it the seeds of its own destruction. Only educated, informed and moral people can control democracy for the benefit of the whole. This is where America is failing today. Moral people are self-governing. Immoral people are doomed to chaos, requiring an oppressive government to bring order, and that is where America is today. This infects both political parties.

A Perfectly Miserable Marriage

As has been jokingly said, the perfect marriage is between a sadist and a masochist. The Left sadists, a collective group of amoral, corrupt hypocrites who are addicted to power, inflict misery upon the masochistic Right, some of whom are so pusillanimous that they seem to love the injustice and pain inflicted upon them by the Left. The Right lacks the will to see their opposition for what and who they are. That's why they keep asking "why?" Republicans argue with the Democrats and conservatives with leftists as if there is moral equivalency. The Right plays by the rules of equivalency, which are flawed and suicidal. Another way of seeing it is how the British in the 1700's fought by lining up on the battlefield. They were easy targets for the Colonialists who fought from the trees.

The Right, more often than not, are like the British, being easy fodder for the Left. There is no equivalency. The Right tend to be the inept moralists, and the Left unapologetically godless hedonists. Both are out to lunch with reality. Yes, again, this is a psychosis, a detachment from reality, the eventuality being the ultimate collapse of the country. In one respect they need each other to keep the public in this perpetual delusion that they are somehow in control, free, and can change things with the next election. Inevitably, both will embrace corruption and sacrifice principles, to become part of a homogenized governing elite where they selfishly find protection while the rest of the country decays. Some call it the "Uni-party." Yes, the idiots of society will and are voting them in and will live under their oppressive rule.

Bringing it Back to the "Why?"

Nothing drives me to distraction and outrage quicker than those possessed of some "common sense," and normal cognition who reflexively ask "why" about the psychotic behavior and plans of the sadistic Left. If it were possible, I would ban the use of the word "why" from the masochistic Right's glossary.

As I just established, the Left is on a dangerous path to replace our democratic republic with socialism and a full-blown totalitarian state, and all the while the Right acts like it enjoys the punishments inflicted upon it by the Left. They truly are perplexed by the wickedness and evil of the Left. They find it so difficult to tell the public in clear and unambiguous terms what the Left is: wicked, evil, corrupt and every other adjective given us to accurately communicate truths that need to be known, not hidden in word salads that hide and dilute the message.

The Right needs to "know thy enemy." It doesn't get simpler than that. Call them an enemy. Define enemy. If you have ever played a game of chess, did you ever assume that the moves of your opponent were made for your benefit? At times it seems that the Left grew up playing the life game of chess and the Right just started yesterday. There are plenty of people on the Right that see what is happening and doing the yeoman's work, but many of those they elect are woefully ineffective. Of course, how effective can you be when your constituency does business with and financially supports the woke corporations that heavily donate and fund the Left?

There is an applicable allegory that has many derivations, but you will get the point. An Indian was walking through the desert one night, the kind of desert where it gets bitterly cold once the sun goes down. The Indian happens upon a shivering snake curled up by the trail who looks up at the Indian and says, "Will you please warm me up by placing me in your shirt? I promise I will not harm you." The Indian thought for a while, and then out of compassion said, "Okay." He decided to trust the snake and placed the snake in his shirt. A few minutes later down the trail, the Indian felt the pain of two fangs sinking into his side. With that the Indian pulls the snake out and shouts, "I saved you from the cold of the night and you promised not to harm me, yet you bit me anyway! Why did you do that?" The snake replied, "Because I'm a snake, that's what I do."

When will the Right ever learn? Again, light has nothing in common with darkness and bad company corrupts good character. Stop asking why to what should be obvious. Stop associating, collaborating, and engaging with those you know to be wicked. You only give them an ostensible credibility they don't deserve. Do not dignify them with an equivalency.

The Indian knew better yet he too asked, "Why?" a question where the answer was already clear. Know thy enemy. And yes, there are such things as "enemies." In America today we have an abundance of home-grown, groomed, educated, and financed enemies. They are the enemies of freedom, life, liberty, property, and humanity. They were created in clear sight. They were created and bore the fruit of chaos because they had the fertilizer of indifference and sloth.

Speaking of sloth, that's one of the reasons for the "whys." Nothing is new under the sun, and even in Christ's time one of the biggest problems among His people was that of sloth. If you are too lazy to build a fence around your vineyard, you'll have no wine because the wild animals will come in and destroy the vines. The wild animals of today are destroying all the foundations aided by the addictions of convenience, comfort, and the desire for security over freedom. Don't ask why. You know why. That is what the wild animal anarchists do. That is what a sadist does. That is what a Marxist does. That is what the Left does and continues to do. It's either you or them. They will not leave you alone to live your life. It is not in their character. It is the only means they have to quench their darkened souls living in futility.

The problem for the Right is they didn't take the threat seriously and didn't build the wall of protection that was needed. They fail to realize there is no co-existence with the Left, whose minds are so toxic and psychotic. There is no equivalence, no commonality. It is just phony, emotional, and irrational outrage that drives the Left. Likewise, it is irrational to sit by and allow the destruction to happen.

What To Do Instead of Asking Why

Instead of asking "why," the Right must label and define the Left with words that accurately describe them. This has nothing to do with "healthy debate," but rather the need for brutally honest and accurate assessments as well as truthful characterizations. The Right needs to remember that there is no moral equivalency between those who want to turn us into a socialist dystopia and those who don't. Antiquated notions about civil discourse cannot be worth more than life itself. We cannot effectively combat the coming nightmare with one hand tied behind our backs. It's an inexplicable disconnect on the Right, and unless it changes, we are doomed. They must stop playing by the British rules of engagement or the country will collapse.

For example, in leftist, Democrat-dominated Delaware, they have proposed legislation that children can have abortions and gender changes without notice to the parents. Now, if that doesn't activate your survival instinct of "kill or be killed," then nothing will. If you are not totally exercised and enraged to the point of saying "Discussion over, touch my kid and that will be the last thing you touch," then you have lost your humanity. Your children are not objects for negotiation. If they are, you have abandoned all that makes us different from the lower life forms. In fact, that places you beneath them—just watch the ferocity of a mother lioness protecting her cubs from the father lion.

So, it's time to stop asking why and start fighting back. What does this look like? It looks like aggressively targeting the minority communities held hostage to the lies of the Left, and helping them wake up and see who really represents their interests.

It starts with defining what the Left is really doing—trying to turn us into a socialist hellscape. Leaders need to help people in general connect the dots with clear and blunt language, not confused double speak, and not with the word salads that they have so cowardly come to use to cover their own asses.

We need to forget about the concerns for "civil discourse" and call out the enemies of freedom for who they are and what they are doing. Some may say that it is so harsh and mean, but at night when people lay their heads down on their pillows and they don't have to strike a pose, they start thinking about what was said, and it begins to percolate. It gnaws at them, and they begin to realize that you just might be right and then they consider how the Left might be a threat to them. You cannot unhear something. They may reject the truth at first, but they have heard it, and just like a seed, it takes time to germinate, but it will sprout. However, if you don't plant the seed, it won't. The seeds of truth as to the danger of the Left must be planted because the Left poses an existential threat—and it's time we treat it as such. History is our proof.

What does it look like to fight back? You may even have to fight back against your own team, your own party, when they are the ones being infected by systemic psychosis. Let me share a personal story that I humbly hope shows what this might look like.

When I Stopped Asking Why and Fought Back Against My Own Party

I had my own battles with the political system when I served as Chairman of the Louisville, Kentucky Republican Party. First of all, I'm registered Republican, not because I need to be Republican or because that is my identity, or because it was my life's ambition. I'm only Republican because the positions they take on issues are beneficial to the nation as a whole. The moment they depart from their principles, so too will I depart from the party.

Nevertheless, one battle in particular, nearly 20 years ago, was a defining moment for me. We had positioned the party to become the majority party for the first time in 100 years. However, the Republican governor, the first in almost 40 years, kept delivering his party and constituents defeat on a silver platter. He had an ego, and he was surrounded by a company of fools. Even as I worked on his transition team interviewing candidates for appointments, I knew at the outset something was amiss. He and his staff had troubling visions of grandeur, already thinking that his next stop was the presidency. I was astounded by that since he hadn't even proven himself in the governorship he had just won.

Early on in his administration he fumbled the ball. Now, there was an incredibly corrupt leftist attorney general whose agenda was to destroy the governor instead of protecting the people, but the Republican governor was doing fine on his own destroying himself. Ego, pride, and stubbornness, combined with ineptness, compounded by the fools around him, laid a foundation for failure. His numbers crashed, affecting the whole party.

One night he called me for support, and in a ninety-minute conversation, I listed all the areas in which he was failing and where there had been missteps. He agreed with my analysis. I was shocked. I asked, "Well governor, what is your plan to deal with the problems?" To my shock again, he had none. I recall standing in my house with the phone to my ear in stunned silence with what I had just heard. He just wanted to keep doing the same thing over and over expecting different results, but with my support. When I hung up the phone that night, I was dismayed but knew what I was going to have to do.

Now mind you, previous to the call there had been months and months of missteps and errors by the governor and numerous pleas and attempts to get him to correct course to no avail. This was in part due to the fact, as mentioned, some of those advisors surrounding the governor filled the air with an arrogance so thick that you could cut it with a knife. I told the governor that they were neither serving him nor the Commonwealth well. Yet he made no staffing changes. Clearly, the arrogance in his administration was trickling down from the top.

In advance of our discussion, I had given him a book by John C. Maxwell, *The Journey from Success to Significance*. I hoped he would get the message since the main theme of the book was that, "the definition of success is when you add value to yourself, and the definition of significance is when you add value to others." I wanted him to start doing his job, which was serving the people of the Commonwealth, adding value to them, and to stop thinking about his delirious desire to pursue another office. It was to no avail. I could tell he had not read the book nor gotten the message.

Thus, my mind was made up: The governor had to go. I would support him in the general election, which I did and was duty bound to do, but would not support him in a primary to run for a second term. Having discussed my plans with leadership a few months earlier, I called a press conference. Within an hour I had calls pouring in from the state capital and the governor's office trying to shut me down.

I took refuge and avoided calls until the press conference. When I entered the large conference room it was packed shoulder-to-shoulder with reporters and cameras. I stood in front of the cameras as Chairman of the party, and called on the Republican governor not to run for re-election. Demands also had been made by the president of the state senate, and I was followed by a Republican U.S. Congresswoman who did end up primarying the governor. These were extraordinary times. I had seen the numbers, statistics, and projections, and knew he had so damaged himself that he was not going to win re-election and was going to take the party down with him, but more importantly ruin an agenda designed to lift the state from the bottom of the list of states where the Democrats had kept us for 100 years.

The story was front page news for about 48 hours, followed by interviews and talk-shows. I tried to explain that saving the important legislative agenda, designed to help the people of Kentucky who suffered at the hands of "good old boy" Democrat politics for 100 years, that had resulted in the state being at the bottom in almost every category and measurement, was more important than one man, the governor, in spite of the fact that he was a member of my party. It was a very unpopular decision, but the correct one. The less informed in the party, living in denial, wanted to go down with the ship—oblivious of the consequences for the state and its people. I saw the same numbers as did leadership. I was proven right in the end. I stopped asking "why" and started fighting back, even if that meant fighting my own team, so to speak. It took courage, and it was costly, but it was worth it. In spite of the governor being very unpopular, he still wielded a lot of power, and I felt it. They tried to remove me from my office. It was a miserable 10 weeks until a Republican Congresswoman challenged the governor in the primary. That November he lost re-election as did others in the party, just as I had predicted, and I remained chairman.

One final anecdote on standing your ground and fighting back occurred in 2004. The local party had placed a bumper sticker in the window of the party headquarters saying, "Kerry is Bin Laden's Man, President Bush is Mine." It became a national story and demands came pouring in that I pull down the sticker (mostly from Democrats, but some from weak Republicans). Demands even came in from the chairman of the DNC and Democrat U.S. senators for me to resign. When asked by the media if I would comply, I responded, "Hell no." It was a fake controversy but a controversy, nevertheless. I was going to stand my ground, and stand I did, even with some in my party wanting me to capitulate. The sweet dessert came four months later when Bin Laden essentially supported Kerry by saying that he would be the better president. Many of the weak people who opposed me were left with egg on their faces after Bin Laden's announcement. That's the price you pay for cowardice in leadership. Lead or leave.

When your title becomes your identity, you and those you serve suffer. The governor and those around him were clearly not in touch with reality. They were in denial. Most troubling was that he was offered the best advice in the country, but refused it. Detachment from reality always has dire consequences.

I give this account to emphasize how power corrupts and blinds us, and how we must face reality and act accordingly, not in denial. The task of standing up to a governor was basically laying everything on the line. I was all in, but in order to do so, your cause must be greater than you. Ten years later the Republicans recovered, and now the people of the state are seeing massive improvements as we position the state to be able to compete with its neighbors. Our legislature is becoming a model for the nation, but not without some struggle.

No more "why" and whining. Now it's time for the "how" of, how to fight back! Kentucky is now on track, and the citizens are reaping the benefits.

CHAPTER 16:

The Cure: Ten Steps to Take to Regain Reality

"We all want progress, but if you're on the wrong road, progress means doing an about-turn and walking back to the right road; in that case, the man who turns back soonest is the most progressive."

C.S. Lewis

The word progressive used to mean something good, like in the way Lewis used it in the quote above. However, the leftist linguists have turned it into camouflaging something bad to deceive the people. When their "liberal" label became so toxic during Walter Mondale's run for the presidency they changed to calling themselves "progressives," as did the Marxists to "socialists." They didn't change their pathological ideology, just their moniker, so as to deceive the people. More recently "globalism" is the euphemistic term for global totalitarianism. Another title for this book could be "America's Slide into Marxism," for that truly is at the root of the psychosis, the detachment from reality, and the suffering we are experiencing as the country and society collapses.

Something is indeed rotten in the state of America. What that is, as I have proposed in this book, is a widespread suppression of the truth, a detachment from reality—a systemic psychosis, and a mass formation psychosis prompted by the most corrupt who are pushing a Marxist agenda. They confuse you with so many nice words and terms, but the core and agenda are, as you read in Cronkite's quote, a new world order devoid of individual rights.

The resulting psychosis is one that has been taught, implemented according to a pathological ideology, and imposed upon you to fundamentally change you and your country in ways that, if you were given the truth, you would never accept. It's a mass formation event that decouples people from the truth. In fact, it prevents you from recognizing the truth.

Earlier you met Mattias Desmet, a professor of psychology at Ghent University and author of *The Psychology of Totalitarianism*. His interview with Tucker Carlson is one of the most important interviews of the 21st century as it relates to an impending authoritarian world order devoid of personal freedoms. He explained this psychosis, this mass formation in this way:

> "Mass formation is in essence, a kind of group hypnosis that destroys individuals' self-awareness and robs them of their ability to think critically. This process is insidious in nature. Populations fall prey to it unsuspectingly. To put it in the words of Yuval Noah Harari, "Most people wouldn't even notice the shift toward a totalitarian regime."[54]

Keep in mind that this was prompted by COVID. In response to COVID, Desmet also notably said: "The fear of the virus is worse than the virus itself." Much has been written on how the corrupt elite weaponize fear to seize power and control the populace. That move is afoot in this country and has reached a critical mass which may not be reversible.

Desmet continued, explaining that the faulty COVID modeling prompted him to focus on this phenomenon; he says, "I decided to focus on the psychological mechanisms that could explain why an entire society couldn't see that the narrative they believed in was blatantly absurd in many respects."[55]

---

54 Mattias Desmet, "Tucker Carlson Today - Mattias Desmet - September 1, 2022," Tucker Carlson Today, YouTube, accessed on December 15, 2022, https://www.youtube.com/watch?v=nQQi_d6H_YU.

55 Desmet, Tucker Carlson Today.

Then it was Dr. Robert Malone who picked up on this concept and added a direct connection to psychosis. Malone said that:

> "mass formation psychosis is when society becomes decoupled from each other and has free-floating anxiety in a sense that things don't make sense. ... Then their attention gets focused by a leader or series of events on one small point, just like hypnosis. They literally become hypnotized and can be led anywhere ... They will follow that person – it doesn't matter whether they lie to them or whatever, the data are irrelevant."

Mass formation, mass formation psychosis, or systemic psychosis— it's all the same thing. It has caused this great societal detachment from the truth that America and the world is experiencing. And it is having disastrous consequences.

You've journeyed with me as I have reviewed how this psychosis has impacted America, and in far more ways than just the COVID pandemic and the responses thereto. I have attempted to connect the dots and thread the needle for you. This systemic psychosis didn't start with the pandemic. Rather, the pandemic just poured gas on the fire. It was a tool. And in some ways, in the light cast from the flames of our society, we caught a better glimpse of the rotten roots underneath. No one is free of blame in this humanitarian disaster.

Now you know what the problem is. You know that the very future of our country is at stake. You know that if we cannot find a way to anchor ourselves yet again to the rock of reason, reality, and truth, then we will be dashed to pieces on the shores of subjectivism and madness.

So, what now? Well, I promised I would give something of a cure. Here it is. Here are 10 steps to help take your mind back, to regain your mental autonomy, get your feet planted on solid ground, and come back to reality. I'm a man of action—I always have been. I trust you are a man or woman of action, too. While not a perfect cure, if we all start putting these ten suggestions into practice, I believe it will go a long way towards ending this national nightmare and bring hope back to America again; hope for a new century and bright future, should the Lord tarry.

1. Question Everything.

In our age of advanced digital technology, the means of deception and manipulation have never been greater. You need to know this: there is not a day that goes by that you are not being deceived or manipulated. Big Tech and other platforms censor speech every day. We have just seen this in the recent explosive revelations from Twitter. It should not have taken Elon Musk buying the company to disclose the truth. Any discerning person should have been able to do that or know that on their own.

Big Tech is not censoring lies, they censor the truth. This is why we must be so skeptical. True science has skepticism at its foundation. Science doesn't prove what is true, it proves what is false, yet without questioning, testing, interrogation, and investigation, one will never discover what is false. I recall sitting in a lecture at Cambridge University by the professor in charge of the doctoral program at that time, and he said that to be successful in the doctoral program one had to learn how to suspend judgment and not accept or believe everything you read that is in print or what is said in lectures until you have thoroughly investigated the matter at hand.

During COVID inquiry was suppressed, censored, and canceled. The falsity of all the claims was never revealed, resulting in great harm to millions. Those who took part in such suppression of the truth are criminals in my opinion and should never be allowed on a public platform again. While they rightly should be prosecuted for crimes against humanity, I don't expect to see that happen.

An American Nuremberg style investigation and trial needs to commence to indict those in Big Tech, the media, institutions of science, medicine and yes, those in our governmental agencies who have methodically suppressed the truth all in furtherance of establishing authoritarian governance in this country accompanied by the suppression of everyone's constitutional rights. It is not enough to stop what they are doing, they must be exposed, purged, ostracized, delegitimized, and never allowed near the levers of power again. Their conduct and complicity in the COVID debacle, which resulted in a mass loss of life and wealth, and is the single greatest fraud in human history, is proof and justification enough for an international trial of those complicit.

The first and most important exercise for taking our country back, as well as our freedoms, is to question EVERYTHING. Distrust anything coming from the government or any governmental agency. Question any article, news, content, or opinion, as in doing so it will bring you wisdom and knowledge. I have always contended that naiveté is a sin, but whether it is or isn't, you will be the first one to pay the consequences for being fooled. So, you would be a fool not to question everything, and I mean everything that you hear these days.

As in communist countries, lying has become a societal norm as a means of individual self-preservation. If ever there is a lesson that you should never forget for the rest of your life, it should be the criminal suppression of the truth around COVID and the mass suffering that occurred. This is your generation's Great Depression. Too few questioned the science or the authoritarian overreach of the government. And those that did were canceled, shut down, and suppressed. The useful idiots, the blindly obedient, submissive, and compliant were in plentiful supply.

Consider this: You already exercise a healthy skepticism every day. After all, you weren't born yesterday. Remember how we used to be towards the internet? It's time to revisit old habits. It's time to treat the internet like the unproven wild west that it always has been.

If you remember anything from this book, remember this: Truth is often hidden like the roots of a plant: you won't see it until you dig for it. Truth, from time immemorial, has been suppressed by those who stand to gain from its absence. The lie is like weeds in a garden, choking out the good plants. Weeds frequently mimic the real plant, but it is only the real plant that produces fruit. Discernment is needed to distinguish the difference. The weed, like the lie, brings famine and death. The plant that produces fruit, as with truth, brings nourishment and prosperity. Healthy skepticism is your friend.

Once you begin to recognize the truth and learn about the lies you believed, your life will change dramatically. You will see the world as it really is, and you will see yourself as you truly are. Your mental autonomy is life-giving. Be free in your own mind and never let anyone occupy that space. There is no greater or faster working pain pill for the social anxiety we are experiencing in psychotic America today than to become a healthy skeptic of all you're told. It triggers thinking, provokes thought and energizes your mental autonomy. It feels wonderful to be free between your ears and in your own mind. It will allow you to make healthy, wise, correct, and productive decisions.

The truth brings freedom. It will fix the compass of your life, bringing with it peace, inner security, and contentment. You will then be in control, not the frauds that keep you discontented, frightened, concerned, and angry. Either you control yourself or others will. And oh, how they want to control you. Any politician who proposes legislation that takes from you or demands something of you is not to be trusted. Remember, they are flawed and sinful men and women, and more often than not, less intelligent than you. They are essentially your employees. Again, as previously stated by Carl Jung, "Those who promise everything are sure to fulfill nothing."

Question everything. Be skeptical of everything. Those who pretend to have all the answers are imposters and are already lost.

2. Seek and Speak the Truth.

The point of questioning everything isn't to be contrary; it's to get somewhere, specifically, to the truth. Why? Because the truth will set you free. Truth, since the beginning of time, has never laid unexposed on the surface; and if it did, man would bury it. There has been and is a war on the truth from the beginning of time, but it is even more intense today than ever before due to technology. It's been captured, suppressed and hidden behind enemy lines. Allowing the truth to roam free goes against the agenda the Left wants to impose upon the people. They have won, so far, as there has been little resistance. So, you must fight for the truth. You have to dig for it. You must first seek it and then speak it. It starts with skepticism as the lie cannot prove itself.

The truth demands action. When you come across a golden nugget of truth, and it opens your mind, you must act on it right away. For example, the moment you finally realize you need to lose weight, or stop smoking or drinking, whatever the matter, don't set a future date or wait till the first of the year to start. Do it immediately. There is never a better time than now. Your resolve is never greater or stronger than at the moment conviction comes your way.

Back when I was counseling people in some of my courses, people who were burdened by problems and sin, and had become convicted of it would say to me, "I know I need to quit doing such and such, but what do I do and when do I start?" I would tell them that they will never have more spiritual strength, power, and determination to stop or to change an action or belief than at that very moment of conviction. Time will only weaken your resolve. So, in today's world, you must act now! Your starting point is the very moment you realize something needs to be done, that something needs to change. Your house of freedom is on fire. Act as you would if your physical home were on fire.

Seek truth while it can be found. There are many sources but too many rely on technology that can be manipulated or canceled or censored. One practical way to do this is to buy real books. Don't get comfortable or confident buying electronic books or simply reading the news online. Buy real books. They can't be canceled or erased. Read them. Don't just accept one source or opinion. Then act. Investigate your news sources and their history and accuracy. Develop a keen skill of observation to detect embedded bias. Look at everyone who espouses an opinion and research their background before you absorb what they say or propose so you can discern if there is a bias.

I said that you need to seek the truth *and* speak the truth. Never be afraid to say what you know is true, even if you are worried that it won't be popular. Remember, when you are told you can't say something, that's tyranny. Be part of the change in this country, helping return it and yourself to sanity. Break free from the falsehoods of the past that have kept you a prisoner. Exercise your rights, don't just talk about them. Truth and freedom are two sides of the same coin. If you are criticized for speaking the truth, consider it not only a badge of honor and courage but let it be confirmation to you that you are over the target. Fire away!

Remember, lies have no rights. Call the liars out. Expose them so others will not fall prey. Don't worry if people disagree with you. It has more impact on them than they want you to know. By speaking the truth, you have thrown the hot potato into their lap and now they must deal with it. They have a much more difficult time lying to themselves in the quiet of their homes than they do publicly to you. You cannot unhear something, so speak up.

3. Get Involved in Politics

Your participation in the body politic is required. You have a responsibility as a citizen, and particularly a voting citizen, not only to cast an informed vote but to know the issues and specifically those running for office. Scrutinize them. It's a job interview, a job where once employed they get to tell you what to do. Would you ever give anyone in your life that power without thorough scrutiny? Politicians do not own this country, you do, so exercise your ownership. The property you own doesn't manage itself, you have to manage it. So, it goes with politics.

When people come to me for estate planning advice, one of the things I might recommend is that they have a power of attorney wherein they name and give someone broad powers to act on their behalf if they are incapacitated. When they hear that, there is an immediate pause and silence in the conversation. You can tell the gears in their mind are turning and searching for the one person they trust to act in their best interests. Why should electing someone to a powerful office be any different? Consider all the power they have. They can tax you, determine what your kids are taught, what kind of medical care you will have, or be able to determine if you must fight in a war. How reckless can anyone be to vote for a party label or vote for someone not knowing what they stand for and believe?

Your current circumstances and the state of the nation could not be any more of a poignant example as to how important it is to know who you are voting for and what they believe. If there are any accurate history books published in the future (that don't revise history), they will look back to today and note with astonishment how a people and a nation went from the peak of its power and wealth to nearly losing it all in just 2 years with one fateful election in 2020. Some say the election was stolen. Well, I say the election never should have been that close for that many votes to have been able to be stolen. In a healthy nation and electorate, the psycho Left should have barely registered any votes. Therein lies the barometer of illness in the nation. With the corruption so rampant the elections shouldn't have been a contest. It's a testimony as to the diminished mental state of the electorate. The illiterate in the country is steering the ship of state. Socrates was correct.

Too many people want to stay out of politics. Or they don't want to fight the culture wars. Well, you might want to stay out of politics, but politics will not stay out of you. You might not want to fight the culture war, but the culture war is coming for you—and for your kids. In fact, it is coming for your life, liberty, happiness, and property. You win on offense, not defense. Our current decay is no fad, it's real and there is not much time left.

The luxury of living life as a disengaged citizen is over. As the church in this country decayed, so did moral standards which kept people within normative lanes that created stability and prosperity for all. Psychosis is infecting everyone today. You must actively resist it. One of the ways you do that is through re-engagement. Avoid isolation. Start community groups and parallel structures. I cannot overemphasize the need to create other structures that challenge the Left, no matter how small.

Isn't it interesting how so many school boards around the country are populated by degenerates more interested in indoctrinating and sexualizing your children than educating them? This didn't happen by coincidence. I doubt that more than 10% of the people who voted for a school board member knew who they were voting for or what that candidate believed. I can assure you that the leftist unions knew and heavily supported their election financially.

Engage in politics by electing the right people to office. Not just "any warm body." Elect people who still have a moral code by which they live, not one they just conjured up. Look for those who love God, family, and country. Educate yourselves on the issues, and those running for office. Again, question everything.

Voting is the least you can do. Maybe you should run for school board. Maybe you should organize a group of concerned citizens to petition your city council on a critical issue. You will have the greatest impact with your state legislators. They have no choice but to listen to you. I have counseled many of them and heard their concerns about what their constituents think or how they may act if the legislator doesn't perform. Sadly, the only ones bending their ears are those on the Left. Maybe you need to help fellow church members get a better handle on pressing policy matters. Maybe you—yes, even you—need to run for office.

This is an "all hands on deck" moment in our republic. Make sure yours are accounted for—and get involved in politics.

4. Don't let Christians Vote for Democrats/Leftists/ Socialists

Now, again this sounds politically biased, but judge not so quickly. Speaking of politics, something needs to stop. That something is Christians pretending that it's okay for them to vote for a party platform that is antithetical to every Christian belief they profess. The Democrat party is no longer the Democrat Party of old, but only in name. It is completely beholden to the pro-abortion, pro-transgender, pro-gay, pro-porn in schools, pro-men in girls' sports, anti-free speech, anti-police, anti-Christian ideology lobbies that are infecting every institution in our nation. And what fellowship can light have with darkness? None! There is no debate as to what side of the moral divide the Left belongs. Simply look at the issues, the facts, and their stance.

Speaking about the Democrat Party of old and why you should not judge me too quickly as a partisan; I first remind you of my previous anecdotes establishing that I'm anything but a rubber stamp, but here's another short anecdote to prove the point. Years ago, I was appointed by a former Democrat Governor to a committee to preserve and prevent historical books from being removed from school curriculum simply because they contained historical references to religion and religious influence in our history. This was called the PERK committee. The governor was a godly man and I worked side by side with him for a year and a half. He was patriotic and loved his country and state. It was a pleasure working with him as well as an honor. The work of the committee resulted in proposed legislation to prevent the removal of historical documents simply because they may contain religious content or reference to religion.

Now, back to the point. As Dr. Albert Mohler, president of the Southern Baptist Theological Seminary, the largest seminary in the world, recently said in his 2022 speech to the Family Resource Council's Pray, Vote, Stand, Summit, "there is a way to vote that is both faithful and unfaithful. Voting for Democrats is unfaithful, before God." This sounds political too, but when you think about it and know your history, it really isn't and that's because those in control of that party are not really traditional Democrats, per se. No, they are mostly insurgent atheists, agnostics, hedonists, socialists, authoritarians, and Marxists that have taken control and have supported nearly every perverse measure designated as evil by not only Christianity, but every other major religion in the world. This is not just a Christian bias they have; it is a bias against all faiths, and against humanity. As recently stated to me by an immigrant from Cuba, "There is nothing in the Democratic Platform that unites it with any of the major religions of the world." How profound that it comes from someone who escaped communism. If anyone should know, they do, having suffered the consequences of those in power on the Left.

Finally, it seems that some in church leadership recognize that the platform promoted by the Democrat Party makes it impossible for one to reconcile Christian doctrine, or those of the other major religions, with the evil that has taken over that party. Truth does not reside in the Democrat Party and has not for a very long time. I know, I was in Washington D.C. back in the '70s, and knew some godly, freedom-loving, and America-loving Democrats at that time. They were the salt of the earth. I knew Senators Sparkman, Allen, and Humphrey, and they never would have tolerated what is now the misnamed Democrat Party. That party needs a name change as its name no longer connotes what it used to stand for. Its name is deceiving.

If Christians across our nation were consistent with their faith and never voted again for the party trying to destroy their faith, we just might have a chance. A key part of this, of course, is that pastors must be willing to inform their members about the moral atrocities of the Democrats/the Left, socialists, Marxists, and how they stand against God and His Word on every major issue. Frankly, this shouldn't be hard to do since Democrats essentially took the sins and perversions of Romans 1 and turned them into a policy platform and a campaign slogan.

No, It doesn't take smarts, it just takes a spine. Pray God gives more pastors the backbone they need to make this clear. It will also take pastors who are informed and not woke. Wokeness is an accurate litmus test of a deficient intellect and mental illness. It is time for the men of the cloth to get with the program or be forced out, and you can make that happen, but not if you are not involved. Once again, WOKE is the "Willful Overlooking of Known Evil.

Let's not leave this topic too quickly. I definitely don't think Republicans are saintly or all godly. Now, many are, and still impact the direction of their party and the nation in a good way, but even that party is infected with some really bad actors that need to be purged. Liz Cheney (whose globalist father I sadly supported one time, more out of a lack of

244 | America's Systemic Psychosis

choice than anything else), was rightly swept out of office by a tidal wave of Wyoming citizens who woke up to her duplicity. She was a fraud and a fake Republican. She was, like her father, a globalist.

Then there is Adam Kinzinger. Mr. fake-pouty face, a virtue signaling former Representative who was no statesman but a crass fame seeker. He was and is a glory hog. He was a fraud and narcissist who wrapped himself up in false virtue, nauseating sanctimony and false piety that was on full display. He was an embarrassingly poor actor.

As Tucker Carlson noted in a monologue on Kinzinger: "This is what happens to a man when a man stops acting like a man." There are a handful of others I could name to which people need to awaken. I would like to specifically mention those who are still in office, but it would serve only to distract from the message of the book. All that one needs to do is look at the voting record of a candidate to reveal who they are. If their kind is allowed to take over the Republican Party, they will destroy it, leaving the people with no choice. A healthy competitive two-party system goes a long way in keeping people honest and is beneficial for the country—and it would be so much better if we had two good parties grounded in God, family, and country.

5. Maintain a Healthy Skepticism Toward All Government

This may be hard to hear, but if you are going to shake off the systemic psychosis, you must come to grips with the fact that every governmental agency and institution is corrupt and cannot be trusted. That is not to say that all the people in those agencies are corrupt, but they are infested with corrupt leadership and agendas.

This is where we are today. The government (particularly the federal government), but also state and local as well, has grown so large bureaucratically and become so unaccountable, that there can be no doubt many portions of it exist to serve its own self-interests, and not yours.

I don't believe every claim of corruption I hear. I do believe that just about any conspiracy theory could be true or has some truth mixed in. Our government has done terrible things in pursuit of its own ends, things that they have covered up. Some have come to light, such as MK Ultra, an "illegal human experimentation program designed and undertaken by the U.S. Central Intelligence Agency (CIA), intended to develop procedures and identify drugs that could be used in interrogations to weaken individuals and force confessions through brainwashing and psychological torture."[56] Or consider the Tuskegee Study, a "study conducted between 1932 and 1972 by the United States Public Health Service (PHS) and the Centers for Disease Control and Prevention (CDC) on a group of nearly 400 African Americans with syphilis. The purpose of the study was to observe the effects of the disease when untreated, though by the end of the study medical advancements meant it was entirely treatable. The men were not informed of the nature of the experiment, and more than 100 died as a result."[57]

As we go deeper down the rabbit hole, we are now learning from different sources, and via the Nixon tapes, that the CIA was involved with the Kennedy assassination. Still after 60 years, your government wants to keep thousands of pages of facts and evidence a secret. No one in government should have the power or authority to suppress the truth from the people. Suffice it to say your skepticism should be on full time, and if ever there was a time to question everything, it's now.

Has anything really changed? The same government that committed the horrors of MK Ultra and the Tuskegee Study (which is just the tip of the iceberg) is still in charge today. The cover-ups today are so profound it is an indictment not only of the corrupt actors themselves, but also upon the whole of the country for not rising up to forcefully purge what is inexcusably and profoundly wrong.

If you have lived anywhere other than under a rock, you've experienced the insanity of dealing with governmental bureaucracy or been subject to unfair treatment by the gears of government. Many have been victims of retribution. People lose their jobs, they are denied certain rights, and some get their homes raided by unlawful government officials. Most end up exonerated, but only after lengthy and expensive, bankrupting trials or court proceedings. This is all a result of power improperly placed into the hands of unaccountable and unelected bureaucrats given to them by the people we elect who haven't the ability to conduct them-

---

56 MKUltra, Wikipedia, accessed on January 6, 2023, https://en.wikipedia.org/wiki/MKUltra.
57 Tuskegee Syphilis Study, Wikipedia, accessed on January 6, 2023, https://en.wikipedia.org/wiki/Tuskegee_Syphilis_Study.

selves properly. Welcome to authoritarian hell. Cause and effect! Know it or live it. Think or feel.

You know the problem with giving unaccomplished people a little bit of power? It goes right to their head. It is the only thing that gives them any esteem or status. They use it to run roughshod over others. This was never intended by our Founding Fathers, but in our laziness, we delegated too much power and responsibility to people who are incapable of faithfully administering the responsibilities of public office. So, you will have to stand up to the tyranny of governmental institutions and expose them publicly. It will not be easy, but then we have only ourselves to blame since through our laziness, we allowed this situation to grow out of control.

Nothing worthwhile in this life is easy; you cannot delegate to others what you should do, and it is that reckless delegation that has caused many of the problems of governmental overreach. Only you can stop it.

6. Know That Most News Is Controlled and Biased – And Fight Back

Remember, press reporters and media figures are not neutral observers simply reporting what they saw. They are promoting a viewpoint.

Less than a handful of people and/or mega-corporations in the world control our flow of information. The evidence is overwhelming. Vast numbers of disseminators of our news and information are liars and truth suppressors with political agendas. Your news and information are controlled by those who only want you to know "their" truth, but not "the" truth. What can you do about it?

Of course, we know you can't trust the media. They are lying to you in service of the regime. They are the mouthpiece of the elite, the psychotics and the propagandists. Yes, it's a racket. You can fight back. Start at the local level, where your local broadcasters, reporters, and announcers live. They are more sensitive because they are closer to their local sponsors that keep them on air. So, start there. Also, there can no longer be sanctuaries or havens for those who use the mass media to spread lies, deception, hate, and manipulation to the community.

Demand accountability. Organize and go after the sponsors and advertisers of your newspapers, television, and radio stations who spread misinformation. The Left has been doing this very effectively because those on the Right (for the most part) did nothing. Look what was accomplished in the boycott of Bud Lite. It was a massive nationwide backlash and reaction to their wokeness costing the company billions and resulting in the firing of those who caused and promoted the transgender messaging. This needs to occur each and every time a woke company attempts social engineering. On a more national level, elect politicians who will reign in Big Tech and bring antitrust cases against them. The problem is whether the people will ever discipline themselves to stay the course.

As an example, when Target caved to the transgender movement as it related to their bathrooms, I stopped shopping there and have not for years now. When Bed, Bath and Beyond went woke, I shut down my account. The same with Coke. I, along with many of my restaurant owner friends, stopped serving Coke. Personally, I liked the taste of Coke better, but out of principle I switched. Now I've come to like Pepsi. This is not to say Pepsi is any better on the woke scale, they just have not been as in your face about it. The power to do something and change things is yours. It's in your wallet and your choices. "Bud Lite" every woke company.

This is so simple it shouldn't need any further explanation, but let's take this one step further. If the Right and those opposed to woke corporate collusion with the government would make several painful examples of these woke companies, driving them to near bankruptcy, you will see DEI, ESG, and other woke administrators, who are being paid billions, be fired en masse. This will save companies billions, making their products cheaper to purchase. Their stock value will increase as well as your retirement portfolios.

Hit them where it hurts—in the wallet. They cannot exist without advertising revenue. If companies who sponsor the media pull their advertising dollars for fear of losing business on a particular network associated with bad conduct, misinformation, disinformation, bias, etc., that media outlet will be forced to reform their practices or go out of business, as they will not be able to pay the bills. Wake up. The left has been unopposed in this practice for years while the Right sat back and did nothing even when the Right had the greater financial power and resources. Had the Right flexed their financial muscles years ago the Left never would have had the influence over the media, corporations, and the sponsors as they do today.

It does not take a large organization to make a big difference. Small groups and parallel structures can be very effective. These companies are more sensitive to opinion than you know. As a rule of thumb and an example, in the restaurant industry, if someone is displeased with service or has a complaint, large or small, they are "comped," which is an industry term whereby the dissatisfied customer's meal is free and other offers are made even if the customer is wrong. Why? Because one happy customer will tell on average 7 others. One unhappy customer will tell 11 others. With the postings and ratings online today, it can be multiples of that.

You actually can shut down a business. The Left did that and consequently imposed upon you their ideology all because you, or the Right didn't do likewise. They sat back and did nothing. You didn't fight fire with fire. You could have but you didn't. In part, the Right gave corporate America no choice because the Right didn't show up for the fight. Now, I have spoken broadly and generally about the Right, but I acknowledge that there are some great institutions and organizations on the Right that have emerged fighting the good fight for freedom, but so many in middle America are doing nothing.

You have the tools and the means to make a difference. The country is in chaos because people simply would rather complain than inconvenience themselves by acting. We are now seeing the deadly consequences of inaction.

7. As Much as You Can, Boycott Big Tech and Woke Corporations

As previously addressed in dealing with the media and Big Tech, big corporations need to face mass boycotts. We have seen the impact on Disney, and it has been profound. Soon stockholders will start firing woke CEOs and Boards, if not suing them for malfeasance. Again, look at the massive backlash against Anheuser Busch and Bud Lite for promoting and partnering with the "trans-queen" Dylan Mulvaney. The company lost billions in stock value. If this message gets through to the other woke companies that this will happen to them if they continue with their wokeness and social engineering, then their corporation will face the prospect of losing billions and the leadership fired for malfeasance.

You must vote with your wallet as corporations have joined hands with the Left in service to their revolution. What is so essential for you to know is that they have no interest in the betterment of mankind, only a dystopian goal and their financial bottom line, which ultimately cannot co-exist. They are mutually destructive. Both have been infected with leadership no more capable of steering their corporate ship than a deckhand being given the controls of an aircraft carrier. I've known too many of them.

The Marxist march through the institutions has reached the corporate world, even though so many once thought them to be immune. Now, in collaboration with an unresponsive and non representative government, they have gone woke and are trying to enforce Diversity, Equity, and Inclusion (DEI), as well as Environmental, Social, and Governance (ESG), designed to exert maximum control over your lives. If you don't comply, they can and will deny you services. They will redline you, as I addressed previously. It seems so counterintuitive, but these morally rudderless leaders don't fear the destruction they are bringing; after all, they are part of the elite, and they have their reserved seat on the ark, or so they think.

Americans who love their freedoms and want to be left alone must use their economic and financial muscle. If the big corporations recoil and comply with every little complaint and threat of the Left (who are not the economic engine of this country), then the Right, who have the greater financial advantage, can make the corporations and big tech bow to their demands as economics will force it upon them. The stockholders are always asleep at the switch until you start cutting their dividends. Most never respond to ethics, only economics. So, give them a painful economic lesson and then they will remove the woke board and replace them with adults who will and should refocus on the primary mission of their company. As I said earlier, if you're Coke Cola, then make Coke and shut up. No one is buying your political opinions.

A great example of how to fight back came from Sen. Tom Cotton, who, when addressing the CEO of Kroger, the giant grocery store chain, recounted to the CEO how big companies would censor and cancel conservatives, but when Democrats were going to burden those same companies with more regulations, those woke companies would run to Republicans for help. Cotton metaphorically slapped the CEO in the face with their hypocrisy and duplicity. With that, Sen. Cotton simply looked at the CEO and said, "good luck," and turned off the microphone. The message was deafening: don't come to me for help when you cancel and censor us. Booyah!! Time for Republicans, conservatives, and Santas of the Right to ask, "Have you been naughty or nice?" And the answer will determine what you get.

8. Reform, Recapture, or Reject Schools and Universities

Many notable scholars, particularly those keenly aware of the corrupt nature of the world and those who desire to dominate us, know that children are the key to the future, particularly if the corrupt want to control the decisions of future voters. We were warned to question the value of compulsory education, which we refer to as public education today, thinking it to be a great thing for equal opportunity. As we see today, education is not meant to enlighten the students but to instill a form of social compliance, mind control, and obedience to the governing elite.

As H.L. Mencken also argued, the aim of public education is not to spread enlightenment, but rather to reduce as many people as possible, a controlling majority, to the same, safe level. Like breeding cattle, the corrupt elite who want unchallenged and permanent control of your lives need a standard citizenry to put down dissent and originality.

Rid yourself of the notion that all the billions that leftist politicians want to keep funneling into public education have anything to do with what is good for your children and raising the intellect of the students. We spend more on education each year per student than any other nation on earth, yet we have the lowest test scores and achievements. Intelligence quotients are dropping and standard test scores across the United States have been declining for years. It never has been for a lack of money. The money was earmarked for expenditures on programs to indoctrinate and create a compliant future electorate.

As I have contended in this book, the institutions of education in this country are no more than institutions of brainwashing and indoctrination. Even Martin Luther back in the 1500s saw public schools would be used by the powerful to indoctrinate citizens into a specific worldview.

Again, Soviet Leader Lenin, murderer of millions, said, "give me a child until he is five and the seeds that I plant will never be uprooted." Oh, how true and how stupid of us not to realize what was going on in the public schools in this country and to your children. What's even worse is that you paid for it.

Again, our insidious disease of mass formation psychosis is being imposed through the education system. It is another poisonous import that our border controls allowed to pass into this country, particularly from the Prussians whose very intent was to preserve their establishment's power in the 1700s. It caught on in the United States with those in power who saw the benefit of maintaining their power by indoctrinating and guiding public opinion of their future voters in a direction more favorable to them. The eventual goal, which is foreseeable (as the elites in the country and government battles against homeschooling) is that as with the Spartans, who would take the child from the parents and raise it in accordance with the ideas of the state, we are not too far off from parents becoming nothing more than Petri dishes, and their children will be taken at a certain age to be developed as the state dictates.

There's no doubt about it, the schools are a disaster. If you want to get back to reality, get your kids out of public schools. Christian theologian, blogger, and author Douglas Wilson has argued that if all Christians took their kids out of public schools at once, public schools would collapse. And what a sight that would be. Furthermore, refuse to pay for tuition at woke universities that are teaching your children that 2+2=5, that men can be women, or other equally insane theories and concepts.

In his recent book *The College Scam*, Charlie Kirk argues that perhaps it might be better not to go to college at all. He writes, "Students literally go through the college system and emerge having learned nothing at all. As a result, employers are concluding, 'We can't hire college grads. They can't do the job. College has ruined them as potential employees.'"[58]

---

58   Paul Bedard, "Charlie Kirk: College is a 'scam'," Washington Examiner, accessed on November 02, 2022, https://www.washingtonexaminer.com/news/washington-secrets/charlie-kirk-college-is-a-scam.

Schools were meant to be institutions of moral formation. Now they are the exact opposite—they deform our children's hearts and minds and even seek to warp their bodies with radical gender ideology. It's time to confront them. Call them out. Expose them to the light and to the masses as to what they are doing. Let your community know of the perverts, sociopaths and deviants who are teaching your children and where they live and their associations just like you would do with a sexual predator. Expose who they are and what they are teaching your children. Humiliate and delegitimize them publicly. And make sure to also expose politicians giving cover to these teachers and the school boards pushing woke ideologies and indoctrinating your children.

These monsters who are mentally abusing your children live amongst you. Give no quarter to anyone physically or mentally abusing your children. They are operating outside of civil and normal society and have no business being around normal adults, let alone your kids. They need to be treated like sex offenders who must register with the state, be put on a list, and cannot live within a certain distance from schools.

If America is to win, it cannot afford to let the next generation get brainwashed. Reform the schools if you can, recapture the ones that you can, but reject the ones that you can't. Too much is on the line. Until then, it would be recommended that every child going off to college should be warned and tutored as to what to expect from college professors. Look up the background of every professor your child may come into contact with, and teach your child in advance who those professors are so that they can filter what the professor says. Get to your child first before the professor or teacher does. Be able to instantly spot a woke message coming from their college and denounce it. Delegitimize professors before your kid gets to the classroom. Build in healthy skepticism beforehand. Let your child know that you have their back to stand up against woke teachers and professors. As a parent it's your right – you are paying the bills, and it's your responsibility.

Grant no automatic respect to instructors, as respect, like trust, must be earned. Finally, programs need to be developed for deprograming kids after college. Metaphorically, vaccinate your children before college and then rehabilitate them again after. In fact, one Fox News report detailed how, "New York City pharmaceutical heiress Annabella Rockwell is claiming that her mother paid a $300-a-day 'deprogrammer' after believing her daughter had been 'brainwashed' by attending an all-female elite liberal college that left the young woman 'totally indoctrinated' and estranged from the parents who raised her."[59] Not all of us have that kind of cash to help purge our kids' brains of the woke mind virus, so maybe the real moral of this story is that you shouldn't send your kids to these liberal indoctrination centers in the first place (this is the "reject" option, if the "reform" and "recapture" fails), but if you do send your child to college, immunize them in advance.

9. Get Local: Focus on State Legislatures

As someone who has worked in local politics for decades, I can assure you that your state legislatures will be more responsive than anyone you find in the D.C. Swamp. Unfortunately, state legislatures hear from only one side. In working with many legislators in Kentucky on various issues, particularly bringing an end to the political indoctrination of students as opposed to educating them, the one complaint that sympathetic legislators had was that they have no support from those who elected them. They complain that once elected they are abandoned by their conservative voters and left to the mercy of wild-eyed, yelling, screaming, threatening, and name-calling leftist activists who teach your children. If you could only see how crazed these people act and look, you would feel more comfortable around a rabid dog. Never let your children near them. Make yourself known and heard. Scream louder than the lunatics. Many of the good legislators need their constituents to back them up. Don't just vote them in, throw the keys to them and say, good luck. Your responsibility doesn't end at the ballot box.

At times I have to question whether those who are passively allowing all of this to unfold are not lunatics themselves. I know from personal experience the impact of your opinions on legislators and their decisions. You have the greatest impact and power at the state level. Use it. If community groups worked for the Left, it can work for the Right, and it has at

---

59 Danielle Wallace, "Mother of NYC heiress paid 'deprogrammer' big bucks after daughter 'brainwashed' by college's woke agenda," FoxNews.com, accessed on February 13, 2023, https://www.foxnews.com/us/mother-nyc-heiress-paid-deprogrammer-big-bucks-daughter-brainwashed-college-woke-agenda.

times but inconsistently. The playbook already has been drawn up by the Left. Just use their tactics. You have the truth and the facts on your side.

You must be confrontational. The time for civil discourse is over because we are dealing with a mass of educated idiots, fools, and violent psychopaths who are harming you, your children, and your nation. You cannot reason with them, and you cannot argue with them. They have been groomed and brainwashed such that they are not rational and cannot exercise cognition in a syllogistic way. There is no logic, or deductive reasoning present, so you are left to try and simply stand your ground. Where once civil discourse was the preferred way, the social chemical reaction has reached such a toxic and critical mass that more abrupt, blunt methods are required. This is the consequence of decades of doing nothing.

Organize! There is strength in numbers. One of the best bits of advice I ever received as a new Chairman was: "Nothing is more powerful than a constituency." It truly gives you a seat at the table from which the Left and the Psychos want to exclude you because they cannot handle the truth you can speak. They are dark and you are light. Fight for your rights—or you will lose them. Remember what Alexander Hamilton said:

"Unjust authority confers no obligation for obedience."

The government owes us justice—at the local, state, and federal levels, but don't expect it today. Never forget that one tool we have in our toolbelt to fight back with is civil disobedience, but a last resort which can be avoided by becoming active in defending your rights and simply speaking the truth. Sometimes, defying tyrants is obedience to God. We must be ready to make that choice. This is a choice I hope will never have to be made, but based upon the mental illness I have seen in the Left, you are now left with having to defend your life, liberty and property as the government, in the hands of the Left, has become your enemy. Let's also talk about the church.

10. Get Back to God – Get Back to Church

Finally, none of this will matter if we don't get back to God. When I say the truth will set you free, I mean more than you know. I belong to no woke church and certainly no Westboro Baptist church either, but this I know, the Jesus (Yeshua) to come will not be the Jesus that was. He won't be hanging on a cross when He comes, nor will He be meeting with us at the corner Starbucks to speak to us in gentle tones. In fact, if you see Him again in this mortal body, it will be an awfully bad day. At the core of all the Left's psychosis is the antipathy they have for God. They know the truth and they suppress it, but that does not alleviate their anxiety. So, they rage and contort society as if large numbers will insulate them from any judgment to come.

Getting back to God means grounding yourself in eternal truths. It means embracing the metaphysical realities that come from a life lived before the face of God, *Coram Deo*. For there to be a moral law, there must be a moral lawgiver. Without God, there is nothing to conserve, and there is ultimately no conservatism. Indeed, without God life is meaningless and futile.

There is a God. And that means that life is meaningful and therefore to be conserved. It also means that life is consequential. There is a consequence to life and that is what the Left suppresses the most. Yes, how you live will have a consequence, as that is the only way it will have meaning, and it does. That's the only means to ultimate justice, and there is one. Live daily with this thought: "you have an expiration date." Live accordingly. The Left does not and that is why they rage.

When you are at home, 99% of people behave rationally. We have schedules to meet, we sleep at normal times, the kids go to bed at normal times and get up to go to school. You are careful as you prepare your food, you clean your house, mow the lawn and take safety precautions. You insure your house and your car and practice good health measures. Life is conservative in so many ways if you desire to prosper. As comedian Joan Rivers once said to a liberal interviewer who was chagrined over the fact that Rivers was conservative and asked why. Rivers said, "Because life is conservative." And indeed, it is.

What this means is that no matter how much you may want to "break all the boundaries," there are just some fixed limits that you cannot transgress without facing serious consequences. If you are so woke that you think you should have the bodily right to fly, then no one is holding you back—except for gravity. If you are that psychotic, do us all a favor and jump off that ten-story building and exercise your right to fly without wings. Nature will cure you of your psychosis.

Though not too many people are throwing themselves off of buildings, many are doing so metaphorically in lots of other areas of life. This disconnect is due to the spread of cognitive dissonance, which is inconsistent thoughts, beliefs, or attitudes, especially as relating to behavioral decisions and attitude change. Today, so many act one way at home but then act almost suicidally once they get away from the home, supporting policies that would be destructive of their personal ordered life. This is the product of systemic psychosis.

Adhering to reality also means taking action. As stated previously, just as so many on the conservative side want to protect their rights to bear arms to protect themselves from this evil world, they do so with false security. If they won't get off the couch to protect their rights, particularly their freedom of speech, then they will never use the arms they horde, should that time ever come, because they have never practiced or exercised their freedoms otherwise in the face of those who would take them away. This takes courage that we can only find in God. God is not a pacifist, and He will ultimately destroy all disorder.

Our Founders dared to forge a new country because they were men of faith. In the pulpits on Sunday, they had their clerical robes on over their military fatigues. If you will not go out and stand up in the public square against tyranny, then you are all talk and no action. Just as you defend all you have acquired and possess, whether it be with locks on the doors, insurance, or any other protective measure, you must actively and passionately defend your constitutional rights, not privately, but publicly and openly. If you do not defend your rights in that way, you will lose them and you will eventually lose everything you have. Remember, the constitution is just a piece of paper. The radical Left knows it and disdains it. Only you can make it mean something and put some teeth and power behind it.

Nature has its limits and if you abuse it, there is no forgiveness. If you abuse your body, it will limit you no matter what you think, or feel is your right. You may think you have the right to be free to drink a whole bottle of vodka at one time, and you are, but your body has an absolute veto regardless of what you think you have a right to do, and you will suffer the effects. Nature holds the ultimate veto. There are myriad public examples where nature forces you into conservatism, rationalism, common sense, and reason because otherwise the penalties are severe. In one sense nature has a way of eliminating the deviant. If we get back to just looking at nature and realizing how orderly it is, how reasonable it is, how it is your reality with limits and parameters to life, then therein is your guide to mental health and a recovery from the psychosis pandemic.

As a man thinks, so he becomes. It can either be destructive or productive. If we live within life's parameters – if we live in truth, we will be happier, healthier, safer, and more joyous and prosperous. Tend to yourself and leave others alone. And, as the Bible teaches us, love your neighbor as yourself. Many Christians today misinterpret Scripture in a way so as to allow evil free reign over the world. Toxic toleration is not biblical, nor is passivity.

The safest and most assured way out of psychosis and back to normalcy is back to church and God. Because without God there is no truth and without truth, there is no order and without order, there is no freedom, only chaos.

Remember: The psychosis truly sets in when you begin to worship false gods. After all, what is a detachment from reality if not, most fundamentally and tragically, a detachment from the One who made all of reality?

All of us, every single one, will only know the truth and be cured of this systemic psychosis when we come back to the way, the truth, and the life. And those three things are found in God. Which means we need to get back to God. Get over this psychosis. And get out there and help others do the same. Quite frankly, you have no choice, assuming you desire your life, liberty, and happiness.

EPILOGUE:
Don't Be Late For The Revolution

The admonition of this title is itself a bit late, especially for the audience to which this book is intended in that the Left has been engaged in the fight against God and country, life, liberty, and the pursuit of happiness for decades. As stated earlier, never underestimate the power of denial. Denial has been the Right's companion long enough. And in their denial, they have imperiled the country and the world, through their failure to act.

The Left's greatest strategy has been against your mind. It was never guns and bullets, although considering the lateness of the hour it is more likely now to come to the latter. The Left, like the Devil they please, infiltrated your minds and corrupted your programing and normal thought processing. As mentioned, the greatest freedom in the world is your mental autonomy. No one can touch or take away what you control between your ears unless you let them.

There is only room for two in the space between your ears: God and you, and in that order. You alone have the key to that door. Never give it away to another, a group, or much less, a government. Other forces may capture your body, but be free in your mind and soul.

The freedom between your ears is worth more than your life, for if you give that up you will have neither a life in this world worth living nor in the next. It is who you are.

Never before in the history of modern man (post flood) has there been more of a singularity of evil on a worldwide scale and of global enslavement of the body and mind than now, and it was all aided with the arrogant advent of technology. If ever there was a cause to devote your life, your physical comfort and convenience, it would be now and in the pursuit of your individual freedoms and mental autonomy.

I speak to those who have the capacity to think, understand, live, and love the truth. Those flourish and thrive in the light of the truth. Most do not and they are perishing, and they will perish. Most of that group know the choices they've made and have done so with unholy relish. Flee not just the allegory of the city of destruction, but flee the world that is in the process of destruction. You do so by engaging in that type of fighting that Solzhenitsyn spoke of regarding the man who simply wanted to be left alone to live his life.

Mentally declare war on those who would deny you your humanity, your freedom, and your mental autonomy. There is no tomorrow for which to wait. You must act now. There is no more time for delay. Choose this day whom you will serve, not only spiritually, but in pursuit of your life, liberty and happiness, or lose it all forever.

This is your moment at Concord where the first shot was fired in this country's battle for independence and freedom. This is now the time to do what you thought you would never have to do or live to see. This is the fight of your life. The revolution is all around you and is no longer hidden. The Left shed its cloak of invisibility long ago and have been daring you to do something about it. Fight the psychosis with all you have, otherwise all that you have will be taken from you. The revolution is upon you, like it or not. If you don't fight, you will be left with nothing in this life, leaving no legacy for your children.

There is a big caveat. Be smart. Remember, one of the main characteristics of the Left is violence. They want to instigate the Right into violence. Do not get drawn into that trap as they are looking for a pretext to shut it all down. They want an excuse to seize ultimate and permanent power. Deny them this.

The revolution we must wage to break the grip of psychosis begins with restoring the truth to our lives. No, not your truth or someone else's truth, but THE TRUTH. Yes, there is a truth and you had better be about finding it, and I've given you a good start in this book. By doing so you can begin to restore your mind, your country, and your world. This is the path out of psychosis and back to sanity—the one paved with truth and lined with those willing to proclaim it loudly, no matter the cost. You have enjoyed the life you have today in America because of the sacrifices of others who came before. Now it's your turn to contribute to the cause of life and liberty, for without it there cannot and will not be any happiness.

ABOUT THE AUTHOR

Jack L. Richardson, IV, is a fourth-generation attorney in one of Kentucky's oldest family law firms, established in 1907. Having practiced law in Kentucky for 43 years, he has argued cases at the appellate levels of both the state and federal judicial system and has accrued extensive legal experience. Jack is well known in the community and among the bar for his extensive and high-profile civic and community activities, as well as his service as a board member for several charitable organizations.

Like his great grandfather, who served in the Kentucky Senate, Jack is also committed to political activism. Shortly before graduating from Samford University, he served as an intern to U. S. Senator Marlo Cook in Washington D.C. During his extensive legal career, Jack worked in several presidential campaigns and has served as a national delegate as well as a Presidential Elector and has been on the statewide executive committee for the Kentucky Republican Party for the last 23 years helping to formulate policy, guide state legislation and give direction to the state party.

As a lawyer, Jack Richardson is trained to argue the point, meaning that one must exclude all that is irrelevant to the issue at hand. Jack has seen on the state and national levels the false narratives used to obfuscate the truth, and was compelled to write this book to expose them. His extensive experience in the law courts began over 40 years ago, but today Jack avidly defends the unmoving common-sense standards in the court of public opinion.

Jack has been a commentator in both television and newspaper, and has published numerous articles, including on his Substack publication at Bluegrassjack.substack.com. He also maintains a high profile in local business affairs, state politics, and community activities, filling out an extensive resume of accomplishment by turning his attention to writing and authoring books and other publications.

A free ebook edition is available with the purchase of this book.

To claim your free ebook edition:

1. Visit MorganJamesBOGO.com
2. Sign your name CLEARLY in the space
3. Complete the form and submit a photo of the entire copyright page
4. You or your friend can download the ebook to your preferred device

Print & Digital Together Forever.

Snap a photo

Free ebook

Read anywhere

Printed in the USA
CPSIA information can be obtained
at www.ICGtesting.com
CBHW020803110624
9872CB00002B/3